Faeries, Bears, and Leathermen

Faeries, Bears, and Leathermen

Men in Community Queering the Masculine

PETER HENNEN

The University of Chicago Press   Chicago and London

PETER HENNEN is assistant professor of sociology at the Ohio State University at Newark.

The University of Chicago Press, Chicago 60637
The University of Chicago Press, Ltd., London
© 2008 by The University of Chicago
All rights reserved. Published 2008
Printed in the United States of America

17 16 15 14 13 12 11 10 09 08   1 2 3 4 5
ISBN-13: 978-0-226-32727-3 (cloth)
ISBN-13: 978-0-226-32728-0 (paper)
ISBN-10: 0-226-32727-2 (cloth)
ISBN-10: 0-226-32728-0 (paper)

Library of Congress Cataloging-in-Publication Data

Hennen, Peter.
    Faeries, bears, and leathermen : men in community
queering the masculine / Peter Hennen.
        p. cm.
    Includes bibliographical references and index.
    ISBN-13: 978-0-226-32727-3 (cloth : alk. paper)
    ISBN-10: 0-226-32727-2 (cloth : alk. paper)
    ISBN-13: 978-0-226-32728-0 (pbk. : alk. paper)
    ISBN-10: 0-226-32728-0 (pbk. : alk. paper)
    1. Gay men—Psychology. 2. Homosexuality, Male. I. Title.
HQ76.H473 2008
306.76'62—dc22
                                                                            2007038591

⊚ The paper used in this publication meets the minimum requirements
of the American National Standard for Information Sciences—
Permanence of Paper for Printed Library Materials, ANSI Z39.48-1992.

FOR STEVE, WHOSE PATIENCE IS APPARENTLY ENDLESS

Contents

Acknowledgments

This book was made possible by the extraordinary generosity of the Faeries, Bears, and leathermen who welcomed me into their communities and who shared so much of themselves in the interviews. I suspect that your abundant goodwill has changed me forever; I know it has inspired me to devote as much care as I could muster to the analysis in this book. Please know that any critical comments contained herein are offered in the context of profound respect and a deepening affection for your respective tribes. You are the lifeblood of this book, and while you have revealed many things to me about gender and sexuality, I am, on a personal level, most enriched by what you have shown me about the power of caring communities. Thank you.

Portions of this book have been published previously. Material from chapter 2 was published under a different title in *Social Thought and Research* ("Powder, Pomp, Power: Toward a Typology and Genealogy of Effeminacies," vol. 24, nos. 1 and 2, September 2002). Abbreviated versions of chapters 3 and 4 have been previously published in the *Journal of Contemporary Ethnography* ("Fae Spirits and Gender Trouble: Resistance and Compliance among the Radical Faeries," vol. 33, no. 5, October 2004) and *Gender & Society* ("Bear Bodies, Bear Masculinity: Recuperation, Resistance, or Retreat?" vol. 19, no. 1, February 2005). I thank these publications for permitting use of this material here.

Jennifer Pierce, my graduate advisor at the University of Minnesota, shepherded this project through its lengthy evolution with unstinting enthusiasm and support. And oh, how I needed that support! Thank you for showing me what ethnography can do, and by extension, what I could do with ethnography. If emotional labor counts, this book is as much your work as it is mine. I would like to thank Doug Hartmann, another member of my doctoral committee, for his sage advice and for always asking the right questions. You and Jennifer have been tireless advocates for my work, and I cannot begin to tell you how much that has meant to me. I am grateful to the other members of my committee, Ron Aminzade, Gary Thomas, and especially Lisa Disch, for challenging and advising me on critical aspects of the project.

I thank the intrepid women of my dissertation support group at the University of Minnesota (the "Piercing Insights") for their audacity and for occasionally reminding me not to take myself too seriously: Karla Erickson, Hokulani Aikau, Wendy Leo Moore, Sara Dorow, Deb Smith, Amy Tyson, and Felicity Schaeffer-Grabiel. In my book you are true academic Amazons (and at long last this *is* my book, thanks in no small part to you). Special thanks to Karla for your lively and constructive critique of chapter 5. Thanks also to my friend Amy Wilkins at the University of Colorado at Boulder for a very thorough and helpful review of chapter 1.

My colleagues at The Ohio State University supported this project in various ways. I greatly appreciate the discussions I've shared with the members of the graduate sexualities reading group, especially Liana Sayer, Griff Tester, and Jason Whitesel. Thank you, Katey Borland, for being there ("there" being Newark, Ohio), and, also there, Newark dean and director, Bill MacDonald.

The fine people at the University of Chicago Press have been a joy to work with. I want especially to thank acquisitions editor Douglas Mitchell, who saw promise in a very rudimentary draft of this work and who has been in my corner ever since. Verta Taylor and Wayne Brekhus reviewed this work at varying stages for the press, and I wish to express my heartfelt thanks for their care and insight. Thanks also to Joel Score and copy editor Joyce Dunne, and also to Tim McGovern, Isaac Tobin, and Joe Claude.

My late parents would not have approved of this book. Nevertheless, I want to acknowledge their years of care and support and to thank them for teaching me how to think, how to work, and how to laugh. As I was growing up, my older sister, Mary Frances, demonstrated that resistance was possible through her late-night arguments with them, and that disagreement need not be fatal to loving family relations. Finally, I want to acknowledge the love and support of my partner, Steve, who has stayed with me through all of the joys and sorrows of the past twenty years. Your wise and courageous spirit informs every word I've written here, and this book is dedicated to you.

In Their Natures: Gay Men, Queer Men, and Gendered Strategies of Resistance

Every summer, the Radical Faeries gather in the forest. As I drive to the gathering in my hopelessly bourgeois Saturn, I am glad to have Hibiscus along for the ride. Although he has been a member of this Radical Faerie band for just over a year, he strikes me as a seasoned and dedicated member of the community. He wears a nondescript T-shirt, a pale blue ruffled peasant skirt, and an orange kerchief on his head. He tells me that in his "clock time" life he works as a life coach. This suits him well, he tells me, because he has a keen appreciation for individual responsibility and knows all of the excuses people make in trying to avoid it. While at this point I do not know much about Faeries, the stern, neoliberal tone of Hibiscus's remarks startles me. Nevertheless our conversation is congenial and lively as we travel down country roads on our way to the secluded sanctuary. He tells me of the history of the sanctuary, how he came to know the Faeries, and how he was given his Faerie name. A moment of panic ensues. "I've already picked a name for myself—is that OK?" He only smiles in response. There are no rules, he tells me. "What name did you choose?" he asks. "Spring Peeper," I reply.

I go on to explain how the name came to me. This seems to pique his interest, and he focuses carefully on my words. I tell him that three hours earlier, as I had been hurriedly stuffing my housedress, Lycra pants, and halter top in among my other essentials, the name came to me from a radio playing in the next room. It was tuned to a National Public Radio program featuring a local authority on nature and the environment. Although I could barely make out what was being said, I assumed it was a discussion of frogs, as I distinctly heard the words "spring peeper" repeated three times in quick succession. Hibiscus seems pleased with this account. "Sometimes Faeries choose a name, sometimes they ask another Faerie to name them, and sometimes their Faerie name finds them." A ponderous silence follows, and soon it is time to leave the road for the wooded path that will lead us to the sanctuary. A brightly colored banner arches across the trees above us. "Welcome Home," it beckons.

As I unpack and pitch my tent I have a chance to introduce myself to my neighbor, Cowslip. Having arrived several hours earlier, Cowslip is still in the process of unloading a series of garish prom dresses from a large rented trailer into his enormous tent. I marvel at his wardrobe and wonder how my frumpy housedress will fare next to this dazzling attire. Hibiscus returns to inform us that we are in for a treat. Lothar, a longtime Faerie, is preparing his famous curry for dinner. I have just enough time for a quick tour of the sanctuary. I follow the path to a nearby clearing. At the perimeter of the clearing sits a small structure labeled "Faerie Pantry." Across the clearing to the left is a cabin; a little further along is a hand-operated water pump. Beginning at the pump the land begins to slope down toward the lake. If you follow the slope you reach the screened-in cookhouse. If you walk the other way you will find a short pathway that leads to the fire circle, surrounded by wooden benches. Behind the cabin you pick up the path to the lake.

A magical feminine spirit is said to watch over the lake. I never quite get the full story on her, but she apparently has an entire family (with whom she occasionally spats), and their story has obviously been changed and embroidered over the years. Just before I reach the lake, I look off the path to the right to find a small shrine attached to a tree. It consists of a small Barbie doll inside a plastic casing and beneath it a small china plate displaying an ode to friendship. This kind of "camp" sensibility contrasts sharply with another feature of the lake: at the far end is a small, picturesque island with room for only a few stately pines. The island is off limits to everyday use and is considered sacred space. The ashes of several deceased Faeries rest there.

Just then I hear several voices join in a spirited shout. The cry "Yooooo-hoooo!" echoes from the clearing and across the lake. A "yoo-hoo" is a Faerie call to attention; this one means dinner is ready. As I arrive at the clearing I notice folks are starting to gather in a circle. Before I join them my eye is drawn to the small deck area surrounding the water pump, where I see something that escaped my notice earlier. There sits a large black phallus, adorned with a garland of brightly colored plastic flowers draped over the shaft and resting on the balls. I pick it up to find that it is made of latex—just a big black dildo really. I wonder if this is meant to communicate something about race, and what it might mean in a community that appears to be almost exclusively white. But the thought is a fleeting one, and easily forgotten. The phallus stays in this same spot, undisturbed and unremarked upon, for the duration of my stay.

I take my place in the dinner circle as all of the attending Faeries join hands. We are a fabulous troupe: some of us naked, some of us in outrageous "trash drag," some of us glittering, some of us in street clothes. I realize at this moment that I have carried a great deal of anxiety into the sanctuary. When I left my house this afternoon I did not know a single Faerie, and I could not help but wonder at all that could go wrong. But now, as I surrender myself to the circle, I feel something within me begin to relax. I do not know what I will find among these friendly fae spirits, but I know, as Hibiscus has so prophetically indicated, that I am in for a treat. I offer a silent prayer of thanks to the goddess for the bounty I am about to receive.

———

Every summer, the Friendly Bears meet in the wilderness. Today is the opening day of the Friendly Bears' annual summer campout at a nearby state park, and what a beautiful day it is. The late afternoon sun shines down on our merry band, bathing this joyous reunion of big, hairy men and their male admirers in a welcoming glow. I arrive a bit later than most, but in plenty of time to enjoy the celebratory energy that so obviously wafts through the camp on the gentle breeze. These men know it is the beginning of a weekend of greeting old friends and meeting new ones, eating, drinking, fellowship, swimming, and sex. Smiles and hugs abound. I register with Burt, a "bear of a man" who is in many ways typical of the men here: stocky, hairy, full bearded, with a ready smile and a warm hug. I make my way down to a picnic table in the clearing just off the parking lot to take in the sights. Several pickup trucks are parked in the lot, some bearing vanity license plates like CUB, LIL CUB, BEAR CKR, and WOOFY.

This last one brings a smile to my face as I remember the first time I was "woofed." I had just finished a flirtatious bar conversation with a handsome bearded man when, upon leaving, he leaned forward and growled low in my ear, "Woof." This reminded me of one of the petty cruelties from my elementary school playground: "barking" at the girls we designated as "dogs." Initially shocked at what I thought was an insult, I was assured by a friend that this was actually a compliment. The man was a Bear and thought I was attractive, or, in other words, "woofy."

Just then my reverie is interrupted as a heavyset man files past me, his hairy belly sticking out from beneath an ill-fitting T-shirt. The shirt reads in large print, "I Have the Body of a God," and beneath it in much smaller print, "Unfortunately, it's Buddha." Other T-shirts adorning other husky frames advertise Bear clubs in nearby cities. One of these reads, "Got Fur? Lone Star Saloon," referencing the San Francisco bar that is reputed to be the birthplace of the Bear movement in the late 1980s. Another T-shirt carries the image of a large, powerfully built, anthropomorphized bear with distinctly human facial features, his warm smile and twinkling eyes belying the intimidating mass of his furry body.

Suddenly I notice that a small group has joined me at the picnic table, just as a red pickup truck barrels through the lot, its cab filled to capacity with loud, beer-drinking Bear men, hooting and gesticulating wildly. A man on my left laughs heartily, pointing out how low the truck is riding, nearly touching the ground at the back. A quiet man who has taken a seat on my right scratches his beard, takes a long draw on his cigarette, and restates the obvious: "Bears in a truck," he mutters slowly. His more boisterous companion lets out a howl of delight. "Hey! You guys look like a takeoff of *Priscilla, Queen of the Desert!*" He is referring to a popular film about drag queens on a cross-country odyssey in a broken-down bus.

But everyone knows this is only a joke. While their carefully studied "regular guy" appearance might be considered a form of drag, these men are anything but queens. In fact, the central principle that unites them in their identification as "Bears" is their collective rejection of stereotypical assumptions about gay men's effeminacy. This is not to say that these Bears are unfriendly. Over the course of the next several days they will generously allow me to share in their play. I'm feeling a bit playful myself just now, as I spot yet another handsome bearded man approaching the table. His eyes are clear and vibrant, and his stern expression breaks into a warm smile as he introduces himself to me. He extends his hand in welcome. I reach out to take it and notice that my own hand is trembling. *Woof.*

———

Every summer, the leathermen of the Sentinels Club meet in the woods. It is Friday evening, and although I have known most of these men for only a few hours, I feel like an old hand. Just now the sun is setting, which seems to cue my fellows that it's time to prepare for the night's revels. As I wander into the sleeping cabin, I find Adam practicing with the flogger. This is a kind of multitasseled whip, a leather-covered stalk with approximately forty leather ribbons attached to it. Each ribbon is about fifteen inches long and an inch thick. As he caresses the cabin wall with a gentle zigzag motion, Adam explains that "somebody's got to get things started." He wears only a pair of leather boots and tight leather shorts. Ted, who has been watching with me, announces that it's time he changed into something "more appropriate." I decide to change as well. I put on a pair of denim shorts, leather boots laced to midcalf, and a leather armband just above each bicep. Another cabinmate, Jack, remains in his T-shirt, jeans, and cowboy boots. When Ted returns he is wearing leather shorts and a matching chest harness. Another man has caught everyone's eye because of his smooth swimmer's build and boyish good looks; his name is Marty. As we move out to the campfire we find Marty shirtless with a pair of silver horns on his head. He looks like a cute, naughty little satyr. He travels around the campfire with a tray of brightly colored Jell-o shots. His traveling companion is a much older man, the gravelly voiced Dino. Dino's warm sociability is a nice counterpoint to Marty's somewhat shy demeanor. This is the second time I have crossed their path; they insist I take another Jell-o shot.

The campfire is stoked and going strong in an area just off the designated "play" cabin. Several men sit on bales of hay and watch the fire. There is a fair amount of traffic throughout the night as people emerge from the intense activity of the play cabin to relax by the fire for awhile. It is a warm evening, and the bugs are not particularly troublesome, so the experience is pleasant. Occasionally a man sitting by the fire gets up and ventures into the play cabin. Moans of pleasure, sounds of spanking, and rough voices issuing orders are all clearly heard at the campfire. An extensive sound system is set up in the cabin, and the music can be heard by the campfire as well. None of this activity interrupts the flow of friendly, mostly mundane conversation.

As I enter the play cabin with Jack and Ted, our threesome immediately disbands as we all check out the ongoing scenes. One area that attracts my attention is a flogging scene that Adam seems to be running. Rob and Lenny are interested in getting flogged, and Adam is accommodating them by rhythmically drawing the flogger across their naked backs. I watch for a while to get a sense of how much pressure he is applying—it is not hard, but it is not exactly gentle either. Rob and Lenny do not seem particularly responsive, yet they occasionally give some sign that they are enjoying this treatment. Adam eventually tires and, to my surprise, hands the flogger to me. I take it a bit reluctantly, but before long I find myself tentatively flogging Rob. This goes on for some time, and I am surprised to find myself completely absorbed in the task. I want to play my role well, but at the same time I do not want to give Rob more than he wants. We do not speak, but I pay close attention to his reactions. I realize that I have been neglecting Lenny, who now tries to work his way back into the scene, and for a while I take turns flogging both of them. Eventually I feel I need a break. As Rob leaves the scene he seems quiet. Sensing my concern he says only, "One thing inexperienced tops need to remember is that the bottom is always in control."

I don't know which alarms me more: the possibility that I may have hurt him, the fact that he can tell that I am inexperienced, his characterization of me as a dominant "top," or the implication that I have somehow broken the rules. When I sheepishly ask Rob about this later, he seems genuinely concerned that his remark has upset me. He explains that all he meant was that I should have done a "check in" with him after Adam handed the flogger off to me. This is how leathermen set up ground rules and lay the foundation for a trust dynamic that both parties can then play with during the scene.

But just now I have little time to consider my mistakes. Jack needs a spanking, and my attention is immediately drawn to the scene in progress behind me. Adam and his partner, Victor, intimated earlier that Jack really likes to be spanked and that "you could break the paddle on his ass," he likes it so much. Adam is using a round wooden paddle, its surface slightly smaller than a dinner plate, which distributes the force of the blow over a wider area. Jack wears only his cowboy boots at this point. He is bent over, holding the back of a chair. Adam asks me to hold him in place while he takes a few spirited whacks at Jack's butt. As I watch Adam work, the scene seems part of a well-rehearsed routine. With a voice soft and low, Adam teases Jack, "Come on now, take your punishment." Jack is trembling slightly, and I notice that he keeps his butt down until he is ready for another hit. Then he raises his buttocks and waits. This, I surmise, is how negotiation enters into the process, while allowing the role play to seem authentic and spontaneous. The butt-down position is time for Adam, as the top in this scene, to engage in some verbal mind play—firmly reminding Jack that he *must* submit, seducing him into accepting the next blow. "You know you love it." The butt-up position is time to actually play with the delivery of pain. It quickly becomes apparent that varying this part of the routine is critical to the erotic energy of the scene. I watch as Adam hesitates with the paddle, sometime for several moments, before his delivery. During the wait, time seems to hang suspended between these two men. It is an intensely intimate moment. With his butt in the air, Jack trembles slightly as he tries to prepare for the next blow, not knowing when it will come. Repeating his earlier pattern, Adam abruptly hands the paddle off to me and we switch places.

As I paddle Jack I think of music, and of theater. Often it is the pause between words, the silence between notes that structure a piece and provide its most powerful effects. This absence is vividly foregrounded as I stand over Jack, the paddle poised to strike. It seems we wait together in absolute silence, despite the variety of raucous activities underway in the cabin. I have known Jack for five hours, yet he and I are connected here, powerfully and ineffably. It is precisely the doing, the being there, the awareness of the moment that make the experience impossible to fully describe.

Much later in the evening I am back at the campfire, exhausted and amazed by what the night has revealed. Rob and his new friend Lance are having an animated discussion. Somehow, their free-ranging exchange settles on arcane points of Christian dogma and biblical interpretation. Both of them demonstrate an amazing knowledge, not only of specific passages from the Bible but also its various editions. They are especially familiar with the subtle differences between the King James and Catholic Bibles, including the deletion of the books of Ruth, Timothy, and Apocrypha from the former. They also reference several ecumenical conferences and councils held throughout history to resolve various theological disputes. Astonished, I ask them how they each know so much about this subject. I learn that Lance is a former seminarian, and Rob tells me that his interest stems from his current religious pursuits.

I want to know more, but the evening is clearly winding down. Several men have already gone to bed, and Marty has mysteriously disappeared, no doubt to a more private encounter. The discussion between Lance and Rob at last winds down, and Lance makes his way to his cabin. As I am saying good night to Rob I realize that he is not quite ready to let the evening go. He sounds wondrous and sad at the same time as he tells me of the invigorating effect Leather Camp has on him and of the evening's sole disappointment: "When I'm away from the city, when I'm in nature, I can go forever." There is a long pause before he adds pensively, "And I really wanted Marty to fuck me."

———

This is a book about Faeries, Bears, and leathermen. It is also a book about gender, sexuality, history, identity, the body, and the complex relationships among them. Somewhere between these two extremes, this book can be read as a series of gendered stories, as three distinct collective responses to a shared history. It includes a focused study of masculinity and the historical construction of its effeminate other, a summary account of the centuries-old social-historical process that has linked effeminacy with male homosexuality, an account of how men affected by this historical product have crafted distinctly different collective responses to it, and how each of these strategies is embodied. In these three cases I examine the gendered legacy that is the peculiar bequest of any man who finds his attraction toward other men leading him outside the carefully patrolled permissions of the homosocial and into the prohibited realm of the homosexual.

Thus, the book includes extensive case studies of three communities of gay/queer men responding in different ways to this gendered bequest linking homosexuality and effeminacy. The first is a group of Radical Faeries, a consensus community that incorporates a great deal of drag and parodic performance in their cultural repertoire, influenced by an eclectic array of neopagan, mythopoetic, and radically queer cultural strands. The second is a Bear community, a much more conventional group whose members are drawn to the company of men who are larger and hairier than the reigning gay aesthetic ideal. Through various cultural practices, most of which are riffs off various identifications with bears in the wild, Bear men seek to naturalize and normalize gay masculinity by striving toward regular guy status. The third case is a community of gay leathermen, who sponsor a diverse and innovative sexual culture that flourishes alongside a demanding and restrictive homage to masculinity. In the following chapters I situate each of these communities in its contemporary history and cast each in turn as a collective cultural response to a much older historical impulse toward the feminization of same-sex desire. How, and to what extent, have these subcultural sexual communities been influenced by this history? How are the politics, lifestyles, and desires of these men shaped by this history? How are their identities constructed in community? What cultural and sexual innovations play a part in this response? How are gender compliance and resistance produced in these communities?

While many of these men may understand themselves as having achieved a kind of personal liberation from its power, all of them inhabit a social landscape of historically sedimented connection between same-sex desire and effeminacy. Each must contend with a resilient social narrative of feminization that continues to shape his social, sexual, and political life in profound and enduring ways. Bears respond with a normalizing strategy, striving to be seen as regular guys who just happen to like other guys. Faeries respond with a gleeful embrace of the feminine, a campy celebration of effeminacy that contests its stigmatizing power. Leathermen respond with an exaggerated masculinity and a hyperextension of masculine power relations, which recasts these relations as "play." Moreover, within the respective communities, their members' responses are written onto bodies. Bear men carries their hirsute, generous frames with pride. Faeries adorn themselves with cheap faux jewelry and thrift-shop dresses as they dance before the goddess. Leathermen place their bodies at the intersection of pleasure and pain in a way that profoundly troubles the distinction between the two.

The Effeminacy Effect

For gay men, effeminate traits are:
Natural (834) 32%
A learned behavior (796) 31%
Not Sure or Depends (923) 36%
—SURVEY RESULTS POSTED ON STRAIGHTACTING.COM

Perhaps more than anything else, this is a book about the tenacious power of gender. With respect to gay- and queer-identified men, the evidence is as close as your local bookstore, television, or computer. In 1982, a novelty book entitled *Real Men Don't Eat Quiche*, by Bruce Feirstein, became an instant best seller. The book is a tongue-in-cheek guide designed to help heterosexual men secure their masculine identity and avoid looking like an effeminate "quiche eater." In addition to quizzes and cartoons, the book is filled with prescriptions and proscriptions, many in the form of lists comparing real men with quiche eaters, for example, "Three things you won't find in a real man's pocket: (1) lip balm; (2) breath freshener; (3) opera tickets" (Feirstein 1982, 42). That the book was enormously successful is perhaps not surprising; its publication seemed perfectly timed to exploit men's burgeoning postfeminist gender anxieties. What is surprising is that 1982 also saw the publication of another guide to masculinity, this one entitled The *Butch Manual,* by Clark Henley, which targeted an exclusively gay male readership. The differences between the two books are not nearly as striking as their similarities. Consider this example from *The Butch Manual:* "Things tricks will not find in butch's bathroom: (1) a soft plastic toilet seat, (2) designer towels with a matching bath mat, (3) a shower curtain" (Henley 1982, 76).

Twenty-five years later this spirited revival of masculinity continues, with the parallels in the gay and straight male communities more apparent than ever. In 1999 a comedy variety show called *The Man Show* debuted on a U.S. cable television channel and enjoyed high ratings throughout its six-season run. Billed as the "anti-Oprah," the show's humor proceeds from an unapologetic recuperation and boisterous celebration of "real" masculinity—political correctness be damned. On *The Man Show* real men are relentlessly heterosexual but denigrate and objectify women (gleefully—each episode ends with images of busty young women jumping on trampolines). Male homosexuality is figured on the show as inherently effeminate, and the show's hosts spend much of their time defining the real man against the affectations and histrionics of the effeminate homosexual. Curiously, at about the same time as *The Man Show* aired, a Web site targeting gay men, straightacting.com, debuted, billing itself as "masculinely politically incorrect" and dedicated to disparaging gay effeminacy. The emergence of straightacting.com can be seen as the crest of a wave of anti-effeminacy that began in reaction to the brief period of post-Stonewall (see below) gender experimentation in the gay community. Since that time, the majority of gay men have been steadily reinvesting themselves in masculinity. Personal ads placed by American gay men now routinely include phrases such as "straight acting and appearing," "no fems," and "masculine GM [gay male] seeks same." Straightacting.com sponsors an ongoing series of "unscientific" polls that are nevertheless instructive for what they reveal about many gay men's continuing concern with the stigma of effeminacy. Despite the powerfully divisive categories of sexual orientation actively sustained by their respective audiences, both *The Man Show* and straightacting.com acknowledge a historical legacy linking male homosexuality with effeminacy. The gender rules proposed are virtually identical in each of these two worlds; both reflect what Brannon (1976) has so succinctly referred to as "the relentless repudiation of the feminine."

The rapidity of this transformation in communities of gay men is thrown into high relief when one considers that as recently as 1968, Quentin Crisp presumed to speak for all homosexual men when he wrote of his doomed search for the "great dark man" of his sexual and romantic fantasies:

[The] problem that confronts homosexuals is that they set out to win the love of a "real" man. If they succeed, they fail. A man who "goes with" other men is not what they would call a real man. This conundrum is incapable of resolution, but that does not make homosexuals give it up. They only search more frantically and with less and less discretion for more and more masculine men. (Crisp 1983, 56–57)

Crisp eventually resigns himself to the fact that "There is no great dark man," a capitulation that draws a sharp rebuke from Michael Bronski just over two decades later. "Quentin Crisp is wrong: We have *become* our own Great Dark Men, our own obscure and not-so-obscure objects of desire" (Bronski 2001, 62). What happened in the intervening years, of course, has everything to do with the Stonewall riots, which took place in New York City in June 1969 and are traditionally considered the beginning of gay liberation. In the years immediately following Stonewall the typical gay man in the United States was perfectly positioned to challenge the reigning gender regime by, as John Stoltenberg (1989) puts it, "refusing to be a man." The riots themselves began when drag queens (the most thoroughly feminized members of the New York gay community) refused to tolerate ongoing police harassment. Their arsenal of resistance included the use of parody, as a line of drag queens kicked up their heels in unison, singing in gleeful defiance to astonished members of the New York Police Department (Duberman 1993, 201):

We are the Stonewall girls
We wear our hair in curls
We wear no underwear
We show our pubic hair
We wear our dungarees
Above our nelly knees!

It makes sense, of course, given the discursive construction of the male homosexual as a "failed" or "feminized" man, that resistance should take this form. In the early part of the twentieth century even the famous sexologist Magnus Hirschfeld, an early advocate of homosexual emancipation, spoke of the homosexual male as the "pitiful effeminate." According to the popular nineteenth-century conception of the homosexual as "invert," gay men were really "women trapped in men's bodies" (Levine 1998, 1). Terms like "variant," "uranian," and Freud's "arrested development" were also popularized during this period (Miller 1995, 13–28). All of these contained some implicit connection between men's same-sex behavior and femininity. Reporting on the key role of drag queens in the Stonewall riots of 1969, one gay publication playfully acknowledged this connection when it referred to the riots as "the hairpin drop heard round the world" (D'Emilio 1983, 232). As I demonstrate in chapter 2, in the decades before Stonewall, the conflation of gender with sexual identity by various experts meant that, come the revolution, "gender trouble"[1] was bound to play an integral part of the movement's tactical repertoire. This tactic was deployed for whimsical purposes (as in the song of the "Stonewall girls" above), but it was also used to make more serious political points in the early phase of gay liberation:

At a session [of the American Psychiatric Association convention in San Francisco] on homosexuality a young bearded gay man danced around the auditorium in a red dress, while other homosexuals and lesbians scattered in the audience shouted "Genocide!" and "Torture!" during the reading of a paper on aversion therapy. (D'Emilio 1983, 235)

Furthermore, these early activists were committed to challenging the gender order in more fundamental ways, as evidenced by lengthy passages in the 1969 "Gay Manifesto," which condemned male chauvinism and challenged gendered stereotypes:

There is a tendency among "homophile" groups to deplore gays who play visible roles—the queens and the nellies. As liberated gays, we must take a clear stand. 1) Gays who stand out have become our first martyrs. They came out and withstood disapproval before the rest of us did. 2) If they have suffered from being open, it is straight society whom we must indict, not the queen. (Miller 1995, 385)

By valorizing the effeminate homosexual, this text radically reinterprets the pre-Stonewall connection between male homosexuality and femininity, just as gay liberation sought to reinterpret homosexuality itself. If Stonewall marked the end of the "gay is sick" paradigm and the beginning of "gay pride," these words in the "Gay Manifesto" sought to instill a lasting pride in, and respect for, the as-yet-unnamed practice of gender trouble.

However, despite a remarkable degree of success in achieving the first of these objectives, the second was easily forgotten as the hypermasculine "clone" image quickly gained status in Greenwich Village during the early 1970s (Levine 1998). The image promoted bodybuilding, sexual promiscuity, and an exaggeratedly masculine dress and appearance (among the most popular clone looks were the construction worker, the military man, and the cowboy). Men who adopted the clone look repudiated femininity and ensured that, at least in terms of the gender order, the struggle for the acceptance of alternative sexual identities would be conducted, as critic Ian Young observes, "on the oppressor's terms" (1995, 100). Henceforth any talk of lionizing the drag queen as the brave revolutionary tenaciously battling an oppressive gender regime would be overwhelmed by a frenzied rush to masculinity on the part of a majority of urban gay men. In short, many gay men in the United States and elsewhere in the industrialized world chose to distance themselves from the most extreme forms of gender trouble as soon as they had the political and economic means to do so. Today, as gay men increasingly seek out other men who are "straight acting and appearing," they distance themselves even further from disruptive gender practice. Connell recently concluded a study of contemporary gay male cultures in Australia by observing the emergence of what she calls "the very straight gay": "The gendered eroticism of these men, the masculine social presence most of them maintain, their focus on privatized couple relationships and their lack of solidarity with feminism point in the same direction. There is no open challenge to the gender order here" (Connell 1995a, 161).

This general cultural backdrop provides the point of departure for each of my case study communities. From this point, each community has crafted its own collective strategy, and each is more complex than it initially appears. While Bears might be seen as most closely approximating the kind of reinvestment in normative masculinity described above, they have also nurtured innovative and resistant sexual practices that cannot be dismissed. Ostensibly, leathermen can be seen as reinforcing certain aspects of normative masculinity. But this characterization is also too simple, as the intensity of their devotion and the radical reinterpretation of the body present startling challenges to normative masculinity. Faeries are seemingly engaged in a gender-bending project directly opposed to the Bear strategy, but as we shall see, this ideological commitment is not without its practical complications.

A "Tool Kit" Approach to Theorizing Gender and Sexuality

As far as I'm concerned, I have a very pragmatic relationship with authors: I turn to them as I would to fellows and craft-masters, in the sense those words had in the mediaeval guild—people you can ask to give you a hand in difficult situations.

—PIERRE BOURDIEU, *IN OTHER WORDS: ESSAYS TOWARDS A REFLEXIVE SOCIOLOGY*

My theoretical approach is pragmatic and might be characterized as casting a wide theoretical net. In terms more familiar to sociologists, I might frame my use of theory as similar to Swidler's (1986) "tool kit" approach. Taking this line of approach I conceive of theories as cultural artifacts that can be used, with varying degrees of success, to help make sense of *some* aspects of *specific* kinds of phenomena. This approach means that

I address some aspects, but probably not others, and implies an idiographic rather than a nomothetic approach to explanation. Furthermore, I do not make any claims to comprehensive explanations, preferring to content myself with partial, contingent explanations. While the analogy with Swidler's tool kit is perhaps the most accessible, it should not be overextended. First, Swidler (1986, 277) assigns the importance of the cultural tool kit to its role in the construction of what she calls "strategies of action," incorporating more or less settled habits, moods, sensibilities, and worldviews, while in my appropriation the tool kit is used for something more like "strategies of explanation" that are necessarily consciously responsive to the novel and fluid characteristics of the object under study. Swidler (1986, 277) writes, "People do not build lines of action from scratch, choosing actions one at a time as efficient means to given ends. Instead, they construct chains of action beginning with at least some pre-fabricated links." I argue that my theoretical tool kit approach obligates the researcher to eschew just such "pre-fabricated links" to ensure an appropriate fit between the particular practice or problem to be explained and the theoretical tool selected for that purpose. Finally, on Swidler's view that the cultural tool kit is used to construct an ostensibly coherent strategy for action, although it is not necessarily rational, it is a course of action that makes holistic sense to the actor himself or herself. Taking the tool kit concept from the level of practical activity to the abstractions of theory, even the most carefully selected tools yield only partial (and contingent) understandings, limited to particular aspects of social phenomena.

This raises larger epistemological questions, which lead to the apparently incongruous intersection of empiricism and postmodernism. While postmodern theorists have made vitally important contributions to our understanding of gendered sexuality, many of the basic assumptions underlying postmodern theorizing make empirical application problematic at best and all but preclude empirical tests. Nevertheless, attempts have been made recently to recast the tension between empiricism and postmodernism in a more productive light. For example, Mirchandani (2005, 86) argues that "sociologists have recognized the potential of a postmodern theory that turns its attention to empirical concerns." With greater "epistemological modesty" this can be accomplished productively in areas such as time-space reorganization, risk society, consumer capitalism, and postmodern ethics. I would add postmodern gender and sexualities studies to this list. Moreover, it strikes me as unlikely that any single theory or even a single theoretical paradigm could adequately address the questions I bring to this study.

Both Text and Practice: The Postmodern Ethnographic Challenge

Furthermore, if the gap between empiricism and postmodernism is to be bridged in any meaningful way, it is probably best to recast the tension as a both/and (Collins 1990) rather than an either/or relationship. Sociologist Ken Plummer lays the groundwork for just such an approach with observations on the analysis of sexual stories:

> There is much in common here with what is often called postmodern social theory except that this sociological approach offers distinctive advantages because it does not stay at the level of textual analysis: it insists that story production and consumption is an empirical social process, involving a stream of joint actions in local contexts themselves bound into wider negotiated social worlds. Texts are connected to lives, actions, contests, and society. It is not a question of "hyperrealities" and "simulacra" but of practical activities, daily doings and contested truths. (Plummer 1995, 24)

Elsewhere Plummer (1995, 19) remarks that "Although recent developments in literary theory and cultural studies will prove useful . . . *it is time to go beyond the text* (emphasis in original), and in a 1994 article with Arlene Stein says, "There is a dangerous tendency for the new queer theorists to ignore 'real' queer life as it is materially experienced across the world, while they play with the free-floating signifiers of texts" (Stein and Plummer 1994, 184). The articulation of this position in turn provoked a spirited critique from Judith Halberstam (1998, 12) in her introduction to *Female Masculinity*: "In an effort to restore sociology to its proper place within the study of sexuality, Stein and Plummer have reinvested here in a clear and verifiable difference between the real and the textual, and they designate textual analysis as a totally insular activity with no referent, no material consequences, and no intellectual gain." While Halberstam admits that Stein and Plummer are "clearly not suggesting merely a quantitative approach to the study of sexuality and queer subcultures," and she eventually advocates an approach that combines "information culled from people with information culled from texts" (Halberstam 1998, 12), she misconstrues Stein and Plummer's position, primarily in attributing an exaggerated polarity to their distinction between texts and lived experience. While I do think Plummer intends to make a distinction between "hyperrealities and simulacra" on the one hand and "practical activities" subject to empirical investigation on the other, I do not hear him asking researchers to abandon textual analysis altogether. Stein and Plummer's position strikes me as a reminder that as researchers of gender and sexuality we have not paid sufficient attention to the *interplay* between both textual representations and empirical practice. It might be argued that the sense of "going beyond" the text clearly privileges empirical/ethnographic modes of knowledge construction at the expense of textual analysis, but the statement might just as easily be interpreted as a testament to the power of texts, hyperrealities, and simulacra to shape practical activity, a reading that would underscore the need to investigate these effects. Moreover, there is not as much distance between the positions advocated by Halberstam and Plummer as Halberstam's remarks might lead one to believe.

Some Useful Theoretical Tools

Two of the communities I studied, the Bears and the leathermen, actively construct masculinity in their communities, while the Radical Faeries are distinguished by their collective rejection of traditional gender arrangements, including normative masculinity. At the same time, each of these groups is evaluated by the larger culture and framed by the hierarchical logic of hegemonic masculinity (Connell 1987, 1995). I am drawn to the concept of hegemonic masculinity because it helps me understand how gender resistance is related to social reproduction.[2] Even as they resist, Bears, Faeries, and leathermen reproduce a gender order that deems them deficient *as men*. This stigmatization fuels their collective resistance and identity work while at the same time reproducing their subordinate status. Branding gay men as insufficiently masculine, usually with the help of broad stereotypes of effeminacy, is an example of this subordinating tendency. Moreover, this ranking tendency broadly reflects Brannon's (1976) "relentless repudiation of the feminine," in that women are subordinated to men, but also men who are deemed feminine are subordinated to normatively masculine men. Men who may identify as heterosexual but deviate in significant ways from the ideal are also stigmatized, which again registers a symbolic blurring with femininity. Of course, homosexuality, and its presumed effeminacy, is not the only axis on which certain groups of men are subordinated. Race, class, and physical ability are also means of ordering and evaluating masculinities.

The concept of gender as an activity, something one *does* rather than something one *is* (West and Zimmerman 1987), continues to suggest compelling explanations and highlights the construction of gender across a vast array of social situations. This concept is eminently practical for looking at the identity work done in Bear, Faerie, and leather communities, as so much of it has to do with constructing gendered identities. While the concept of "doing gender" has little to say about the agency and autonomy of the actors involved, gender performativity (Butler 1990, 1993) problematizes the subjectivities of the "doers" behind such gendered deeds. From this perspective, gendered communities like Bears, Faeries, and leathermen are not so much the result of individual choices freely made as they are the discursive effects of an unstable gender system. Still, Butler's position does allow for some limited agency, achieved through parody and citationality. Bears, Faeries, and leathermen can (in different ways) be seen as engaging in parody and citationality. The extent to which community members see their activities this way is a matter for empirical investigation.

My interest in embodiment is twofold. I am interested first in what Connell has referred to as "body reflexive practices" (1995, 59–64), in that each of these communities is a product of a distinct and fairly recent history, yet these histories have taken up the body of the Bear, the Faerie, and the leatherman in particular ways and with particular consequences. This line of thinking sets up a productive way of considering the body's response to social processes, particularly gendered processes. I find a more elaborate treatment of this idea in the concept of "habitus" (Bourdieu 1977, 1990b), which has a prominent place in my theoretical tool kit. Although he originally proposed the concept as a way of illustrating how social class is "written on the body," toward the end of his life Bourdieu (2001) applied it to gender.

Second, I am interested in how desire, pleasure, and sexuality are embodied. Having witnessed the carnage of the AIDS pandemic, I have often wondered at the heteronormativity of a homosexual erotic that places penetrative sex at the center of its erotic universe. It strikes me as particularly ironic, inasmuch as gay men have clearly demonstrated the protean capacities of the body to produce nonnormative pleasures. In studying an environment where penetrative intercourse is strongly linked with HIV transmission, I am interested in efforts to dislodge penetrative intercourse from its "pride of place." At the same time I am mindful of the logic of prohibition, which endows prohibited practices with fetishistic appeal. In trying to reimagine the body and its pleasures, I am drawn to concepts like the "desiring machine" (Deleuze and Guattari 1977), whereby pleasures are dispersed across the body in a less genitally centered erotic. With his concept of "groupings, " or dissident sexual communities collectively working toward just such an embodied reimagining of the erotic, Hocquenghem (1996) suggests the social, rather than individual, character of this endeavor. While feminists have typically been concerned with how phallic sex reinforces relationships of domination and objectification, my concern is with reordering pleasure in ways that deemphasize phallic sex but maintain a premium on pleasure.

The postmodern process of social saturation, and specifically Gergen's (1991) concept of the saturated self, renders the broad cultural backdrop informing each of my case study communities. Gergen describes a contemporary world of dizzying social stimulation wrought by rapid advances in technology, which opens previously unimagined possibilities for fluid and fractional identity formations. He describes the contemporary self as "populated" through the distinct and often conflicting demands of daily life, and an expansive sense of "multiphrenia," which is "a result of the populated self's efforts to exploit the technologies of relationship" (Gergen 1991, 74). I see each of my case study communities, in various ways, reacting *against* the postmodern conditions Gergen describes. The Faerie's sanctuary, the Bear's bar night, and the leatherman's dungeon each provide an *identity cove*, a calm place of relative stability, safe from the roiling postmodern identity storms described by Gergen. Paradoxically, each of these communities is, in its own way, eminently postmodern.

Finally, the ethnographic travelogue that opens this chapter suggests the importance of place for my research communities. The Faerie sanctuary, Bear Camp, and the leather dungeon all serve as what Brekhus (2003, 25) terms "identity potent," or high density, settings. These are settings that "elicit a greater concentration and higher visibility of marked identities. Such spatial and temporal enclaves serve as 'amplifiers' for identity." They are contrasted with everyday "identity diluted" settings, which "have an overall muting effect on the volume of identity" (Brekhus 2003, 26). All of my subjects, to varying degrees, regularly travel from diluted to potent identity spaces as a part of their community participation, with varying effects. Also relevant are the three fundamental aspects of identity construction posited by Brekhus (2003): density, "how concentrated or diluted an identity trait is, relative to one's overall 'presentation of self'" (24); duration, "the length or percentage of time that one performs a certain facet of an identity" (24); and dominance, a more comprehensive attribute that Brekhus describes as "the product of duration times density, or the degree to which an identity attribute occupies one's whole self" (28).

Nature in Theory and Practice

Recent developments in queer theory have drawn attention to the tendency within identity politics to overemphasize the importance of categories based on sexual orientation ("gay," "lesbian," "bisexual," etc.). To date, these critiques have not been adequately synthesized to reveal the various ways in which gay/queer men's identity as *men* may be affecting their same-sex desires and practices. To the extent that most men (regardless of how they may come to identify themselves with respect to sexual orientation) are socialized under many of the same general norms of masculinity, this socialization remains a neglected topic in the sociology of sexualities. As Connell observes of her interviews with gay men:

> To emphasize this complexity is not to deny the significance of social structure, nor to say we cannot see a shape in what is happening. The same logical moments appear, despite the variety of detail, in all these narratives. They are (a) an engagement with hegemonic masculinity, (b) a closure of sexuality around relationships with men, (c) participation in the collective practices of a gay community. (Connell 1995, 160)

Other scholars have made compelling arguments for "denaturalizing" the taken-for-granted links between biological sex, gender norms, and sexual desire, arguing for a view of these relationships as socially constructed, that is, developed and reinforced primarily through social interaction. This is explicit in Butler's work (1990, 1993) and implicit in the work of most of the theorists who have informed my analysis in this study. Butler's view assumes that the heterosexual matrix is buttressed by a naturalizing narrative that reifies and privileges it in relation to nonnormative sexual practices. Thus, in sexually dissident communities, one might expect to find a rejection of naturalizing narratives in favor of a heightened appreciation of the constructed nature of sexuality. This is an eminently sensible argument; sexual dissidents have for centuries been violated both physically and psychologically by physicians, politicians, and religious authorities speaking in the defense of "nature" and the "natural order."

However, this assumption is confounded by a robust array of naturalizing narratives emanating from various gay and ostensibly queer cultures. How to explain, for example, the strong allegiance to essentialist/naturalistic narratives evidenced by gay activists who emphasize that their sexual preference is "not a choice" and that they were "born that way"? The naturalistic narratives buttressing identities like "top" and "bottom"? Even the rhetoric of "barebacking" (anal sex without a condom) incorporates naturalizing narratives, as evidenced by the following excerpts from a popular barebacking Web site targeting gay men (barebackjack.com 2001):

Leading gay men back to *real* sex since 1998.

Nearly 1,000,000 raw-fuckin' men have come into this backroom cruising for *skin to skin* sex.

Rubbers are left outside, because in Jack's back room *we fuck like men*!

And *true men* fuck bareback.

Barebacking is considered taboo even though it is the *most natural act of intimacy* two people can enjoy.

They thought by getting men to don condoms and creating aggressive safe-sex awareness programs they would keep people from *doing what comes naturally*.

The act of inseminating your partner seems to bring up some kind *of ancient human connection* within us. I think that's *pretty basic*. (Emphases added)

This reconfiguration of barebacking reenlists nature in support of a practice that has more typically been constructed as an abomination *against* nature. While I sing in the chorus critiquing "the voice of the natural," (i.e., those strategic and selective deployments of nature that endorse particular practices, moral values, or institutions over others), I also argue that any project to denaturalize the complex relationships between sex, gender, and sexuality is problematic precisely because in practice we *always* construct some understanding of our relationship with nature. Thus I investigate empirically how attempts to denaturalize heteronormative and patriarchal notions of sex and gender fare in actual practice in communities that ostensibly are the sites of sexual dissidence and gender trouble. My particular focus is on how these naturalizing narratives are constructed among Radical Faeries, Bears, and gay leathermen as they attempt to negotiate their problematic, feminized positions, and how certain gendered and masculinist assumptions are smuggled back into these narrative constructions. Moreover, I hope to demonstrate that the presence of these resilient naturalizing narratives in nonnormative sexual communities suggests their importance in the construction of both garden-variety and "exotic" sexual experience and points to a neglected link between normative and nonnormative sexual cultures. If they are to succeed, theoretical projects that seek to denaturalize sex and gender need to acknowledge this.

Identity in Community

One of the mainstays of new social movement theory is that identities like "Bear," "Faerie," or "leatherman" do not precede, but rather are actively constructed and sustained through, participation in social movement communities (Taylor and Whittier 1992; Laraña, Johnston, and Gusfield,

1994). Social movement scholars have recently observed that "the collective search for identity is a central aspect of movement formation" (Johnston, Laraña, and Gusfield, 1994, 10). This insight is confirmed by a number of empirical studies investigating identity construction in a variety of contexts.[3] Two sociologists who have written extensively on the subject of gay/queer identity formation are Steven Seidman (1988, 1993, 1994, 2001, 2003) and Joshua Gamson (1995, 1996, 1997, 2000).

Seidman (1993, 1994, 2001) has made important contributions in meticulously chronicling the social and political transformations in gay identities in American politics, from the essentialism of the homophile period through the liberationist phase to the rise of identity politics and the ethnic model and finally to more recent poststructuralist and queer perspectives. He observes that over time, the sense of solidarity offered by the ethnic model began to splinter, as it became clear that it served to marginalize the experiences of some gays and lesbians while it celebrated others. Accompanying this development was scholarship questioning the unity and relativizing the existence of gay identity. This led to a renewed interest in the social construction of identity and eventually to the subversion of identity itself, which stands at the center of queer anti-identity projects. In response to the challenges posed by queer theory, Seidman (1993, 137) calls for a shift away from a preoccupation with self and identity and toward a perspective that takes into account the self's embeddedness in a matrix of cultural and institutional practices. In his more recent work, Seidman (2003) detects a move toward the normalization of gay and lesbian identities, arguing that the social and cultural conditions supporting the closet have attenuated significantly over the past several decades. However, even as they enjoy greater social acceptance, gay men and lesbians continue to negotiate a thoroughly heteronormative social environment. Throughout his work, Seidman reminds us that gay identities are responsive to particular social and historical circumstances, not the least of which have to do with the problematic relations between communities of sexual difference and a mainstream sexual politics seeking to erase this difference.

Gamson's work, on the other hand, concentrates on the internal dynamics of movement communities themselves and how these symbolic and political struggles yield varying identity outcomes. In what is arguably his most familiar work, Gamson (1995) explores the contradictory tensions within identity movements embracing a dissident sexual politics that increasingly seeks to dismantle and undermine stable identity categories. The dilemma is an exquisite one, as identity categories enable both political oppression and empowerment. But Gamson is less concerned with discerning which of the identity productive/deconstructive moves represents the more effective political strategy than he is in determining how this tension plays itself out, and to what effect. For example, in an article on two gay film festival groups fostering distinctly different types of identity work, Gamson (1996) demonstrates how the festival organizations mediate collective identity. While the Experimental Festival sponsors a deconstructive identity narrative, across town the New Festival is engaged in more traditional identity construction. Again, Gamson resists adjudicating between these two strategies and concentrates on the organizational environments informing each group. This same concern with internal dynamics informs a later article (Gamson 1997) detailing the boundary work performed by identity movements when they encounter problematic membership claims. The article examines processes of inclusion and exclusion accompanying the expulsion of the North American Man/Boy Love Association from the International Lesbian and Gay Association and the decision of the Michigan Womyn's Music Festival to exclude male-to-female transsexuals. Gamson concludes that these exclusionary moves are best understood as public statements, designed to clarify the symbolic boundaries of legitimate movement membership for particular audiences, and that a full explanation for the tone and timing of such moves requires a consideration of the communicative context informing the movement.

While neither Seidman nor Gamson ignores the subjective orientations of identity movement participants, subjective dispositions are not their primary source of data. Their work emphasizes the larger cultural and institutional arrangements bearing on the identity work being done in these movements, and their analysis is framed primarily in terms of political implications. The task I have taken up is somewhat different in that my primary focus is on how the identity narratives produced in each of my communities meet specific emotional needs (rather than political objectives) for participants. Thus I am more concerned with analyzing microsocial settings, interpersonal processes, and intrapersonal matters like embodiment than I am with the meso- and macro-level relationships that concern Seidman and Gamson. This is not to imply that these emotional needs are not, in and of themselves, political in some important respects or that the groups themselves are apolitical. Indeed, the reason I spend so much time establishing historical context (chapter 2) for my case studies is to foreground the politics of gender that constitute these three communities. But my analysis remains anchored in the subjective understanding of participants, who for the most part, when speaking about community membership, do not speak about politics. In this limited sense my approach may be characterized as Weberian, but this is certainly not the only theoretical perspective informing my work (see previous section). Moreover, while both Seidman and Gamson are keenly attuned to the tension between poststructuralist anti-identity narratives and more traditional essentialist narratives, my approach assumes that this tension has been (at least provisionally) resolved by community members. While the three distinct identity narratives I document here may be understood by academics outside these communities as evidence of the fluid, contingent, and protean nature of postmodern identities, the point I emphasize here is that from the perspective of participants themselves, quite the opposite is the case. Membership in these communities represents a refuge from, rather than an embrace of, the destabilized identities posited by poststructuralist theorists. Against the grain of the deconstructionist impulse, my research subjects actively embrace identity and "renaturalize" stigmatized subjectivities. In the context of postmodernity, community narratives become a vital source of refuge from the uncertainties and knowledge shifts in the larger social world, most significantly as a source of stable knowledge of the self and reality. Again, this refuge cannot help but have political implications, and I trust that in what follows that I have not ignored these, but my primary concern is with capturing the subjective orientations of the participants themselves. This approach reveals that, despite the gender politics informing each of their communities (Bears are interested in repudiating effeminacy and capturing "authentic" masculinity, leathermen respond to the stigma of effeminacy with an exaggerated masculinity, and Faeries celebrate and embrace the feminine), members understand themselves as responding to nonpolitical cues. This identification is undoubtedly related to matters of privilege and how it shapes consciousness; each of these communities is overwhelmingly white, male, and middle class. However, the fact remains that identities fostered in these communities are understood by participants as authentic and, to a surprising degree, essential.

Doing It: Methods, Data, and Positionality

A queer methodology, in a way, is a scavenger methodology that uses different methods to collect and produce information on subjects who have been deliberately or accidentally excluded from traditional studies of human behavior. The queer methodology attempts to combine methods that are often cast as being at odds with each other, and it refuses the academic compulsion toward disciplinary coherence.

—JUDITH HALBERSTAM, *FEMALE MASCULINITY*

In the past, sexological studies have typically investigated the role of gender through a narrow empirical focus on quantifiable survey data. These studies have generally failed to adequately contextualize same-sex behavior in terms of the gendered meanings that contribute to sexual desire. Furthermore, these studies typically failed to place gendered sexuality in historical context, paying little if any attention to the sociocultural development of masculinity norms and their changing relationship to sexual behaviors across a variety of cultural and historical settings. My research addresses these deficiencies by combining an in-depth, qualitative assessment of gay/queer subcultures with detailed historical context. Furthermore, I exploit my own position in the field as a source of data.

My case study communities were chosen for their suitability along several dimensions, the most prominent being theoretical relevance. I used a number of data collection methods, including participant and nonparticipant observation (Lofland and Lofland 1995; Pierce 1995; Burawoy, 1991), semistructured in-depth interviews (Seidman 1991; Briggs 1986; Douglas 1985), and historical-comparative research (Kiser and Hechter 1991; Quadagno and Knapp 1992; Tilly 1984). All names of research subjects included in the book are pseudonyms.

Historical data were gleaned primarily from secondary sources through library research, supplemented by archival material for the leather and Faerie case histories. Ethnographic data were drawn from fieldwork and supplemented with twenty-three in-depth interviews. Although I did not carry a journal with me at all times during my time in the field, I found opportunities to take notes in private settings from time to time. These notes were immediately transcribed upon my return home. Interviews ranged from one to four hours in length, with the average interview running between ninety minutes and two hours. Interview subjects were chosen carefully, based on observations in the field. I strove for subjects who varied on as many dimensions as I thought theoretically relevant—support for/dissent from prevailing group norms, length of time of association with the community, my estimate of the subject's level of sexual activity, traditional/nontraditional gender attitudes, and so forth. In each community I made a special effort to interview the recognized leaders. I was able to interview the presidents of both the Bear and the leather organizations. The Faeries eschew this kind of formal organization and have no "official" leaders; in this case I interviewed several "grannies," the designation given to members who have been active in this particular Faerie band for many years.

No one approached for an interview declined my request. To my surprise, I generally had very little trouble scheduling interviews. I had anticipated a great deal of difficulty in this area, due to the sensitive nature of the interviews. I attribute the fact that I did not encounter these problems to my time spent in the field and the rapport I was able to build with members of each community. I found all three communities welcoming and extremely supportive of my research. Interview subjects were told little about the study beyond the fact that it concerned gender and gay subcultures. All interview subjects came from middle-class backgrounds; all were white. This was a fair reflection of the overwhelmingly white, middle-class composition of the communities from which they came.

During my graduate career my attention to issues of self in research had been primed most effectively by two life-history studies that address the interaction of social forces on specific researchers and their careers. The first is Laslett's (1990) study of William Fielding Ogburn, a major figure in American sociology. In her study Laslett shows how the course of Ogburn's career was largely determined by prevailing norms of masculinity, and how these norms privileged scientific sociology while feminizing Ogburn's early interests in applied sociology and social work. The second study is my own investigation of the life of Dr. Edward Sagarin (1913–1986), a sociologist of deviance who wrote more than thirty-five books and seventy-five research essays during his long career (Hennen 1996). Sagarin was also a gay man who, early in his career, critiqued the prevailing "gay is sick" paradigm in his then groundbreaking book *The Homosexual in America: A Subjective Approach* (1951), writing under the pseudonym Donald Webster Cory. His subsequent disagreement with members of the New York Mattachine Society (an early homophile organization) caused him to completely reverse his position. He renounced not only his earlier work but also his own homosexuality. He insisted that sociologists should cease researching homosexuality since it was nothing more than a reification. He went on to write disparagingly of the nascent gay community, consistently emphasizing its pathological character. This spiteful move apparently provided Sagarin with a strategy for distancing himself from Donald Webster Cory and the emotional pain suffered at the hands of the Mattachine militants, while at the same time offering a way to rebuild a sense of personal efficacy and influence within the academic profession of sociology. Sagarin clearly associated homosexuality with subjectivity, uncontrolled emotion, impotence, and weakness, while he associated heterosexuality with objectivity, control, virility, and power.

Both studies serve as cautionary tales for my work as an ethnographer. From them I have gained an appreciation of the *positive* role of emotion in fieldwork, and I have tried to put this appreciation to practical use with what I call the "emotional interrogation" of field notes. The method involves rereading field notes, sometime after they have been composed and after the experiences recorded therein have presumably been fully assimilated. The method requires a high degree of self-monitoring, as the objective is to take careful notice of emotional responses triggered by the text, with special attention paid to gaps, silences, and the exclusion of material deemed too emotionally "hot" yet still within memory. With this method of interrogating my prior choices, I feel I have been able to extend my analysis and open my research to new questions.[4]

Two specific issues bearing on this project have to do with the sexual content of my interviews and the fact that the study is centered on gay/queer communities. Plummer (1995) touches on both of these issues when he remarks that "Stories of 'homosexuality' have recently changed" (81), concurrent with the formation of new communities to hear them. Plummer sees this relationship as symbiotic: "For narratives to flourish there must be a community to hear . . . for communities to hear there must be stories which weave together their history, their identity, their politics. The one—community—feeds upon and into the other—story" (87). Thus, for Plummer, storytelling is intimately related to identity formation. "Of course," he concedes, "this is just what the medical practitioners were doing in the nineteenth century when they created their rogue's gallery of perverts. But now the identity is no longer imposed, stigmatizingly, from without. It is instead embraced, willingly, from within" (86). The case studies that follow richly illustrate this process of identity in community through storytelling, and I feel my interviews have proven effective in capturing this phenomenon.

Against the positive science emphasis on distance and objectivity, a number of gay/lesbian ethnographers have written recently of the advantages of, as one such writer put it, "being gay and doing field work" (Williams 1996). Citing Jackson (1989), Williams discusses the positive rapport that gay/lesbian ethnographers may enjoy when researching not only queer cultures but other types of marginalized communities as well.[5] Roscoe attributes this rapport to a sensitivity to borders:

Ultimately, I believe the gay affinity for borders derives from the fundamental experience of being outsiders. Gay men and lesbians are participant-observers in heterosexual culture, whether in the field or at home. They survive by being sensitive to all borders—whether social conventions or rules of discourse. In short, the postmodern subject, whose identity is divided and dispersed, whose subject position is multiply determined and constituted, might very well be a lesbian or gay anthropologist writing lesbian and gay cultures. (Roscoe 1996, 204)

Burkhart (1996) chronicles the changes in his research interests and success in the field in terms of a growing acceptance of his same-sex orientation. He writes of the "costly stance of emotional neutrality" (34) early in his career, as contrasted with the insights of his later career, wherein he cautions against reveling in the "outsider" status that Williams and Roscoe seem to celebrate: "A rhetorical marking of anthropologists in general, and of lesbian and gay anthropologists in particular, is counterproductive. Such psychologistic notions frame collective issues as idiosyncratic, personal conflicts. Thus, they serve to dissipate critiques of the profession as tied problematically to the larger society" (Burkhart 1996, 42).

My own experiences in the field confirm the wisdom of these contrasting perspectives. On the one hand, I felt that my willingness to freely identify myself with the communities I researched (which to some extent involved acknowledging my own subjectivity as "multiply determined and constituted") carried with it an enormous amount of goodwill and definitely contributed to rapport in the interviews I conducted. Like Williams, I was amazed at the ease with which I was able to extract some of the most intimate details of my subjects' sex lives. On the other hand, I have also seen how this same rapport can lead to insularity and a conviction that the topics of study are unconnected to the larger social world.

Finally, my own position in the field became a rich source of data. As Behar (1993, 338) observes, "With all the discussion of ethnographic writing going on at the moment, so little is said about how each of us comes to the pen and the computer and the authority to speak and author texts." I would like to briefly address these issues here, including how my privilege as an author is "constituted by [my] gender, sociohistorical background, and class origins" (Behar 1993, 338). For example, my conviction that gender is an understudied aspect of communities like Bears, Faeries, and leathermen is undoubtedly an effect of the particular intersection from which I examine my data. For the most part, my research subjects occupy this same intersection. My status as a white, middle-class, gay/queer male is mirrored in the communities I chronicle in this book. Including all three communities, I can count the number of nonwhite members on one hand, and although not all members could be classified as middle class, no divisive issues arose in the field around social class. For the most part Bears, Faeries, and leathermen maintain the same silence around class issues as the larger culture, with the assumption that in the United States, everyone is middle class. I am therefore intrigued by the various ways that whiteness and middle-class values may enable the foregrounding gender and effeminacy, both in the communities I have visited and in my analysis.[6] I am thinking here, for example, of those African American men who must choose between an identification as "gay" and an identification as "black." It would be foolish to assume that the stigma of effeminacy carries the same force for them as it does for white men. Similarly, among the working class and working poor, men may read "gayness" in classed terms that remain invisible to those comfortably ensconced in the bourgeoisie. It is unlikely, for example, that working-class men read popular media representations like the television series *Will and Grace* or *Queer Eye for the Straight Guy* in the same way as middle-class men. But for their sexual difference, which remains haunted by the specter of effeminacy, white, middle-class, gay men occupy a social space of premium privilege. Thus race and class help to explain why the effeminacy effect represents such a formative influence in these cultures while suggesting the need for an intersectional analysis. In the chapters that follow I have tried to include race and class in my analysis wherever the data allow; I begin here with a bit more about my own social location.

I am a white, middle-aged man from a large, lower-middle-class family. I grew up in an overwhelmingly white suburb of Milwaukee, a city that still ranks among the most segregated in the United States. My father worked as a pharmacist, and my mother, who never attended college, was a full-time homemaker. Despite my father's professional status, I was profoundly affected by the working-class values of my Depression-era parents. Their devout Catholicism and reticence in discussing anything related to sex or sexuality has undoubtedly contributed to my current fascination with these topics. I currently identify myself as gay/queer, benefiting from an exposure to an array of critical perspectives on sex and gender through the privileges that come with education. I came of age and have lived most of my adult life in the shadow of the AIDS pandemic, having thus far escaped its ravages. AIDS has nevertheless fostered my critical consciousness of the social organization of sexuality, particularly with respect to intersections of gender and sexuality.

As a child my imagination vacillated between flights of fancy and an annoying literalism, the latter exhibited in my pedantic reaction on the fateful morning I first encountered this infernal playground taunt:

Peter, Peter Pumpkin Eater,
Had a wife and couldn't keep her
Put her in a pumpkin shell,
And there he kept her very well.

Why, in the first place, did I need a wife? Second, assuming I did need a wife, why would I need to "keep" her? (Although I was a precocious child, I was completely clueless at this point about the sexual connotations involved in "wife keeping.") Finally, assuming I had a problem with keeping my wife, how would forcible imprisonment solve the problem? Thus was my feminist consciousness awakened by Mother Goose. I would likely not have been moved to ask such penetrating questions had it not been for the influence of strong and capable women in my early life: my mother, my sisters, and my tomboy friend, Tillie Buchowski, from down the street. Tillie's delight in beating up her younger brother and the many adventures we embarked on together showed me that there were many ways to be female. I went on to meet several accomplished women in high school and college, leaving little room for personal sexism despite the evidence of its existence all around me. Eventually, as I began to explore my sexual interests in other men, I carried these gendered insights into my queer life as well.

When I began having sex with adult men in the late 1970s I was puzzled to find such escapades commonly dismissed as "meaningless casual sex." What I was experiencing was deeply meaningful and empowering, with strong spiritual intimations. Thus I have been especially attuned to cultural messages linking sex with guilt and shame. In graduate school I began to understand, by reading Foucault (1990a), how even in transgression, sexuality can reproduce mechanisms of discipline and social control.

As a white boy living in an exclusively white suburb, attending almost exclusively white schools (I remember exactly two students of color during my entire high school career), I remained blithely unconcerned with race until my late teens. Coming out, which in Milwaukee meant spending a lot of time in gay bars, marked the turning point. My downtown excursions on the number 57 bus marked the first time I met and socialized with men of color. Nothing was easy about these exchanges, as I was negotiating both my racial and sexual anxieties simultaneously. In retrospect I can see that this eroticized setting was probably the perfect antidote for the passive racism of my childhood, but at the time I was terrified. Still, I did not get a clear sense of the power of race until later in my college career, when I began working closely with "at risk" high school students who were overwhelmingly students of color. Only then was I obliged to think seriously about how whiteness had privileged my life. More recently, as an educator I have continued to learn from my students how race structures experience, and especially how whiteness comes to be so easily ignored.

Class consciousness also arrived in my college years. My parents had given me years of advance notice of their very limited ability to support my educational aspirations, and I probably would not have attended college at all were it not for a generous scholarship from Coe College in Cedar Rapids, Iowa. When I received word that I had won the scholarship, I remember that the news was absolutely decisive. This was free money. The thought of weighing competing offers from other schools never occurred to me, nor to my parents. Early in my first year my own class position was revealed to me during a conversation with a group of friends about our favorite family vacations. All of my classmates had not only traveled on airplanes but had all been to Disneyworld. This was out of the question for my family. On that day I began to think about how the college itself was structured by social class, and about what it meant to be a "scholarship student." The education I received at Coe was a good one, which prepared me for an eventual return to graduate school and helped place me into a solidly middle-class existence as a degreed academic.

Cedar Rapids had a surprisingly lively gay community and provided some spirited distractions from my studies. But the party came to a crashing halt one evening in early 1982, just before I was set to leave for a semester in New York City. I was in a 7-Eleven convenience store with my friend Lauren when she approached me with a copy of *Rolling Stone* that included an article about cases of a new "gay cancer" recently diagnosed in New York and Los Angeles. With the arrival of AIDS I began to think seriously about the complicated connections between death and desire, intimacy and masculinity, and, much later, about how all of these elements figure into the way heteronormativity shapes gay/queer sexual cultures. Over the years my thoughts have followed the ensemble of desires associated with penetrative intercourse, the most efficient method of HIV transmission. What kind of intervention is possible at this level? How is gender implicated in desire, and why? Is it possible to reorient the body to new desires? Is it possible that a decentering of penetrative intercourse might increase, rather than diminish, pleasure?

These are the questions I bring to this book, and how I came to ask them.

Plan of the Book

Broadly speaking, these questions concern human agency and the limits of subversive and resistant gender practices. I argue that while each of the three communities I have studied exhibits impressive evidence of innovation, both in terms of gender revisions and the invention of new pleasures, hegemonic notions of masculinity continue to constrain participants in important ways. My objective is not to generalize about all gay/queer men but rather to apply existing theory about the various ways in which sex, gender, and desire interact with and are shaped by communal processes.

In chapter 2 I survey various cultural and historical perspectives on effeminacy and develop a four-point typology of effeminacies. I then use this typology to augment and clarify an argument advanced by historian Randolph Trumbach explaining the historical "marriage" of effeminacy and homosexuality. I identify the historical legacy of this association and its continuing hold on men's social and sexual behavior as "the effeminacy effect."

Chapters 3, 4, and 5 comprise my case studies. In each of these chapters I begin with a brief history of the community under study, highlighting its problematic association with hegemonic masculinity and its collective, strategic response to the effeminacy effect. As much of this response is tied up with the particular identities enabled in each community, I devote a significant amount of attention to what it means to be a Radical Faerie, Bear, and gay leatherman. Sexual culture is another topic I explore across each of the three cases. Moreover, each community has drawn my attention to certain case-specific topics. Thus, in chapter 3, as I commune with the Radical Faeries I pay particular attention to an overarching Faerie belief in "subject-subject consciousness," how power and authority are uniquely reconfigured within the group, and the distinctive deployment of drag and parody among the Faeries. In chapter 4, as I hunt for the truth about Bears, issues of embodied gender are brought into sharper focus. In chapter 5 I am consigned to the dungeon and the world of gay leathermen. Here I am particularly fascinated with the way an amplification of masculinity seems to allow at least some members of this community to transcend the limitations of gendered sexuality. Those not enamored of theory, or who are already familiar with the theoretical concepts in my tool kit, will be happy to discover that I have relegated much of this material to the latter sections of the empirical chapters or to the notes.

In chapter 6 I return to some of the issues raised here and offer some concluding thoughts in light of the empirical and theoretical material presented in chapters 2 through 5.

TWO

Girlymen: Cultural and Historical Perspectives on Effeminacy

Among the Mehinaku, an Indian tribe of the Brazilian Amazon, a vigorous misogyny structures the "anxious pleasures" of a surprisingly open sexual culture (Gregor 1985). Here "A man who admits to even a hint of femininity repudiates his own nature" (184). A time-honored Mehinaku myth provides a concise illustration of the culture's attitude toward women. Among these people the tapir, a large animal related to both the horse and rhinoceros, is featured in a number of scatological jokes because of its enormous output of feces. The tapir is also known for "blindly running through the forest no matter what obstacles may be in its way" (178). While tapirs are real animals, the Tapir Woman is pure myth. According to this tale, a young boy, left alone by his mother, begins to cry out for her. The mysterious Tapir Woman approaches and tries to comfort him: "Don't you know me? I am just like your mother. Don't cry." She approaches him tenderly, "Put your arm into my rectum," she pleads. The young boy at first recoils in horror but is eventually convinced to enter the Tapir Woman up to his shoulder, whereupon she tightens her grip and spirits him off through the forest. There the young boy, whose now shriveled arm has ruined his chances of ever becoming a man, lives with the Tapir Woman. To sustain himself he occasionally reaches back into her rectum to feed on the fruit that she has eaten. This perverse specter warns of the unwholesome consequences of male regression to a feminine world of ease and comfort (Gilmore 1990, 97). As such it serves as a ghastly cautionary tale for Mehinaku boys and young men, as well as mothers. Masculinity is not to be tainted by the feminine—the alluring yet dirty, foolish, deceitful feminine.[1] The myth of the Tapir Woman is but one of a number of cultural narratives throughout history and across the globe that impart the same admonition. Moreover, it is an example of an effeminacy narrative absent any association with homosexuality.

The Sambia of Papua New Guinea have developed a virulently misogynistic culture characterized by an aggressive, militaristic masculinity that can only be cultivated through extended mentorship from older men in the tribe, including a series of ritual initiations (Herdt 1981). One of these involves a painful bloodletting procedure, wherein "sharp grasses are thrust up the nostrils until the blood flows profusely" (Gilmore 1990, 156). This is done to cleanse the boy of "feminine" fluids, which he has acquired in part via feeding at his mother's breast. Another ritual involves the activation of the *tingu,* a bodily organ that will remain inactive without physical intervention (Gilmore 1990, 152). The *tingu*'s activation is accomplished through a practice that serves to initiate all Sambian boys into manhood involving a sustained sexual relationship with an adult man of the tribe, during which the older man's penis is sucked and the semen swallowed. Again the emphasis is placed on replacing feminine fluid (breast milk) with masculine fluid (semen), and the penis symbolically supplants the breast as a source of sustenance. Left to themselves, according to this way of thinking, boys will not masculinize. Semen is the essence of masculinity and must be transmitted between generations of men to ensure the survival of the tribe. "If a boy doesn't 'eat' semen, he remains small and weak" (Herdt 1981, 1). This is an example of a homosexuality narrative absent any association with effeminacy.

Effeminacy, then, has often proved useful in devaluing women and socializing men (or perhaps more to the point, socializing men into the devaluation of women), but it has not always been associated with homosexuality. In this chapter I set the stage for a discussion of my case study data with an analysis of some of the varying historical and cross-cultural meanings of effeminacy and their relationship to hegemonic masculinity, that is, how effeminacy is employed in structuring the distribution of power both between men and between men and women (Connell 1987, 1995). I also consider the historical conflation of effeminacy and male homosexuality that I maintain deeply affects the organization and practices within each of the communities I studied. Moreover, while effeminacy as a cultural concept has been a popular topic among scholars working in history and cultural studies (Sinfield 1994; Trumbach 1977, 1989, 1991, 1998; Bray 1982; Dowling 1993; Erber 1996), among sociologists it has not attracted the attention it deserves. This is unfortunate, as a given society's concept and deployment of effeminacy reveals a great deal about the practical and symbolic aspects of gender relations within it, particularly assumptions about and attitudes toward women.

I begin by expanding upon aspects of effeminacy that I hope will serve to better define the concept. From there I move to a brief review of the historical uses of effeminacy in Europe and the United States and develop a four-point typology. My historical survey reveals a plethora of meanings, linking effeminacy alternately with deficient citizenship, a general lack of sexual restraint, excessive heterosexual behavior, and exclusive connection with passive homosexual activity, as well as an incorrigible proposition that uses a naturalizing narrative to link it with homosexual orientation regardless of sexual role. I then employ my typology to expand and augment an argument advanced by Randolph Trumbach to explain the emergence of the strong cultural link between effeminacy and homosexuality that developed during the eighteenth century. Finally, I look at some more recent disciplinary deployments of effeminacy that consistently conflate it with homosexuality and introduce what I call "the effeminacy effect."

Aspects of Definition

In attempting to devise any meaningful definition of effeminacy, the first issue to be addressed is the misogyny inherent in the term itself. The Oxford English Dictionary (online version 2006) makes it clear that the effeminate is one who has become "like a woman," "womanish, unmanly, enervated, feeble; self-indulgent, voluptuous; unbecomingly delicate or over-refined." Effeminacy is a quality of "unmanly weakness, softness, or delicacy." What is startling here is how little this definition actually reveals. Many of the attributes included in these definitions could easily be recast in a positive light: "softness" becomes "sensitive and understanding"; "delicacy" becomes "refinement"; "unbecomingly delicate or over-refined" indicates the cultured man of good breeding; "self-indulgence" translates to something like "taking care of oneself." The critical component of this definition seems to be "womanish," along with the fact that the term is used almost exclusively as a pejorative and, in most contemporary usage, strongly suggests homosexuality. Far from implying that a person actually *is* a woman, effeminacy signals the fact that a man is "womanlike." Thus the tension between the "reality" of biological sex and the prescribed gender performance is transformed into a personal failing. The fact that this charge is, in the majority of cases in which it is deployed, extraordinarily effective in bringing about a desired change in behavior is just one more indication of what psychologist Robert Brannon (1976) terms "the relentless repudiation of the feminine" at work in most Western conceptions of effeminacy.

Because of their relevance to my case study communities, these Western conceptions of effeminacy are my focus. But before I turn to an extended treatment of them, I review some intriguing cross-cultural data that challenge these Western conceptions. In preparation I first identify four abstract aspects of effeminacy that vary (or at least might vary) from one culture to the next: polarity, universalizing versus minoritizing tendencies, associations with homosexuality, and effeminacy's intersections with race and class.

Polarity

Polarity indicates the degree to which the effeminate man is understood as the polar opposite of the authentic or "real" man. This is undoubtedly informed by broader views of gender describing the degree of difference between men and women.[2] At its most extreme, this gender polarity implies mutual exclusivity between effeminacy and masculinity. More commonly the presence of feminine traits automatically implies a deficiency in masculine traits. On this view femininity and masculinity form a kind of "zero sum game" in that an increase in one quality necessitates a decrease in the other. With the exception of what I refer to as "appended effeminacy" (see below), effeminacy is currently positioned as polarized in most of the industrialized West. A nonpolarized understanding of gender would allow masculinity and effeminacy to vary independently of one another. By this logic one person could be both more masculine *and* more feminine than another, a position advanced by Lindy, a gender-bending character in the 1976 film *Car Wash* when he confronts one of his detractors with the quip, "Honey, I'm more man than you'll ever be and more woman than you'll ever have!"

Universalizing versus Minoritizing Tendencies

Sedgwick's (1990) binary can be applied to the way a given society views effeminacy. Does the society adopt a universalizing view (whereby *any* man is understood as vulnerable to the temptations of effeminacy, which then figures as a generalized social threat) or a minoritizing view (whereby a relatively small number of men are invested with the qualities of effeminacy and the concept of *the* effeminate figures prominently)? While most societies probably exhibit a bit of both tendencies, the empirical question remains as to which of these prevails. Related to this question, how does a given society deploy effeminacy? To what extent is the specter of effeminacy used to discipline the conduct of men? Is it applied to all men with equal vigor? Are some men simply beyond the pale, not worth the trouble? Moreover, in those societies where the effeminate figures as a distinct type of person, to what extent does this structure self-concept? Is one's effeminacy experienced as a "master status" (Hughes 1945) or as a less influential set of secondary characteristics?[3] Furthermore, does the charge of effeminacy automatically cancel what Connell (1995, 148) refers to as the "patriarchal dividend"? As I demonstrate in the next section, even where it was seen as undesirable, effeminacy has not always disqualified the bearer from male privilege. Historically, this has been particularly true of elite and aristocratic men.

Moreover, effeminacy is commonly attributed either to one's environment or to a fixed internal disposition. The inversion paradigm is an essentialist concept that ascribes effeminacy to some kind of physiological "mistake." Here the effeminate is to some degree understood as a woman trapped in a man's body. Variations on this idea attribute insufficient masculinity to a deficiency in testosterone (or testicular fortitude), chromosomal or genital deficiency, the presence of female hormones, gonads, and so forth. This is often extended in an attempt to "explain" same-sex attraction. In this view, effeminacy is a characteristic ascribed at birth. Conversely, the environment paradigm attributes effeminacy to some aspect of social or physical conditioning (poor diet, lack of exercise or fresh air, too much reading, poor parenting, too much time spent with females). In this latter view, effeminacy is understood as an achieved characteristic.

Association with Homosexuality

Effeminacy is sometimes associated with same-sex interests, but it has also been interpreted as the result of a too-ardent interest in the opposite sex. Also, during much of the history of the West, effeminacy and homosexuality were understood as contemporaneous but unrelated vices. Of course, given the intricate historical associations between gender and sexuality in many cultures it is not surprising that gender variation is often associated with variation in sexual practice and that some degree of association between effeminacy and homosexuality can be detected. But the presence or absence of such a link—and, if present, its strength and substance—is a matter that must be investigated empirically, on a case-by-case basis.

Intersections with Class and Race

Effeminacy intersects broadly with both class and race. In much of the West the masculinity of working-class men has traditionally been understood as authentic, with doubts about manliness sown generously as one moves up the class ladder. At the very top, the effeminacy of the effete, elite patrician signals his decadence and insulation from the harsh realities that constitute everyday existence for the less privileged. Similarly, in racialized societies entire races may be feminized in the popular imagination, such as the feminization of Asian men in many Western cultures.

"Other" Effeminacies: Racialized, Cross-Cultural, and Historical Interpretations

The feminization of certain races suggests that one way hegemonic masculinity subordinates different groups of men is by race (Connell 1995, 80). In the United States, this subordination is not accomplished with an even hand. While the logic of hegemonic masculinity consigns all nonwhite men to subordinate status in relation to white men, it also sets up a hierarchy of racialized masculinities. This hierarchy posits a dangerous and hypersexual African American masculinity at one extreme (Collins 2005; Oliver 2003; Kelley 2004) and a passive, asexual Asian American masculinity at the other (Espiritu 2004; Fung 2004; Chen 1996). The polarity helps to constitute the "normality" of white masculinities, which occupy the sexual middle ground. Thus, inasmuch as effeminacy functions as masculinity's "other," it makes sense to look at effeminacy through a racialized lens as well.

Collins (2005, 171) writes about this in terms of the black "sissy," tracing his roots to the emasculated image of Uncle Tom but also attributing a specific meaning to the image in post–civil rights America. "Representations of 'sissies' and 'Negro faggots' suggest a deviancy that lies not in Black male promiscuity but in a seeming emasculation that is *chosen*" (Collins 2005, 172; emphasis added). While this is probably also true of white attitudes toward effeminacy, the ostensibly voluntary adoption of an effeminate disposition may be perceived as particularly repellant among poor and disenfranchised black men whose emasculation is experienced as coerced. Denizet-Lewis (2003, 30) speculates that this distaste may be contributing to the "down low" phenomenon: "Rejecting a gay culture they perceive as white and effeminate, many black men have settled on a new identity . . . Down Low. There have always been men—black and white—who have had secret lives with men. But the creation of an organized, underground subculture largely made up of black men who otherwise live straight lives is a phenomenon of the last decade."

Espiritu (2004) traces the feminization of Asian American men through their experiences in the labor market; beginning at the turn of the twentieth century, Japanese, Chinese, Korean, and Filipino men entered feminized professions like laundering and domestic service in significant numbers. In addition, she shows how immigration policies and the American job market have tended to create gendered tensions within many traditionally patriarchal Asian American families, leading to a loss of status and power among male heads of household. Fung (2004) articulates the feminization of Asian American men in a radically different context—in the world of gay porn. His research suggests that even among gay men, Asian American men are consistently feminized. He concludes that the result of this "double effeminacy" is that, for many gay Asian American men, mainstream gay culture becomes "a site of racial, cultural, *and* sexual alienation sometimes more pronounced than in straight society" (Fung 2004, 550; emphasis in original).

Finally, Almaguer (1991) outlines the distinctive conceptions of effeminacy that inform the sexuality of Chicano men. He observes that although stigma accompanies homosexual practices in many Latino cultures, it does not equally adhere to both partners. It is primarily the anal-passive individual (the *cochón* or *pasivo*) who is stigmatized for playing the subservient, feminine role. He cites Lancaster (1987, 113), who observes that the insertive partner (the *activo* or *machista*) typically "is not stigmatized at all and, moreover, no clear category exists in the popular language to classify him. For all intents and purposes, he is just a normal male." In fact, the active partner in a homosexual encounter often gains status among his peers in precisely the same way that one derives status from seducing many women:

Consider for a moment the meaning associated with the passive homosexual in Nicaragua, the *cochón*. The term is derived from the word *colchón* or mattress, implying that one man gets on top of another as one would a mattress, and thereby symbolically affirms the former's superior masculine power and male status over the other, who is feminized and indeed objectified. (Lancaster 1987, 112)

In stark contrast to the North American gender order, Nicaraguan men are free to enjoy same-sex relations with impunity, provided they limit themselves to the active role. Kulick's (2002) study of transgendered Brazilian prostitutes elaborates this alternative system in vivid ethnographic detail and argues that in Latin American cultures it is sexuality (and what one *does* sexually) that accounts for gender in the popular imagination, rather than the North American preference for imagining gender as an extension of the sexed body.

All of these raced inflections of effeminacy can be found within the United States, and taken together they suggest that the conception of effeminacy that emerges from the history I provide below is shaped in important but largely unacknowledged ways by whiteness. This conviction becomes even more apparent when cross-cultural and historical cases are taken into account. I turn now to a brief consideration of effeminacy in three very different international contexts: in Africa's Hausaland, in Qing dynasty China, and in sixth-century Arabia.

Speakers of the Hausa language comprise a community in northern Nigeria and southern Niger (Salamone 2005). As Salamone notes, the shared Hausa language only partially obscures a number of internal differences and tensions within this diverse community, most notably between Muslim and pagan Hausa (*maguzawa*). The latter are much more liberal with respect to the public profile of women, allowing them to travel freely through public spaces and allowing for the public display of the female breast without reproach (Salamone 2005, 78). However, ideal masculinity among the culturally dominant Muslim Hausa demands complete mastery of the household, including wife seclusion (financially supporting a wife who is confined to the home). The ideal Muslim Hausa man is allowed up to four wives and numerous concubines, provided he has sex with each and provides them with children. This ideal is rarely realized however, as wife seclusion is expensive and few Hausa men can afford it. Consequently the typical Hausa wife, who is fully protected in her society only when she has a fully grown son, has a vital practical interest in her husband's sexual performance, sometimes prompting humiliating public declarations of her husband's deficiencies. Salamone (2005, 83) notes that "It is a pressure from which many Hausa males seek to escape in various ways."

In this fascinating and unstable cultural context the '*yan daudu*, usually translated as "homosexuals," "transvestites" (Gaudio 1998, 116), or "men who talk like women" (Salamone 2005, 75), fulfill a function integral to the workings of hegemonic Hausa masculinity. Associated with the pagan Bori cult, which is "widely understood as a refuge from the strongly patriarchal ideal of Hausa Islam" (Salamone 2005, 81), the *'yan daudu* represent a group of feminized men. Gaudio (2001, 37) notes that in addition to the variable use of "women's talk," the *'yan daudu* position themselves as feminine in the work they do cooking and selling food and in their role as intermediaries or "go betweens" for men seeking prostitutes. But this public role is complex, as *'yan daudu* also "attract otherwise unidentifiable 'men who seek men' (*maza masu neman maza*) and permit them to meet and socialize without having to blow their cover" (Gaudio 1998, 116).

The social profile of *'yan daudu* differs markedly from that of effeminates in most Western societies. Their self-concept differs in that, despite their stigmatization, they understand themselves as men fully entitled to the patriarchal dividend. This is because, as Gaudio notes,[4] among the Hausa it is the biological ability to father children that provides the basis for the *'yan daudu*'s claim to patriarchal power, despite their flagrant violation of masculinity norms. This is at least partially a consequence of religious culture, as many *'yan daudu* share a profound faith in Allah and the prophet Muhammad with other Hausa Muslims. Gaudio observes that "being a *ɗan daudu* [the singular of *'yan daudu*] in no way precludes an individual's participation in the same cultural and religious practices that other Hausa [Muslim men] perform. For example, many *'yan daudu* marry women in traditional ceremonies conducted by imams, and keep their wives in seclusion."[5]

Unlike effeminate men in the industrialized West, the *'yan daudu* are fully integrated into the gender order of the Hausa, and as Salamone (2005, 75) notes, in contemporary contexts the *'yan daudu* represent both a challenge to and a means of reinforcing normative masculinity among the Hausa by virtue of the escape (albeit temporary) that they provide conventionally masculine Muslim men from the demands of their home life. Finally, in marked contrast to the subjectivities of many Western effeminates, the *'yan daudu* do not understand their feminine behaviors in essentialist terms, but as elements of surface play, as more or less arbitrary and relatively inconsequential components of their identities.

Qing dynasty China (1644–1911) provides another fascinating departure from Western concepts of effeminacy. Louie (2002, 14) argues that it is not possible to fully grasp the complexities of Chinese masculinities without an appreciation of *wen*, "generally understood to refer to those genteel, refined qualities that were associated with literary and artistic pursuits of the classical scholars," and *wu*, "attributes of physical strength and military prowess . . . but also the wisdom to know when and when not to deploy it." Historically, leadership in China was demonstrated by men who were able to maintain a harmonious balance between *wen* and *wu*, "because it evokes both the authority of the scholar and that of the soldier" (Louie 2002, 11).

Throughout Chinese history the preferred form of masculinity has varied greatly, but the essential *wen-wu* ingredients remained the same, and either one was considered normative. "Indeed, at certain points in history the ideal man would be expected to embody a balance of *wen* and *wu*. At other times only one or the other was expected, but importantly *either* was considered acceptably manly" (Louie 2002, 11, emphasis in original). However, Louie argues that historical events tended to tip the balance slightly in favor of *wen*.

One implication of this idea is that for Chinese men, effeminacy in the sense of being womanlike simply does not resonate within Chinese society. Historical data from the Qing dynasty lend some support to this idea. As Louie (2002, 18) states, "*wu* became associated with non-elite masculinity at various points in China's past, while *wen* was often a more elite masculine form." The Qing dynasty was one such historical point. In her analysis of what she terms "anti-masculine taste" among the elite in Qing China, Wu (2003, 22) presents dozens of descriptions drawn from the contemporary literature describing men "as beautiful as white jade," "delicate as a flower, soft like powder," and "beautiful boys made up as beautiful girls." Interestingly, this feminine deportment made such men more, rather than less, attractive to women. "As her ladyship gazed upon Langzi she found him to be just like a beautiful woman, sporting an ivory complexion and fine features, returning her look with a dreamy smile. Uncontrollable passions flooded over her."

It should be noted that this feminization was an elite phenomenon, associated with the cultivation of *wen* qualities. Commoners in China were held to much stricter standards during the Qing dynasty (Sommer 2002), and *wu* masculinity was considered to be the preferred form of masculinity among non-elite men. Still, it presents a profile of the womanlike man that differs radically from familiar Western conceptions.

Evidence of an institutionalized class of effeminates known as *mukhannathūn* in pre-Islamic and first-century Islamic Arabian society is inconclusive but intriguing. Medieval Islamic scholar Everett K. Rowson (1991) has completed the most exhaustive study to date. His painstaking attention to a number of obscure, anecdotal, and often conflicting sources yields a number of tentative conclusions.

Prophetic *hadith* regarding the *mukhannathūn* emphasize their effeminacy, including the use of henna dye for the feet and hands. Rowson

(1991, 675) concludes that this feminine adornment probably extended to the wearing of feminine clothing and jewelry as well. Unlike other men, *mukhannathūn* "were permitted to associate freely with women, on the assumption that they had no sexual interest in them, and often acted as marriage brokers or, less legitimately, as go-betweens" (671). Other anecdotal sources closely associate the *mukhannathūn* with music, particularly the singing of "light songs" and their expertise with the *duff*, a kind of square tambourine (679). Such skills attracted elite interest, and anecdotal evidence suggests that several successful *mukhannathūn* enjoyed a degree of celebrity in elite circles. Despite this status, it is clear that the *mukhannathūn* were stigmatized, as sources indicate that punishment could be imposed for using the term to insult a conventionally gendered male (677).

Exactly how the *mukhannathūn* were regarded sexually is unclear. Some sources unequivocally indicate that they were involved in same-sex activities; others stress only that they were among "those lacking interest in women" (Rowson 1991, 674). Furthermore, it is unclear whether the low social status of *mukhannathūn* derived from their femininity, their presumed homosexuality, or (in an explanation that Rowson apparently favors) because their status as go-betweens and their role as entertainers "associated [them] with wine, sexual license, and the frivolous pursuit of pleasure" (671–72).

Perhaps the most intriguing attribute of the *mukhannathūn* is suggested by numerous anecdotes that record a distinctively flippant, irreverent, and defiant attitude toward authority. While many *mukhannathūn* were prized for their wit and humor, they often angered officials who interpreted their behavior as blasphemous. Rowson (1991, 680) records numerous incidents like the following, wherein a notorious *mukhannathūn* by the name of Tuways ("little peacock") demonstrated irreverent behavior during a pilgrimage stoning ritual wherein Muslims throw stones at a larger stone meant to represent the devil. When asked why he had coated his stones with sugar and saffron, Tuways replied, "I owed the devil a favor, and I'm making up for it." Elsewhere Rowson (1991, 683) recounts the crude humor of another famous *mukhannathūn* by the name of al-Dalāl, who, after allegedly farting during prayers, proclaimed loudly, "I praise Thee fore and aft!" On another occasion al-Dalāl brought worshippers to raucous laughter when he responded to the imam's rhetorical question, "And why should I not serve Him Who created me?" with a deadpan, "I don't know."

I am struck by the alacrity with which the *mukhannathūn* apparently embraced their role as reprobates and blasphemers through their caustic, often crude, and very public response to authority, even during periods of brutal persecution. It may be that, lacking any effective defense when cornered, they simply decided to refuse to acknowledge their offenses as serious. Although it is probably tempting for many Western researchers, it is almost certainly a mistake to equate the flippancy of the *mukhannathūn* and the "non-serious" attitude of the *'yan daudu* with contemporary Western concepts of gay "camp" sensibility. A fine-grain analysis of the differences in how humor, satire, and parody are deployed in each of the three cultures would likely be instructive and reveal significant differences. However, it might also reveal some surprising common ground with respect to cross-cultural links between effeminacy and humor, or more broadly with respect to the use of humor among oppressed or stigmatized populations.

––––––

The data in this section introduce a note of caution to my analysis. It seems clear from the American and cross-cultural cases detailed here that whiteness plays a significant and underacknowledged role in the construction of popular Western concepts of effeminacy. If this is true, it may help to explain why the Faerie, Bear, and leather communities I studied are overwhelmingly white, despite their deliberate attempts to attract more men of color. If the gender stigma they are responding to (i.e., a very specific construction of effeminacy) is also structured by race, it makes sense that the response will resonate along racial lines as well. Having underscored this important caveat, I turn now to the history of effeminacy's dominant Western form.

A Brief History of Western Effeminacy

Effeminacies currently circulating in the industrialized West reflect a high degree of gender polarity, a minoritizing perspective that nevertheless operates as a nearly universal disciplinary mechanism exacting an impressive level of gender conformity among most men because of effeminacies' strong association with homosexuality. To understand how this particular combination of meanings came about, a brief historical review is in order.[6] Foucault (1990b, 85) observes that today "no one would be tempted to label as effeminate a man whose love for women leads to immoderation." However, in ancient Greece this is precisely the measure taken of men who indulged themselves "immoderately" (either in same- *or* in opposite-sex relations). This is because the virtue of "moderation" was understood as an inherently masculine trait. According to the ancient Greeks, "immoderation derives from a passivity that relates to femininity. To be immoderate was to be in a state of nonresistance with regard to the force of pleasures, and in a position of weakness and submission" (Foucault 1990b, 84). Thus, "the dividing line between a virile man and an effeminate man did not coincide with our opposition between hetero- and homosexuality; nor was it confined to the opposition between active and passive homosexuality" (85). The objects of normative sexual desire for adult male Greek citizens ranged from women to boys, slaves (male or female), and noncitizens (male or female). As long as the same-sex relations of the adult male citizen occurred with these partners assuming the passive role in any form of intercourse, and as long as the activity was considered "moderate," there was little stigmatization attached to the behavior and the charge of effeminacy simply did not apply. On the other hand, for adult male citizens of ancient Greece this equation between effeminacy and immoderation was of monumental importance with respect to their participation in the public life of the *polis*. The effeminate was understood as one who had allowed himself, through immoderate sexual activity of virtually *any* kind, to be distracted from his public duties.

Interestingly, the Greeks formulated an early version of the inversion paradigm as an explanation for the effeminate male. Such a man exhibited a "mismatch" between the gendered agents of biological reproduction: "*Androgynoi* [effeminate men] are produced when male seed from the female parent overpowers female seed from the male parent" (Gleason 1990, 394). Consequently, the body "naturally" displayed the truth of a man's effeminacy in a way that was easily recognizable:

You may recognize him by his provocatively melting glance and by the rapid movement of his intensely staring eyes. His brow is furrowed while his eyebrows and cheeks are in constant motion. His head is tilted to the side, his loins do not hold still, and his slack limbs never stay in one position. He minces along with little jumping steps; his knees knock together. He carries his hands with his palms turned upward. He has a shifting gaze, and his voice is thin, weepy, shrill and drawling. (Gleason 1990, 395)

But the relationship between the effeminate *androgynos* and same-sex preference seems ill defined at best. While *androgynos* denotes "the appearance of gender-indeterminacy," the more specific term, *cinaedus*, implies sexual deviance, "in its most specific sense referring to males who prefer to play a feminine (receptive) role in intercourse with other men" (Gleason 1990, 396). While Gleason asserts that "the two terms become virtually indistinguishable when used to describe men of effeminate appearance and behavior," there is reason to suspect that the average Greek did not consider the terms to be synonymous. First, the use of two separate terms implies as much. Second, it is clear that the more sexualized term, *cinaedus*, was often used as a general term of derision in nonsexual contexts: "Apparently one could hurl the epithet *cinaedus* as an all-purpose term of abuse to express generalized, not specifically sexual, moral reproach. In such cases, *cinaedus* functions as the equivalent of terms like 'loathsome,' 'licentious,' or 'reprehensible' (Gleason 1990, 396).

Halperin (2002b) argues that even in sexualized contexts, effeminacy was more about citizenship than sexuality per se. He observes that the young male prostitutes of classical Athens were disqualified from citizenship not so much for what they did as for what their activity implied:

The city as a collective entity was vulnerable in the person of such a citizen, vulnerable to penetration, corruption, foreign influence. No person who prostituted himself could be allowed to speak before the people in the public assembly because his words might not be is own; he might have been hired to say them by someone else, someone whose interests did not coincide with those of Athens. (Halperin 2002b, 73)

The poor male citizen who consented to being penetrated for money was thus "effeminized by poverty" as much as by his passive sexual activity. Halperin observes that one of the reforms carried out by the famous Athenian statesman Solon (c. 638–558 BCE) was the establishment of inexpensive brothels staffed by slave women. Thus, for poor citizens, a major temptation to dishonor their masculinity, and thus their citizenship, was removed:

The disenfranchisement of male prostitutes and the cheap provision of female prostitutes beg to be seen together as complementary aspects of a single democratizing initiative intended to shore up the masculine dignity of the poorer citizens . . . and to promote a new collective image of the citizen body as masculine and assertive, as master of its pleasures, and as perpetually on the superordinate side of a series of hierarchical and roughly congruent distinctions in status: master vs. slave, free vs. unfree, dominant vs. submissive, active vs. passive, insertive vs. receptive, customer vs. prostitute, citizen vs. noncitizen. (Halperin 2002b, 74)

Sinfield (1994) provides what amounts to an extended history of effeminacy in western Europe. His major claim is that the connection between effeminacy and homosexuality, advanced as necessary and natural by much of our contemporary culture, is in fact a fairly recent (and socially constructed) phenomenon. He cites dozens of examples from European literature of the seventeenth, eighteenth, and nineteenth centuries to illustrate his point. His research reveals that, in fact, the very meaning of the word "effeminate" has changed dramatically in the past three centuries. Originally the word indicated an overabundance of feminine sentimentality and emotion. The object of the effeminate man's affection could be either male or female; this had essentially no bearing on his gender status. The critical feature was the fact that he was womanlike in his emotional attachment. Thus, during the eighteenth century men were sometimes warned to limit their contact with women lest it make them "effeminate." Certain stock characters appearing in European plays written during this period (e.g., the fop, the dandy, the beau) were readily understood by audiences as both heterosexual *and* effeminate.

According to Trumbach (1989), by the dawn of the eighteenth century in England the fop, the dandy, and the beau were already coming to be replaced by the "molly," an effeminate male presumed to be interested exclusively in other (masculine) men. Drawing on a range of cross-cultural evidence, Trumbach argues that roles such as the molly appear in societies as a kind of bridge between binary sex roles in societies where those roles are in the process of moving toward similarity. Trumbach attributes the emergence of the molly in England to certain broad-based structural changes that were taking place with respect to marriage and the family and to a growing recognition that these changes were in some appreciable way moving British society in the direction of gender equity. Thus the molly served the interests of hegemonic masculinity in that he clearly demonstrated the distinction between those men who were quite literally "becoming women" and those whose masculinity remained untainted.

Sinfield (1994) takes a different approach, arguing that the sensational series of trials that put Oscar Wilde's homosexual affairs on public display in England functioned as a kind of historical catalyst that forever cemented the connection between effeminacy and male homosexuality in the public's mind. Unlike Trumbach, Sinfield argues that before the trials the kind of "decadence" displayed by Wilde would have been more likely interpreted as evidence of heterosexual licentiousness than homosexuality. Wilde's effeminacy allowed for an understanding of homosexual behavior that left the sex/gender system unchallenged. Although it might be stigmatized and publicly condemned, a "womanish" man's desire for another man served to bolster Victorian assumptions about the necessary and "natural" connections between sex, gender, and sexual object choice.

Kimmel (1996, 19) comments on the political uses of effeminacy in the days leading up to the American Revolution. The aristocratic world of Great Britain was understood as effete, impotent, and soft in comparison with the rugged individualism of the evolving American consciousness. "American men faced a choice between effeminacy and manliness, between aristocracy and republicanism." In later years effeminacy was enlisted to assuage white men's anxieties centered around race and class, as in the "effeminate progeny of mixed races, half Indian, half Negro, sprinkled with white blood" (Kimmel 1996, 92). Effeminacy became something of a fashion statement during the early twentieth century; in fact it was all the rage during the "pansy craze" in New York City during the 1920s. Ironically, the pansy craze was fueled by Prohibition (originally designed to *control* morally suspect forms of entertainment), which allowed for the expansion of a sexual underworld in New York City that was closely associated with illegal speakeasies. The upper crust flocked to Times Square to see all manner of "gay" entertainments featuring flamboyant, effeminate (and presumably homosexual) men in various clubs and theaters (Chauncey 1994, 305–6). After a subsequent crackdown on such entertainment in the early 1930s, many otherwise "conventionally gendered" gay men continued to advertise themselves sexually to other men by adopting an aggressively effeminate persona in public. Thus an ascendant public perception that linked effeminacy with homosexuality was immediately exploited for practical purposes by gay men themselves.

Cold war America saw one of the most effective political deployments of effeminacy with McCarthyism's portrait of the homosexual as "security risk" (Corber 1997). This equation revived the classical Greek notion of the effeminate as failed citizen, with at least one important change: the logic of hegemonic masculinity confidently assumed that the link between effeminacy and homosexuality was both "natural" and necessary, a situation that continued until the years immediately following the Stonewall rebellion of 1969.

In his study of gay masculinity, Levine (1998) reveals that an authentic challenge to this idea was launched by the more radical wing of the gay movement in the years immediately following Stonewall, but its appeal was short lived:

Gay activists formulated radically different images of the postcloset homosexual. Some gay liberationists viewed this man as a politicized hippie who eschewed traditional manliness, conventional aspirations, and established institutions. He avoided the quick sex associated with the sexual marketplace and formed instead lasting relationships. And he wore "gender fuck" attire that mixed masculine and feminine (beards and dresses). Gay reformists, by contrast, viewed the postcloset homosexual as a "butch" rebel who had sex with "anyone, any way, any time." He actively participated in the sexual marketplace, "cruising" and "tricking" in gay bars, bathhouses, and porno-graphic bookstores. The liberationist image gathered few converts as most gay men found gender fuck too radical. They opted instead for the reformist image of the post-closet homosexual. (Levine 1998, 28)

This flight from effeminacy is supported in the following excerpt from one of Levine's field interviews. Here an aging member of the gay com-munity in New York (c. 1975) casts a jaundiced glance backward as he assesses some of the changes in gay culture during the early 1970s:

Honey, when you have been around as long as I have, you get to know a lot of men. Over the last few years, I have watched many of these girls change as the times changed. A couple of years ago, they had puny bodies, lisping voices, and elegant clothes. At parties or Tea Dances, they came in dresses, swooning over Garbo and Davis. Now, they've "butched up," giving up limp wrists and mincing gaits for bulg-ing muscles and manly handshakes, giving up fancy clothes and posh pubs for faded jeans and raunchy discos. (Levine 1998, 55–56)

From the preceding historical survey we see that effeminacy has alter-nately been understood as (1) a passive disposition toward pleasure and self-discipline that was perceived as womanish; (2) a moral failure result-ing from a kind of "contamination" by the feminine; (3) a willingness toward objectification in sex; (4) a means of resolving tensions within a particular gender narrative; and (5) a way of presenting oneself to the world, through either a style of dress or movement (or both) that is un-derstood as womanly. Although they do not correspond exactly, I use these observations to develop a four-point typology of effeminacy in the next section. I conclude this section by offering the following (pro-visional) definition of effeminacy: effeminacy is a historically varying concept deployed primarily as a means of stabilizing a given society's concept of masculinity and controlling the conduct of its men, based upon a repudiation of the feminine that recognizes it as a "present ab-sence."[7] It is present in that it marks an all-pervasive fear that informs nearly all aspects of masculine identity construction and absent in the sense that it suggests a lack or deficiency in qualities presumed to be critical to gender competence.

Thus effeminacy can be seen as a disciplinary development within hegemonic masculinity, a mechanism that, despite its widely varying cultural and historical manifestations, provides a remarkably effective means of policing the boundaries of acceptably masculine behavior. Furthermore, the concept of effeminacy encodes some of the central paradoxes of masculinity as it currently operates in most industrialized cultures. Real men are never feminine, yet real men must remain ever vigilant against the feminine. Masculinity is an essential and natural consequence of biological sex, yet it must be carefully taught and learned. Authentic masculinity implies freedom and control, yet anything marked as feminine is strictly proscribed.

A Typology of Effeminacies

En route to the marriage of effeminacy and homosexuality, I want to make a brief stop to propose a typology of effeminacies that may help illuminate some aspects of this historical coupling. This typology is not meant to identify "types of people" but rather, on Becker's (1998b, 45) advice, to describe socially intelligible types of activities that certain people occasionally engage in. Furthermore, in my reading across a fairly wide variety of sources, I have recognized these types consistently. The distinctions I make here have emerged from the data, and I am confident that they have been tacitly operating as social types for some time. Although I have made an attempt to construct an exhaustive typology (perhaps a chimerical pursuit, given the protean nature of effeminacy), I do not in any way see these forms of effeminacy as mutually exclusive. A great deal of overlap between these types should be expected when considering any specific historical case. In fact, the argument might be made that they are, in some sense, cumulative forms (i.e., each type builds upon, or is in some sense dependent upon, the prior form). While I do not pursue that argument here, I have presented these distinctions in a way that is conducive to this view.

Political

Political effeminacy represents a lack of fitness for citizenship and the demands of involvement in state activities. This type predominates in ancient Greece (Dover 1989). Where the political view of effeminacy prevails, it may or may not be associated with same-sex desires, or it may pertain only to specific practices, regardless of sexual object. For example, in ancient Greece, same-sex desire and behavior are neither proscribed nor feminized; rather, *any* indicator of submission among male citizens (including but by no means limited to passive anal sexuality) is marked as effeminate and condemned as evidence of poor citizenship. On this reading effeminacy represents a significant danger to the political health of the *polis*. As with nonsexual forms of passive behavior, the male citizen's active involvement in affairs of state is threatened by adopting a passive sexual role.

Moral

Moral effeminacy registers as a form of moral or ethical weakness, specifically a "softness" with respect to pleasure. The effeminate man is prey to his passions, for food and creature comforts as well as sexual gratification. An inability to reign in these passions is understood as womanlike and provides a sharp commentary on the debased status of women with respect to morality. This form of effeminacy is decidedly not associated with exclusive homosexuality. Rather, it assumes that all men must remain vigilant against the temptations of excessive sexual activity *in general*. This form of effeminacy makes no distinctions between women, men, animals, or the effeminate's own body as sexual objects. Lack of self-control (rather than sexual object choice) is the critical factor, and this version of effeminacy assumes that all men are equally vulnerable to temptation from women and men. The "homosexual" as a separate species is not acknowledged. During the Renaissance, this type of effeminacy was more closely associated with debauchery and in other periods was articulated in terms of class (particularly with respect to the "debauchery" of the aristocracy).[8]

Cosmetic

The cosmetic form of effeminacy emphasizes outward appearance as an indicator of the womanly man. Specifically, the use of women's clothing, jewelry, and makeup is understood as signaling effeminacy. Thus, this type of effeminacy is employed in categorizing a wide range of men who alter their appearance in violation of conventional norms of masculine dress and grooming. Transvestism, the most extreme case of cosmetic effeminacy, was understood as a vice in its own right during the Renaissance, entirely independent of same-sex desire. It was not until the eighteenth century that this form became closely associated with homosexuality.

Somatic

The somatic form reads the body itself (rather than the accoutrements of dress and makeup) as evidence of effeminacy. It can be further divided into *kinesthetic* effeminacy, wherein a man is judged by prevailing standards as either moving or using his voice "like a woman," and *anatomical* effeminacy, wherein a man's genitals, build, or facial features are interpreted as feminine or less than masculine. The relationship between somatic effeminacy and homosexuality is complex. While in some deployments this relationship may be heavily implied, somatic effeminacy is only occasionally regarded as conclusive proof of same-sex interest among boys and men. More often it extends and underscores the importance of repudiating the feminine as it may be expressed by (or read into) the movement and appearance of the male body. In contemporary societies, then, its primary purpose seems to be surveillance and discipline (Foucault 1995).

The Marriage of Effeminacy and Homosexuality

I turn now to an application of this typology to a specific historical puzzle. The preceding examples raise a number of interesting questions: When and where was the dominant meaning of effeminacy transformed to indicate homosexuality? Why did this transformation occur when and where it did? Randolph Trumbach (1977, 1991, 1998) provides the most comprehensive account in response to these questions with his study of the sodomitical cultures of Enlightenment England.

While several scholars have placed the "wedding date" for effeminacy and homosexuality sometime in the middle to latter half of the nineteenth century (Sinfield 1994; Dowling 1993; Erber 1996), Trumbach (1977, 11) traces the relationship back much further. He finds evidence from as early as the twelfth century that "whenever homosexual behavior surfaced at the royal courts . . . it was accompanied by what contemporaries viewed as markedly effeminate behavior." Here is the first instance in which distinctions between types of effeminacy may be of use. I would suggest that aristocratic effeminacy is best understood as a subset of what I have identified above as moral effeminacy, with one important caveat: the immorality of this particular form of aristocratic behavior is attributed to it from outside of elite circles, and it is understood as an aristocratic indulgence unto itself, quite separable in the popular imagination from the aristocratic indulgence in same-sex passion. Aristocrats themselves undoubtedly held a different view of their effeminate behaviors (although to the extent that they were aware of the negative moral judgments of their social inferiors, they may have relished the "naughtiness" of effeminacy).

First, despite the fact that both effeminacy and sodomy were associated with the aristocracy, they were not necessarily correlated with each other. As Sinfield (1994, 41) points out, "The aristocrat was expected to be effeminate, so same-sex passion was not foregrounded by his manner." He goes on to cite an example that suggests that among the elite, effeminate behavior (including transvestism) may have been understood as "good clean fun," part of the privilege accorded those with high social standing, appreciated even by those aristocrats who explicitly scorned same-sex activity (42). From the perspective of the aristocrats engaged in it, then, effeminacy may perhaps be best described as a kind of carnival. In the terms I've introduced here it was more likely understood as something closer to cosmetic, or perhaps even somatic, effeminacy than moral effeminacy.

This explanation, of course, provides us with only part of the picture. Nevertheless, Trumbach makes it clear that the association between homosexuality and effeminacy was not completely secured in the popular imagination until the eighteenth century. He explains this as a reaction to the confluence of two distinct historical trends. The first trend is the development of a distinctly homosexual subculture at least partially reliant upon secret meeting places throughout London and the popular descriptions of these places that emphasized the effeminate behavior of their patrons. The second trend is the reaction against the "sentimental movement" that increasingly came to bear on heterosexual gender relations during the eighteenth century. We can trace the first trend to 1699, when the London authorities began raiding "molly houses" in various parts of the city, raids they conducted again in 1707 and 1726 (Bray 1982).[9] These houses were scattered across an area north of the Thames, providing clandestine meeting places for men with same-sex interests. They were also the site of flamboyant displays of transvestism and effeminacy. An agent who had visited a molly house in advance of a raid left this account as part of a court transcript:

On Wednesday the 17th November last I went to the prisoner's house in Beech Lane, and there I found a company of men fiddling and dancing and singing bawdy songs, kissing and using their hands in a very unseemly manner . . . In a large room there we found one a-fiddling and eight more a-dancing country dances . . . Then they sat in one another's lap, talked bawdy, and practiced a great many indecencies. There was a door in the great room, which opened into a little room, where there was a bed, and into this little room several of the company went. (Bray 1982, 82)

Elsewhere in the transcript we find a vivid description of a drag ball at the molly house in the Old Bailey:

They had no sooner entered but the Marshal was complemented by the company with the titles of Madam and Ladyship. The man asking the occasion of these uncommon devoirs, the Marshal said it was a familiar language peculiar to the house. The man was not long there before he was more surprised than at first. The men calling one another "my dear" and hugging, kissing, and tickling each other as if they were a mixture of wanton males and females, and assuming effeminate voices and airs; some telling others that they ought to be whipped for not coming to school more frequently . . . Some were completely rigged in gowns, petticoats, headcloths, fine laced shoes, furbelowed scarves, and masks; some had riding hoods; some were dressed like milkmaids, others like shepherdesses with green hats, waistcoats, and petticoats; and others had their faces patched and painted and wore very extensive hoop petticoats, which had been very lately introduced. (Bray 1982, 87)

These descriptions are interesting, both for what is said and what is not said. To a twenty-first-century audience, perhaps most salient are the descriptions of cosmetic effeminacy ("fine laced shoes, furbelowed scarves, and masks"; "extensive hoop petticoats, which had been very lately introduced") and somatic effeminacy ("using their hands in a very unseemly manner"; "assuming effeminate voices and airs"). This may be because they conform so well to our already formed understanding of the stereotypically effeminate homosexual. But Sinfield warns against such a reading:

How rash it might be to assimilate these men to modern patterns is suggested by reports, dating from 1709 and 1813, that mollies mimicked not just marriage but childbearing—with a midwife, nurse, and doll to represent the child. It is very hard to imagine "childbearing" scenes in twentieth-century queer or gay culture; there are breaks as well as continuities in the transmission of the molly-house model. (Sinfield 1994, 39)[10]

What is not mentioned in the preceding description, and what surely went without saying at the time (given the fact that these descriptions are taken from criminal court proceedings), is that all of this activity would undoubtedly have evoked a powerful and an extremely negative set of moral associations from its contemporary audience.

The existence of the London molly houses shows that a subculture of men with same-sex interests existed as early as the late seventeenth century, and Trumbach (1977, 17) notes that "descriptions of the subculture which were intended for the general public always emphasized its effeminacy." However, a wide discrepancy seems to exist between the interpretations encouraged by such popular accounts and the understandings of the mollies themselves. The key to understanding this discrepancy may lie in an appreciation of the particular *type* of effeminacy celebrated in the molly houses. Trumbach (1977) notes that the London mollies were primarily drawn from the middle and lower classes; he further indicates that popular opinion held (erroneously) that molly houses were frequented primarily by aristocrats. Thus the flamboyant displays of effeminacy in the London molly houses may easily have been understood by their lower- and middle-class patrons as little more than a playful and theatrical form of social climbing, one perhaps designed to assuage misgivings these men may have had about the legitimacy of their desires and the community they were forming:

To people of the lower class, a noble—powdered, pomaded, refined—was both elegant and effeminate; but that bothered no one as long as the mode of attire remained faithful to the specific superior social condition which its wearer represented. If someone lower on the social scale assumed this costume . . . not only did he betray his social condition, but in addition, his effeminacy, by losing its accepted association with elegance and the upper class, became an indication of the wearer's *real* effeminacy. (Rey 1988, 189; emphasis added)

Thus, using the typology introduced here, we might say that while the mollies were engaged in an enthusiastic embrace and celebration of the "lighter" side of cosmetic and perhaps somatic effeminacies—as a theatrical pretense to a higher social standing than they actually enjoyed—the general public interpreted the whole affair in starkly moralistic terms.[11] It is important to remember that although public concern with the existence of the molly houses waxed and waned during the eighteenth century, when the crackdowns came they were swift and terrible. The raids (particularly the one in 1726, involving some twenty houses) resulted in executions, imprisonment, and suicides (Bray 1982, 114).[12] The second trend that helped to secure the relationship between effeminacy and homosexuality, according to Trumbach, is the reaction against the sentimental movement that increasingly came to bear on heterosexual gender relations during the eighteenth century. According to its tenets, married men and women were encouraged to form close bonds that emphasized the intimacy of the marital relationship and introduced an egalitarian element not present in earlier conceptions of marriage. "But it is apparent," remarks Trumbach (1991, 202), "that a married man who went to whores did so in part because he wished to *limit* the degree of intimacy with his wife" (emphasis added). It seems that the gendered sexuality of many eighteenth-century men was still effectively governed by close associations between women, intimacy, and effeminacy. Furthermore, with the vitriolic reaction to effeminacy in London's molly houses, these men may have had an additional reason for patronizing prostitutes:

The man without a wife who went to whores did so for a different but related reason. He was determined to show that his sexual interest was exclusively in women and that he was not an effeminate passive sodomite. Though it may not seem so at first, it is very likely that this fear of male passivity and the new sodomitical role that it produced in the early Enlightenment was also a consequence of the anxieties induced by the new ideal of closer, intimate, more nearly equal relations with women . . . The sodomite and the prostitute guaranteed that ordinary men would never be transformed into women as a result of the intimacy or the passivity that might be produced by more nearly equal relations between men and women. (Trumbach 1991, 202–3)

"What changes, then," remarks Sinfield (1994, 45), "is that male and female become polar opposites." This is in line with the transition among natural scientists investigating the human body, from a one-sex model that emphasized sameness to the two-sex biological model that prevails today (Laqueur 1990).[13] It also marks the beginning of a new understanding of gender wherein masculinity and femininity are interpreted as the essential, natural developments of two radically different sexes:

The best documented [sexual subcultures] are the Molly houses of early-eighteenth century London . . . Historians of the period have noted a shift in medical ideologies of gender, from an earlier period when gender anomalies were freely attributed to hermaphroditic bodies, to a later period when a clear-cut dichotomy of bodies was presumed and anomalies therefore became a question of gender deviance. The requirements that one must have a personal identity as a man or a woman, rather than simply a location in the social order as a person with a male or female (or hermaphroditic) body, gradually hardened in European culture. (Connell 2002, 247)

With this new understanding, effeminacy quickly comes to be deployed as a means of policing the boundaries between effeminate men and real men, between men and women, and between prescribed homosocial relationships and proscribed homosexual relationships. These distinctions continue to be critically important, especially in the case of men who submit to the passive role in anal intercourse. The revised sex/gender system demands that he be feminized. Otherwise, a man who "takes his sex like a woman" might accidentally be treated socially as a real man. Such a man is perfectly positioned to refute the naturalistic narrative that claims that sex is naturally determinative of sexuality and leads inevitably to an eternal and unchanging masculinity or femininity.

Contemporary Uses of the Effeminate Homosexual

Thus effeminacy is historically constructed as a powerful disciplinary force shaping the everyday conduct of men. Since its power is central to the argument I am making with this study, I identify it as the "effeminacy effect." In this section I examine the power of the effeminacy effect in more detail as it relates to homosocial relations and the development of capitalism and to the conduct of war and soldiering.

The effeminate homosexual played a useful role in the development of capitalist economies. As Lofstrom (1997) suggests, the nineteenth century saw the development of a puritanical, bourgeois consciousness that required that the unwholesome figure of the effeminate homosexual as reviled and stigmatized figure be kept close at hand. As a "soft" man, given to self-indulgence, he represented an ever-present threat to the demands of an expanding capitalist system. His lack of productivity and competitiveness, along with presumptions about his excessive sexual desires, imperiled the idealization of economic pursuits and the enthronement of self-restraint as a paramount social and sexual virtue. Kimmel (1996, 144) echoes this sentiment in his description of a 1910 postcard that pictures an "effeminate clerk in a dry goods store who fixes his hair while his customers go unattended." In these contexts, self-restraint meant avoiding sensual pleasure and delaying gratification for the sake of concentrated work toward an instrumental goal; this concept had a specific set of implications for same-sex relationships. Lofstrom (1997, 36) remarks on the conflation of sexual and economic values as he speaks of the emerging middle class's "revulsion toward all forms of pleasure-seeking sexuality including spending one's semen on 'unproductive' purposes, as in homosexuality." Furthermore, with the development of a capitalist economy, relationships between men became increasingly problematic. Business often demanded extremely close relationships between middle-class men, yet these relationships could not become intimate, lest business interests be forced to take a back seat to personal interests. Thus the tabooing of intimate bonds between men is conceived as a functional component of capitalism, and the effeminate homosexual serves as a highly effective admonition against such vice.

Several studies have suggested that masculinity is linked with war and soldiering early in a boy's socialization (Canada 1998; Jordan and Cowan 1998) and that this association continues to hold powerful sway in the lives of adult men (Cohn 2000). The figure of the "draft dodging" effeminate homosexual acts as a foil against which real men define themselves with respect to military service. Conversely, the alleged demoralizing effect of gay men who serve openly in the military presents the danger of discrediting the stereotype while at the same time contradicting the logic whereby, as Connell (2002, 253) observes, "the potential for homoerotic pleasure [is] expelled from the masculine and located in a deviant group, symbolically assimilated to women and beasts." The furor over President Bill Clinton's attempt to allow gays to serve openly in the military illustrates the central importance that American leaders place on the expulsion of the homoerotic from the modern American military. However, as Connell (2002. 253) demonstrates, this position is rife with contradiction: "The contradiction between the purged definition of masculinity, and the actual conditions of emotional life among men in the military and paramilitary groups reached crisis level in fascism. It helped to justify, and possibly to motivate, Hitler's murder of Ernst Rohm, the homosexual leader of the Storm-troopers, in 1934."

Quentin Crisp, whose 1968 autobiography, *The Naked Civil Servant*, chronicled his life as a flamboyantly effeminate homosexual in Great Britain, demonstrates what happens when effeminacy meets the military. When Britain declared war at the onset of World War II, Crisp was living in crushing poverty, and, as "many of my friends were able to find work in camouflage," he decided to enlist. At the induction center, Crisp reports, the first doctor to examine him was so startled that he fainted dead away:

I was surprised. My appearance was at half-mast. I wore no makeup and my hair was hardly more than hooligan length . . . but of course my hair was still crimson from having been persistently hennaed for seven years and, though my eyebrows were no longer in India file, it was obvious that they had been habitually plucked. These and other manifestations of effeminacy disturbed the board deeply. Even while I was merely having my eyes tested, I was told, "You've dyed your hair. This is a sign of sexual perversion. Do you know what those words mean?" (Crisp 1983, 109)

After a considerable amount of whispering among the induction officials, Crisp is unceremoniously dismissed:

A young man appeared holding at arm's length, as though he were about to read
a proclamation, a sheaf of papers which he tore up with a flourish. "You'll never be
wanted," he said and thrust at me a smaller piece of paper. This described me as
being incapable of being graded in grades A, B, etc., because I suffered from sexual
perversion. (Crisp 1983, 110)

———

Effeminacy and homosexuality are two discrete social constructions
with separate histories. However, the social and political developments
I outline in this chapter secured the marriage of the two concepts in the
Western imagination sometime during the eighteenth century. Since
then the effeminate homosexual has acted as a powerful mechanism for
policing hegemonic masculinity.

When the conflation of effeminacy and homosexuality is successfully
challenged, the nature and effects of this disciplinary power become
more apparent. However, as I hope to demonstrate in what follows, just
such a disaggregation—a protracted "divorce" between effeminacy and
homosexuality, if you will—is currently under way. Not surprisingly, it
is proceeding through a range of strategies and in a variety of gay/queer
subcultural contexts. As I take up an examination of these strategies in
the next three chapters I am once again reminded of the astounding
power and scope of gender, but I also hope to suggest new questions
and possibilities for "undoing gender" (Butler 2004). At the very least,
even a partially successful attempt to divorce effeminacy and homosexuality opens a space to investigate the relative stigmatizing effects of
each. I turn now to an in-depth investigation of how each of my three
case study communities has crafted a unique collective response to their
shared historical legacy and to the effeminacy effect.

THREE

Fae Spirits and Gender Trouble: Resistance and Compliance among the Radical Faeries

Faeries are a pale and motley race that flowers in the minds of decent folk. Never will they be entitled to broad daylight, to real sun. But remote in these limbos, they cause curious disasters which are harbingers of new beauty.

—ATTRIBUTED TO JEAN GENET

Part progressive social movement, part countermovement, part spiritual revival, part green political experiment, the Radical Faeries are a tribe of gentle gender warriors, queer folk, self-described "country faggots." Theirs is an eclectic community composed primarily (but not exclusively) of men with same-sex interests who explicitly reject traditional notions of masculinity. This is signaled in part by an active embrace and satire of the historically sedimented associations between same-sex orientation and effeminacy, which is most apparent in the way the community deploys drag. Radical Faerie culture is forged from an astonishingly diverse cultural tool box that includes Marxism, feminism, paganism, Native American and New Age spirituality, anarchism, the mythopoetic men's movement, radical individualism, the therapeutic culture of self-fulfillment and self-actualization, earth-based movements in support of sustainable communities, spiritual solemnity coupled with a camp sensibility, gay

59

liberation, and drag. Like gay leathermen, Radical Faeries exist at the margins of the margins; they are often stigmatized by other members of the queer community. For all these reasons, Radical Faerie culture provides a fascinating site for the study of gender resistance and compliance.

Much of the field research for this study was conducted at a Faerie "sanctuary." This is a beautiful plot of wilderness land, replete with lush forests, a lake, a garden, a cookhouse, and an outhouse. During most of this phase of the study, I, like many of the other Faeries, wore a dress. Mine was a yellow housedress with a pattern of brightly colored flowers that I bought at the Salvation Army for $3.00. "I'm getting in touch with my inner *hausfrau*," I told the other Faeries at the sanctuary. Many of them were wearing much prettier dresses, some were wearing nothing at all, and some simply wore jeans and T-shirts. I spent my time at the sanctuary under an assumed name—but so did all the other Faeries. I chose the name "Spring Peeper"—some at the gathering would say *it* chose *me*. My new Faerie friends went by names like Dragonfly, Zinnia, Lavinia, MoonGaze, PopTart, Aunt Tildy, Witchhazel, and Frankie.

The first gathering of Radical Faeries took place in 1979 when a group of 220 men showed up at the Sri Ram Ashram in Benson, Arizona. This meeting was in response to an ad placed in a magazine with a small but ardent following called *RFD*, an alternative publication that billed itself as "a magazine for country faggots." In his "Call to Gay Brothers," gay activist and former Communist organizer Harry Hay (1979, 20), along with his partner, John Burnside, and friends Don Kilhefner and Mitch Walker, urged gay men to come together to explore the coming "paradigm shift in gay consciousness." During the gathering Hay called on those assembled to "throw off the ugly green frogskin of hetero-imitation to find the shining Faerie prince underneath" (Timmons 1990, 265). The Radical Faerie movement, if it can accurately be described as a movement, can be seen at least in part as a reaction to the culture of commodification and sexual objectification that quickly developed in gay male urban enclaves in the wake of the Stonewall riots and gay liberation. More specifically, the Faeries can be seen as an alternative to the self-presentation and lifestyle of the hypermasculine gay "clone" of the 1970s, a cultural form closely linked with mainstream masculinities. Timmons observes that this connection between straight and gay masculinities was not lost on Faeries attending that first gathering:

The spirit seemed to flow through the circle. A heavy-set, gray-haired man wearing a floppy hat stepped into its midst and told of his career as a lawyer. "I deal every day with people who fight with each other—and they're all he-men. Policemen who abuse power. Judges. And because I am a Faerie, I feel great pain in that world." He struggled momentarily with his emotion, then continued. "All of these people are he-men. I come to my fellow Faeries because I need the love that I get here. And so many times in the gay world, I do not get that. I get the same kind of alienation that I get in the world of he-men." (Timmons 1990, 249)

In their steadfast resistance to definitions and centralized authority structures, the Radical Faeries are in many ways exemplars of postmodern community movements, with all the paradox this implies. For example, there is widespread agreement within the group that Faeries never agree about anything, yet their very existence depends to some degree upon consensus. Most Faeries understand their community as intentional, but exactly what this intentionality consists of is an open question. Refreshingly, Faerie culture seems to continually privilege process over results. Faerie enterprises, from preparing a meal to creating a sanctuary, are notoriously inefficient affairs—and this is just the way most Faeries like it.

The Faerie community I studied had no Faeries living permanently on the land, although sanctuaries in other parts of the United States and the world do offer permanent residence for Faeries. But most who identify with these communities live outside of Faerie space, in nearby rural and urban settings. Based on my observations, rendering a "typical" profile of a Faerie's life outside of sanctuary space is complicated by at least two factors. One is the astonishing diversity (in terms of work and occupations) of the men and women[1] drawn to this community. I encountered two pastors (of traditional religious faiths), a paralegal, an administrative assistant, two professional academics, a retail clerk, a performance artist, a professional photographer, a consultant, a computer graphics artist, and a personal coach. A significant number of Faeries remain committed year-round to simple living, minimal consumption, and as little contact with the capitalist market economy as possible.[2] Some of these Faeries work odd jobs to support their simple lifestyles; others may work part time. Another reason it was difficult for me to get a full picture of "everyday" Faerie life is the reluctance of some members to talk about their more "worldly" work. I learned quickly that asking another Faerie what he or she does for a living is discouraged. This was communicated to me effectively as I watched one of the established members of the community playfully imitate a "bad Faerie." With a glad-handing smile he shook my hand, looked me in the eye, and said, "Hi! Name's Mark—I'm in real estate. And what line are you in?" With respect to political activity, my strong impression is that many Faeries follow politics, and a few are committed to active political participation, but most prefer a lower political profile.

A tantalizing exception to this pattern is worth mentioning here. During my research I caught wind of an incident that had apparently taken place a number of years earlier, in a major city close to the sanctuary. On this occasion, several Faeries, dressed to the nines in "trash drag" (a form of drag often featuring thrift-store castoffs, with no attempt toward the illusion of femininity), paraded through downtown streets, boarded buses, and staged a piece of guerilla theater at a local upscale department store, Neiman Marcus (referred to in every telling of the story that I encountered as "Needless Markup"). Here they enacted a delicious parody of American consumption by making lighthearted fun with sales clerks, shrieking with delight at all the "fabulous" gowns, and interacting with the "legitimate" customers. The Faeries involved were much admired by other members of the community for their participation, but judging from the reactions to retellings of this tale, such high-profile events are not common occurrences. TigerLily, a prominent member of the community, informed me that Faeries in other parts of the country may be more politically active.

Almost thirty years after that first voyage of discovery in Arizona, at least a dozen Faerie gatherings take place every year across the United States; five sanctuary spaces are established in various parts of the country, with one in the works in France; gatherings take place in Europe and Australia; and the Radical Faeries have become a recognizable part of the contemporary queer cultural landscape.

―――

My interactions with the Faerie community spanned approximately fifteen months. I made initial contact with them by mail in early July 2001, telling them of my interest in studying the group, identifying myself as a graduate student in sociology, and expressing a desire to attend their upcoming gathering. Later that month I had a phone conversation with Tiara, the Faerie in charge of registration. We had a friendly chat, ranging over a number of topics related to my attendance in a research capacity. After discussing my training as an ethnographer and the precautions I would be taking with respect to confidentiality and privacy, Tiara intimated that he did not think that my research would present any problems. In fact, I was delighted by his reminder "not to forget about my own pleasure" and to remember to have fun. The gathering itself lasted, as it always does, for ten days, beginning on the first Friday in August 2001. I subsequently returned to the sanctuary in October for a weekend with a smaller group of Faeries and maintained contact with numerous others throughout the coming year as I arranged interviews and traveled to conduct them. During this time I also helped two Faeries with major moving projects and chatted with several informally when I met them at various public venues in a nearby city. I also subscribed to the group's e-mail discussion list, so I was kept up to date on issues of interest to the community.

I had long been intrigued by this group on both a personal and an intellectual level. Prior to this research, my only contact with this group was its appearance each year in the local gay pride parade. Their outrageous trash drag appearance and high spirits never failed to delight the crowd, myself included. At the time I began this research my own experience with drag was limited to several brief attempts in early childhood to pass myself off as sultry Ginger Grant, the castaway movie star of TV's *Gilligan's Island*. This I attempted by wearing my older sister's slip and a simple strand of *faux* pearls borrowed from my mother's jewelry case. Much later, a Halloween appearance as then–first lady Barbara Bush garnered lukewarm reviews during a spirited night on the town.[3] Beyond this, I had little experience with "dress up," but I certainly had no qualms about it. Tiara suggested I visit a local resale shop and "pick up a few things" before attending the gathering.

My ability to identify myself as a researcher and to gauge the group's reaction was greatly facilitated by the Faerie convention of circling (a group meeting wherein participating Faeries sit in a circle and share their thoughts; see below). At my first morning circle, while introducing myself, I "came out" as a researcher to the assembled crowd. If this announcement caused any concern, none was communicated to me. In fact, I was delighted by a gracious offer from one of the longtime members: with a twinkle in his eye and a hearty laugh that shook his ample frame, he informed me that he had "*lots* of stories to tell me." Thus was I welcomed into the heart of this generous community.

A Brief History of the Radical Faeries

Who are we gay people? Where do we come from, in history and in anthropology, and where have we been? What are we for?
—HARRY HAY, "A SEPARATE PEOPLE WHOSE TIME HAS COME"

Many accounts of the early days of the Radical Faeries depict longtime gay activist and political writer Harry Hay as almost single-handedly bringing the organization into being. Although Hay's role was undoubtedly critical to the movement, the development of the Radical Faeries relied upon several concurrent strands coming together. As early as 1976 writer Arthur Evans gave a series of well-attended lectures in San Francisco on the subject of gay spirituality, and his "faery circle" began to meet regularly in his Haight Street apartment (Timmons 1990, 252–53; Thompson 1987, 262). Throughout the 1970s various gay groups attempted to create communities in isolated rural areas of Oregon, Washington, North Carolina, and Tennessee (Thompson 1987, 262). Less permanent assemblies of gay men came together as well. The most ambitious of these was the Faggots and Class Struggle Conference in Wolf Creek, Oregon, during September 1976. Here the word "fairie" was used in a way that signaled its political content (Thompson 1987, 264). It was during that same year that a young neopagan spiritualist and aspiring shaman by the name of Mitch Walker began corresponding with Hay after hearing of his work at one of Evans's lectures (Timmons 1990, 259).

The clearinghouse for all of this activity was a little publication founded outside of Grinnell, Iowa, in October 1974; *RFD* currently maintains a readership of primarily rural gay men. It promotes a vision of queer life that differs sharply from the prevailing urban sensibility that shapes the various meanings of queer in twenty-first- century America[4] During the late 1970s it provided the perfect sounding board for like-minded gays to read each other's work and exchange ideas on gay politics and spirituality. As Rodgers (1993) notes:

These early explorations of gay spirituality documented by *RFD* had no single focus—they were eclectic examinations of paths such as Christianity (Crow 1977; Treelove 1975), Buddhism (Englebert 1977), New Age esotericism (Wittman 1975a), and especially Neo-Paganism (Caradoc 1977; Circle of Loving Companions 1975; Hermsen 1977; Wittman 1975b) from a gay perspective. *Faeries*, as such, had not yet come into existence. (Rodgers 1993, 18; citations in original)

It is worth noting that Harry Hay's philosophical work on what he called "subject-subject consciousness" was rejected by *RFD* in 1976 as "gobbledygook," in spite of his status as putative founder of the Radical Faeries (Timmons 1990, 257). Despite this setback, Hay continued to share his ideas and manuscripts, both with the young Walker and with another gay activist by the name of Don Kilhefner. At the time of their initial collaboration in 1978 Hay was sixty-six, Kilhefner thirty-nine, and Walker twenty-five. Thus, they spanned three generations of gay activism (Timmons 1990, 257). Together these three worked to channel the burgeoning interest in spiritual and political alternatives for gay men into the movement that soon became the Radical Faeries. I turn now to some background on each of these three men.

Harry Hay was the first to associate the word "faerie" with a unique form of same-sex consciousness. This was during his 1970 speech to the Western Regional Homophile Conference: "Let the spirit be betrayed, let coercion of opportunism bind us against our will, and PRESTO, like the faeries of folk-lore, suddenly we are no longer there" (Timmons 1990, 252). By virtue of his long career in activism and his occasional philosophical writings, Hay is often seen as the intellectual anchor of the Faerie movement. But prior to this, he was probably best known for leading the first attempt to formally organize the grievances of an emerging "homosexual minority" in the United States during the early 1950s. His first encounter with the idea of a homosexual organization was the result of a peculiar coincidence. In 1929, a seventeen-year-old Hay had his first homosexual experience with a man named Champ Simmons. Through Simmons, Hay learned of an earlier abortive attempt to organize homosexuals in Chicago during the 1920s. "Champ passed it on to me as if it were too dangerous; the failure of the Chicago group should be a direct warning to anybody trying to do anything like that again" (Katz 1992, 407). Hay apparently interpreted the idea in more optimistic terms. The next year he enrolled at Stanford University, where after a few months he made the then unheard-of decision to declare himself openly as a homosexual: "I declared myself on campus to all the people that I knew: to the eating club I belonged to, the fraternities who were rushing me" (Katz 1992, 407). But Hay's intellectual development did not really begin until he left Stanford. He dropped out after a little more than a year to pursue an acting career. During this period he met actor Will Geer (TV's Grandpa Walton on *The Waltons*), who introduced him to the Communist Party in Los Angeles (Timmons 1990, 64). After a period of initial excitement and active involvement, he came to feel increasingly alienated by the party's policy on homosexuality. He revealed his homosexuality to party superiors, who encouraged him to repress it. Accepting their advice, he married another party member, Anita Platky, in 1938. "I determined that I would simply close the book and never look back. For fourteen years I lived . . . in an exile world" (D'Emilio 1983, 59).[5]

By 1948 Hay was the leader of a group of four gay men who were meeting privately to discuss political issues related to their homosexuality. At this point Hay had been a member of the Communist Party for fifteen years and was supporting himself by teaching at the People's Education Center in Los Angeles. During that year, the discussion group evolved from private meetings to semiprivate events open to all who wished to attend. The original group soon found it necessary to split in half to accommodate the increasing audience, and by 1953 the founding members had set up an organization of cell-like secrecy, with groups meeting in several cities throughout California, as well as in New York City and Chicago.[6] "The important thing to note," writes Licata (1981, 168), "is how quickly the movement spread to the large urban gay ghettos, proof that a gay communication network already existed surreptitiously but effectively in the large cities." Hay chose the name Mattachine Foundation for this new group.[7]

With respect to Mattachine ideology, Timmons (1990, 150) observes that "one central concept was heavily influenced by Marxism: Harry's application of the term 'cultural minority' to homosexuals," ostensibly to make a homosexual identity more intelligible to the other (primarily Marxist) members of the early Mattachine:

Their definition of homosexuals as a minority "unaware" of its existence put the founders on more familiar ground and suggested to them an initial course of action. Their formulation resembled the Marxist distinction between a class "in itself" and a class "for itself." The difference between these two was one of consciousness . . . Homosexuals, too were trapped by false consciousness, by a hegemonic ideology that labeled their eroticism an individual aberration. (D'Emilio 1983, 65–66)

Thus Hay's experience as a movement intellectual (socialist, homophile, and Faerie) provides a concrete example of Eyerman and Jamison's (1991, 63) observation that "particular movements tend to feed off and create each other." Through the language of Marxism, the founders were able to articulate the Mattachine's ideological commitments and determine an initial course of action. These early decisions had far-reaching implications; some even carried over into Faerie culture decades later. Early activities of the Mattachine emphasized the process of changing consciousness and creating what Eyerman and Jamison (1991, 56) call "a new conceptual space." James Gruber, an early Mattachine activist, spoke of this atmosphere in terms that are strikingly similar to those used by many of my Faerie interview subjects:

All of us had known a whole lifetime of not talking, of repression. Just the freedom to open up . . . really, that's what it was all about. We had found a sense of belonging, of camaraderie, of openness in an atmosphere of tension and mistrust . . . Such a great deal of it was a social climate. A family feeling came out of it, a nonsexual emphasis . . . it was a brand new idea. (D'Emilio 1983, 68)

However, as the Mattachine Foundation grew, a number of relatively conservative, middle-class gays were attracted to the movement and began to push for a more open organizational structure and a lower political profile for the group. Trouble soon erupted within the organization. At Mattachine's 1953 convention, middle-class members were furious when they discovered that the group's attorney had recently testified in a hostile manner before the House Un-American Activities Committee. This revelation brought issues of secrecy and Mattachine's ties to communism to the convention floor. A disgruntled Harry Hay saw the handwriting on the wall and decided to cede control of the organization to "the middle-class groups" (Katz 1992, 419). The new leadership of the foundation that emerged after the 1953 convention completely refashioned the organization. Political action was replaced by an emphasis on social support for members, education, and the dissemination of information to the outside world. On March 23, 1954, the Mattachine Foundation was renamed the Mattachine Society to reflect these changes (Licata 1981, 169). At this point the movement began a quiet period of consolidation and cautious growth, for the most part eschewing activism and direct protest. Hay busied himself with other projects, including writing and developing his ideas on subject-subject consciousness.

The second member of the founding triumvirate was West Coast activist Don Kilhefner. Kilhefner grew up in an Amish-Mennonite community in Pennsylvania, which he left at the age of seventeen to attend Howard University.[8] There he came out and was active in the Student Nonviolent Coordinating Committee and antiwar activism. After graduating from Howard he went to Ethiopia with the Peace Corps, and upon his return he decided to move West to attend the University of California, Los Angeles (UCLA). During the late 1960s he joined the Peace and Freedom Party and became a follower of Mao Tse-tung (Timmons 1990, 257–58). Kilhefner was very active in the Los Angeles Gay Liberation Front (GLF) during its short lifespan (1969–1971); he was also active in California GLF efforts to establish a gay colony in Alpine County, California, in 1970 (Teal 1995, 294–98). Eventually, when the Los Angeles GLF evolved into the Los Angeles Gay Community Services Center, Kilhefner was its first executive director. He involved himself in nonprofit organizational work, eventually administering millions of dollars in grants in support of a gay/lesbian alcohol recovery facility. Later he became interested in various human potential movements and developed a growing conviction that something was missing from gay life. He moved into a yoga commune in Los Angeles and began to reassess the movement (Timmons 1990, 257–58). Prior to their collaboration, Kilhefner had met Hay twice during the early 1970s.

However, it was not until a third meeting in 1978, when Hay gave Kilhefner a copy of his position paper on subject-subject consciousness, that the two began to connect on a deeper level (Timmons 1990, 260–61).

Mitch Walker was the youngest member of the founding trio and brought an emphasis on Jungian depth psychology to Faerie culture. Raised in a middle-class Jewish family in suburban Los Angeles during the 1950s and 1960s, he studied psychology at UCLA and later at the University of California, Berkeley. In most of his academic work he concentrated on applying Jung's work to gay culture. Walker was also inspired by the idea of gay shamanism in the tradition outlined by the early twentieth-century British sex radical Edward Carpenter. "I work with the spirit and I'm a gay spirit worker and I'm a gay shaman and that's what I do," he once explained. Walker has been described as having a very intense personality; some in the early days of the group looked upon him as a messiah who blended magic, psychology, and gay liberation. Others thought he was "a mind-tripper with an air of psychological super sophistication and mystical superiority" (Timmons 1990, 259). Upon hearing about Hay's work at one of Arthur Evans's lectures, Walker began a spirited correspondence with Hay, followed by a month-long visit to New Mexico, where Hay lived with his lover, John Burnside, during February 1978.

The collaboration of Hay, Kilhefner, and Walker in the late 1970s generated a great deal of excitement, and soon plans were being made for the first Faerie gathering. These efforts culminated in the 1979 publication of "A Call to Gay Brothers: A Spiritual Conference for Radical Faeries" in issue 20 of *RFD* by Hay and Kilhefner. Not long after that, smiling down upon that small patch of land in Arizona, the universe turned toward the fabulous and opened a space for the Radical Faeries.

What Is a Faerie?

For me [*pause*] being a Faerie has something to do with [*pause*] really wanting to break with convention. That seems to be a unifying theme. When I think of what is a Faerie, I think of, so what can I think of that Faeries would agree on? 'Cause there are lots of Faerie things that not every Faerie would subscribe to. So when I think of "what's a Faerie?" I think, so what would people agree on? And that, wanting to break convention, and some of the key conventions have to do with gender norms and, and, the manifestations of those, so—drag. Um, and it can really even get into a gender question in terms of who are bona fide Faeries. 'Cause there are boy Faeries. There are genetically boy Faeries and genetically girl Faeries in addition to whatever genders they may choose to express. So it's not about biological sex. (Zinnia)

One of the fascinating discoveries I made during my fieldwork was that in Faerie culture, almost thirty years old and having made its mark both nationally and internationally, fundamental questions of identity are still being actively debated. "What is a Faerie?" is a recurring question in the community. In this section I examine this conundrum and analyze its implications for the gender transgression that is a central commitment of Faerie culture. I asked each of my interview subjects to tell me what being a Faerie meant to him:

Peter: Now that you are one, you should be able to answer this question—what is a Faerie? . . . How would you answer that question, right now?

Calliope: Well I appreciate that you put those additions to the definition because they do really make a difference. Everything is a continuum, things change constantly.

Frankie: Yeah, it resurfaces every time there are three new people asking the question. And from what I've heard from other e-lists that, um, and like there's a big national Faerie e-list I guess, that it like once a year crops up and then there's this huge discussion about it.

Wanda Sue: I don't know if a Faerie can be nailed down as "this is what a Faerie is." I think a Faerie, I think Faeries come from, it's almost like there's a space that's opened and for us.

As you can see, there is a curious indeterminacy about Faerie identity, a postmodern emphasis on fluidity and incoherence that paradoxically exists quite comfortably alongside some strongly essentialist notions emphasizing the fixity of Faerie identity.

The strongest indicator of Faerie essentialism is probably the notion of the "fae spirit." This indicates the presence of an internally stable and recognizable "essence" that reveals itself as one goes about the business of living in the world. As Calliope puts it, "Many of my friends have said, 'Well, you are a Radical Faerie, you always have been, you just don't realize to what degree you are.' Well, I knew that to be true, which is why I was seeking in the first place." Furthermore, once one recognizes the fae spirit in oneself, it is easy to recognize it in others, as Petunia indicates: "I don't know, you know, I know one when I see one, I know one when I feel one." Frankie concurs with this assessment: "And people will say, 'Oh, he doesn't know it but he's a Faerie.' So there must be something we recognize beyond a person who comes to the gatherings." This discourse suggests that Faeries exhibit high-identity dominance (Brekhus 2003), since they are essentially Faeries "all the time" (maximum duration). However, I suspect that identity density varies a great deal among Faeries. For some, the sanctuary serves as an identity-potent setting, the only place for some to safely enact their Faerie identity. However, many community members maintain their Faerie identity outside the sanctuary, but my overall impression is that most do this at a significantly lower volume.[9]

In my interviews I found evidence that the fae spirit has a history, and not an altogether happy one. One of my subjects spoke at length of the Faerie diaspora, whereby fae spirits were driven underground for centuries:

I've come to believe that what we're seeing now in the Faerie, I think what we're seeing now is a certain coming of age of the Faerie movement. And in that way what I mean is that we're coming, I think, full circle in a diaspora. That at one point somewhere in human history in various cultures, people who, if we look back on it and we examine their lives and who they were as people, we have an instant, we'd have an instant ah-ha [*assumes falsetto voice*], "Oh! They're Faeries!" But this was hundreds of years ago. In some cases it was dozens of years ago, in other cultural cases it's hundreds of years ago and maybe even thousands of years ago that this happened. And rules were set up, which were in effect a diaspora, that kept us away from each other, you know, that forbid us to have really meaningful contact with each other. And it's not just about the gay thing. 'Cause I don't really believe that Faeries are specifically a sexual identity. It's more a spirit thing. And because we're soooo, to put it in modern terms, out there and weird, and um, eccentric and unique and radically individualized, um, that they—they in the more mainstream cultures, the more mainstream people in various cultures, laid down all sorts of taboos about us being able to hang out together and uh . . . now, thanks to the cultural and political and sexual revolutions that happened in the United States primarily, but also in Europe, in the middle of the twentieth century—the stage was set for us to come back together . . . there is an enormous coming together of fae energy, and maybe we're not, we're somewhere along the way in that process, I think. (TigerLily)

Another strongly essentialist narrative running through my interviews underscores the idea that the sanctuary serves as a highly potent identity setting. This is the idea of "coming home" to the Faerie community. Several of my subjects spoke in very emotional terms of their initial contacts with Faerie culture as a return to a familiar place from which they had been exiled:

But that's what if felt like, when I got there. It felt like coming home. You know we always use that sort of metaphor, and it's because that's what it feels like, even if you've never been there before. (Frankie)

Part of that final piece was that I had found my home. I had found my tribe . . . the Radical Faeries are definitely my home. (Calliope)

I remember it as being a very cleansing time, a very fulfilling time, a very loving time, a very accepting time, a very . . . I was home, I was home. (PopTart)

I think to a degree it just kind of evolves, and you can just kind of, you get to a comfort level where you just feel like, OK, you're at home. (MoonGaze)

What I think about [is] the symbol that draws me back . . . there was a huge arbor that said, "Welcome Home" . . . the whole idea of "welcome home"; it was home in a way that I had never experienced before, and deeply moving, deeply, deeply moving. (Zinnia)

In fact, this sentiment of "coming home" to Faerie space is so common that it has even been incorporated (in a minor way) into the construction of the sanctuary cookhouse. On my way to my first gathering dinner I was stopped dead in my tracks by what looked to be the hateful graffiti of a homophobic vandal. Upon closer inspection, I realized it was just a charming sight gag. Sprawled across a large board in front of one of the cookhouse windows in large spray-painted letters was the simple phrase, "Faggots Come Home!"

Paradoxically, alongside this strong emphasis on a fixed Faerie identity is an enthusiastic embrace of fragmentation and fluidity. As Calliope says, "Every time that I go [to the sanctuary] I know I will have new and different experiences. Some of it I might be able to predict ahead of time, and others I won't. And I look forward to both, and I don't know how much I'm going to change—none of us do." One of the first changes a person experiences when visiting a Faerie sanctuary involves renaming. Almost all Faeries take a second name and use this in interaction with other Faeries. The process of choosing a name is understood as organic. Either a new Faerie discovers his or her name or the responsibility for naming is given to some established member of the community. Either way, the new Faerie name is revealed, rather than simply made up. TigerLily explains it this way:

And all the sudden here everybody is saying, "Be, be, whoever you are, do it, whatever it is! Go unique, be yourself." Naming is an absolute extension of that. It's all about saying, this is me, I'm claiming this identity, and in fact, you know what? I can change this identity and be another one, right here—boom! I'm not, I'm multifaceted. I can be anything I want to be.

Furthermore, the practice of abandoning one Faerie name in favor of another is quite common. Many Faeries in the band I studied have taken several names, abandoning each when the feeling was right, in favor of one that more clearly expressed an emerging identity. This practice has even become the occasion for a fair amount of joking about instituting "name change fees" for Faeries who change their names too often. This dynamic process of evolving identities was put in spatiotemporal terms by Wanda Sue:

I think a Faerie, I think Faeries come from, it's almost like there's a space that's opened and for us here . . . it's [our sanctuary]. And so it's this space that is open and the Faeries here meet in August for a ten-day gathering, and within that space people can start defining and fleshing out, they may have, they may bring themselves a raw potential Faerie type of stuff [*laughs*], but as they're there they can more clearly define what that means for them . . . When I think of what is a Faerie I think of a time and space where people can explore that as opposed to, you know . . . [*trails off*].

But it is important to acknowledge that identity change and fluidity in this community are bounded by certain shared assumptions about what it means to be a Faerie. One is not free, for example, to abandon one's identity as a vegan shaman or star spirit to take up an identity as an investment banker, tobacco lobbyist, or Hummer salesman. The flourishing discourse of identity change and transition obscures this important fact, and I suspect that this freedom within strictly delimited identity boundaries is what qualifies the Faerie community as an identity cove, sheltered from the more perplexing and troubling postmodern identity demands issuing from the surrounding culture (Gergen 1991).

What implications does this paradoxical mix of fixed and fluid identity have for gender subversion within the Faerie community? Essentialist notions of Faerie identity can be traced to Harry Hay's intellectual stewardship of the movement's early days. One can see the precursors of an essential Faerie identity even in his early work with the Mattachine Society, and his separatist bent seems to have reached fruition with the publication of his essay entitled "A Separate People Whose Time Has Come":

I propose that we gay folk, who Great Mother Nature has been assembling as a separate people in these last hundred thousand years, must now prepare to emerge from the shadows of history *because we are a species variant with a particular characteristic adaptation in consciousness whose time has come!* (Hay 1987, 280; emphasis in original)

The Faeries I observed spoke of gender in essentialist terms when they referenced the ideal of the third gender. Although it is probably safe to say that not all Faeries subscribe to the idea, it is clear that Hay conceived of Faeries as neither masculine nor feminine, but as something new:

The Hetero-male, incapable of conceiving that there could possibly be a window on the world other than his own, is equally incapable of perceiving that we Gay People might not fit in either of his Man-Woman categories . . . he might not be able to handle perceiving that the notion that persons are all varying combinations of male and female is simply a Hetero-male derived notion suitable only to Heteros *holding nothing of validity insofar as Gay People are concerned.* Yet we Faeries allow Bully-boy to persuade us to search out the "feminine" in ourselves. (Hay 1980, 33; emphasis in original)

There is more than a hint of misogyny here, along with the strong suggestion that, at least in Hay's mind, the stigma of effeminacy had a powerful effect. Hay seems to be overly concerned that the third gender he is trying to establish escapes the taint of feminization. Elsewhere he writes rather frantically, "No, you're not being feminine. You're being . . . *other.* Not masculine—okay! Agreed! But not feminine either. *Other!*" (Hay 1987, 283; emphasis in original). Furthermore, his anxieties can be traced directly to his lived experience and an early encounter with hegemonic masculinity: "When I was in fourth grade, the boys at school would tell me I threw the ball like a girl, but MaryEllen Fermin and Helen Johnson said, 'No, you don't throw a ball like a girl. You throw it like a sissy!'" (Hay 1987, 282–83). Thus it becomes possible to see this struggling toward "otherness" that is motivated less by concerns with the limits of binary gender thinking than it is with escaping the stigma of feminization—that is, a *gendered* motivation for transcending the gender binary.[10]

Fluidity and fragmentation are more characteristic of the actual day-to-day gender practice of the Faeries. Here the ideal of the third gender is forgone in favor of a kind of "gender pastiche" that involves a shuttling back and forth between the two terms of the binary, between thoroughly established indicators of masculinity and femininity and by the juxtaposition of recognizably masculine and feminine features in novel and sometimes surprising ways. This is perhaps most visible in the way drag is deployed in the community (see below), but it is not limited to dress.

MoonGaze, a photographer who at the time of our interview had recently completed a series of Faerie portraits, comments on this explicitly:

[There is a] balance between the masculine and the feminine in the Faerie portraits, especially. And I think in the people that are drawn to [the sanctuary] in general. I feel like there's a, a very nice balance between the masculine and the feminine, and it's like both are honored and both are embraced and accepted, and it's not just for one side of the teeter-totter more than the other. There's really room for the mixture of everybody's unique mix, and so in fact as I went around to try to ask people what their definition of a Faerie was, it helped me hone my own definition of a Faerie, which is somebody who not only honors but celebrates the unique mix of masculine and feminine within everyone.

What the data reveal is both a postmodern emphasis on the fluidity and fragmentation of identity and an essentialist emphasis on the stable autonomous individual—both views existing within the same community, often expressed by the same person. My sense is that the tension between these two conceptions of the self goes largely unrecognized; further, this lack of awareness obscures the fact that despite a *recognition* of fragmentation and fluidity, in the final analysis the members of this community are likely to return to accounts of their behavior couched in *essentialist* terms—sometimes in the form of the idealized third gender. This ideal is only partially realized in practice, but it is sometimes expressed in ways that reinscribe the notion of a masculine essence, even in this community explicitly committed to radical gender experimentation. As Butler (1993, 133) observes, an awareness and a celebration of gender performativity do not necessarily imply an emancipatory gender politics or consciousness.[11]

TigerLily was the only one of my interview subjects to offer his thoughts on how social class intersects with fae consciousness:

Faeries have got a good, Faeries are pretty good on class. They're, I think Faeries have got a really strong ethic about, I mean, for example, no one ever has to pay if they can't. Nothing, ever. No one ever has to pay a damn bit if they can't afford it . . . and [we're] not that hung up on job status or, or what your daddy did or, there isn't any of that. Classism—I think we've pretty much got that one beat in our community.

Not only were class observations absent from my other interviews but I received few indicators of class consciousness during my time in the field, and only limited information about how most Faeries were employed outside of the sanctuary. Those who did volunteer this information were usually employed in professional or semiprofessional positions (although two Faeries stressed the fact that they had opted out of the mainstream economy and supported themselves through odd jobs). Despite the dearth of data, I encountered a suggestive situation on a chilly fall day at the sanctuary, which I chronicled in my field notes:

After we eat there's time to relax around the stove in the cabin. As we talk, an occasional snowflake drifts past the window. I'm astonished to discover that two Faeries in our group of six have attended private boarding schools. I'm suddenly struck by how inattentive I've been to social class in my field notes. I recall Sun Ray telling me he worked in a professional position. I'm also interested to discover that even in this small group, three of us have pursued graduate studies. Is this a movement fueled by middle/upper-middle class disaffection? I'm tempted to link this with the idealized imaginings of nature I've been encountering among the Faeries, which, it seems to me, could only come out of a background of relative privilege and comfort . . . An example of this romanticizing tendency came about when several Faeries were "grieving" the fact that some peaches had to be thrown out because they were rotting. It seemed to me that this kind of sentiment could only come out of a bourgeois experience—I was amused at the prospect of the pioneers or any other people truly living close to the exigencies of nature "grieving" for spoiled peaches.

TigerLily was also the most forthcoming of my interview subjects regarding race. In sharp contrast to his assessment of social class among the Faeries, he is much less forgiving here:

I think that there's an incredible amount of racism [in our Faerie community] but not nearly so much as there is in the rest of society . . . I mean people don't, I'm the only one I've ever heard, except, no, [names another Faerie] and I are the only two people who've ever expressed dismay about the fact that we just took the name [of our sanctuary from Native Americans]. Nobody else sees it as cultural appropriation . . . But we just took that word, on the basis of what a white guy said, without bothering to go talk to [Native Americans]. We just took their word, your word, your tradition, we're going to, we're going to just pluck it up and use it. And I was part of that whole scene where the naming was taking place, and in the back of my head little red flags were going up saying, what's this? But I didn't say anything.[12]

When I ask him why he thinks more people of color have not found their way to the Faeries, TigerLily responds sensibly, "I don't know, and my first inclination is to go to people of color and ask them, rather than me trying to spend a lot of time trying to predict what it is." Perhaps part of the answer lies in the way whiteness is reflected in the central symbol of the Faerie community. Fairies, those sprightly magical beings of European lore, have until recently been depicted as exclusively white beings. Silver

(1999), in her study of fairies in nineteenth-century Britain, demonstrates their connection with racialized and imperialist anxieties among white, middle-class Victorians. She cites a number of scholars who explicitly interpreted fairies in these terms. In this view, stories of fairies operate as nostalgia narratives, hearkening back to fundamental struggles over culture and civilization: "The clashes between early peoples were not mere power struggles, but conflicts filled with racial and imperial implications; the importance of the fairies is that they were white" (Silver 1999, 46). She goes on to explain how, as a dominant and dominating symbol, fairies were linked to imperialism in the Victorian imagination:

The nature of given concepts was dictated by whether they were believed and enunciated by the conqueror or the conquered. For example, beliefs about fairies and about witches were very similar, said Gomme [Sir George Laurence Gomme (1853–1916), British folklorist and author]. The belief in fairies, however, came from the conquerors; it was a belief about the aborigines from Aryan sources. The belief in witches, on the other hand, came from the conquered aborigines themselves; they believed they had magical powers and tried to spread this belief (in part, to guarantee their survival) among their conquerors. (Silver 1999, 46)

This view suggests that the overwhelming whiteness of my Faerie community might be explained in part by the unconscious adoption of an already racialized symbol. The fact that this move is made without conscious intent (indeed it exists alongside a vigorous discourse of inclusion and racial diversity within Faerie culture) may be read as a consequence of white privilege, a reading encouraged by TigerLily's observations about cultural appropriation.

Changing the Subject: From Gay Clone to Fabulous Fae

Let us gather therefore—in secure and consecrated places . . . to re-invoke from ancient ashes our Faerie Circle. To dance . . . to meditate—not in the singular isolation of hetero subject-OBJECT praxis—but rather in Faerie Circles reaching out to subject-SUBJECT evocation.
—HARRY HAY, "TOWARD THE NEW FRONTIERS OF FAIRY VISION"

In a community as diverse and eclectic as the Radical Faeries, the tendency to resist rigid ideological commitments is perhaps not surprising. Easily a hundred ideological and spiritual flowers have flourished in Faerie space, perhaps many more. Although it is probably safe to say that most of these would be considered "unconventional" (and almost certainly "left of center"), one finds a variety of political, spiritual, and communal beliefs thriving among the Faeries. However, there is one ideological component that almost all Faeries recognize and acknowledge (or are at some point asked to acknowledge) as part of the philosophical and spiritual foundation of the movement: the notion of subject-subject consciousness, as developed by Harry Hay. The concept is fairly simple and to some degree reflects Hay's earlier political commitment to Marxism.[13] Subject-subject consciousness dictates that one must always treat others as subjects like themselves, never as objects or as a means to some instrumental end: "Humanity must expand its experience of thinking of another not as object—to be used, to be manipulated, to be mastered, to be CONSUMED—but as subject—as another like him/her self, another self to be respected, to be appreciated, to be cherished" (Harry Hay, cited in Timmons 1990, 255). Hay clearly saw this as a new form of consciousness and saw gay people as its progenitors. He talked about the early Mattachine Society as enabling this new form of consciousness in terms that explicitly link it to a rejection of the logic of hegemonic masculinity: "The Movement created around itself a free-space, a fire-break if you will, a discontinuity between itself and the ever-oppressing, ever-invading Hetero-male Conglomerate of Domination and Submission Games that we call Society" (Hay 1980, 30).

Hay was convinced that a subject-object orientation (the pattern that results when one person objectifies another and treats that person as a means to some sexual, political, or economic end) is inherent in hetero-sexual relationships and is responsible for a host of evils, including war, slavery, and other forms of oppression. Even aspects of gay culture, particularly its commodified urban forms, were infected with subject-object relations. This situation, argued Hay, was a tragedy, as same-sex relationships offered the promise of a new form of consciousness centered on subject-subject consciousness. Subject-subject consciousness became possible when love and sex happened between what Hay called "two similars," and it had implications for gay people's capacity to forge more authentic and beautiful relationships with nature and ideas:

Relating subject to subject is not limited to one's relationship with a lover, but in fact is widely applicable. Some people are ready to respond at this level, to at least some degree. An opening invitation to relate so might well be offered to all one may encounter . . . if we are not snuffed out while lingering too long immersed in conflict, we shall one day all be related in this great new way to one another and to all living beings. (Burnside 1989, 19–26)

The aspiring shaman and Faerie cofounder Mitch Walker outlines the same concept in terms of "magickal twinning" in a passage that again emphasizes the equality inherent in same-sex relations:

Since Magickal Twinning inheres in the Double, Double projections involving others invoke the Twinning force between people. When this happens, there's a sense . . . of being identical to the other person. If two things are identical, they must be perfectly equal. Since Double-love involves the most intense projections of Double, it gives rise to the clearest, strongest sense of Magickal Twinning. Because of this, Double-love is the source of ideals concerning equality. (Walker 1987, 224–25)[14]

What is perhaps the most striking attribute of subject-subject consciousness in Faerie culture is the way it is linked to the fae spirit. The assumed point of origin for this new form of consciousness is linked with Faerie essentialism, with "being a different species perceiving a different reality" (Hay 1980, 31):

Natural selection, early on in human evolution, set into the evolving whirl a small percentage of beings who appeared to counter-balance a number of prevalent characteristics of the emerging human conformity. Humanity, thus, would be wise to finally give consideration to these deviants in their ranks . . . to begin to grant the GAYS the peace and growing space they will need to display and to further develop in communicable words and in models of activity, the "gift"—the singular mutation we GAYS have been carrying so unfalteringly and preserving so passionately, even over the not infrequent centuries of despair and persecution. (Harry Hay, cited in Timmons 1990, 256)

I offer an alternative to this essentialist narrative that highlights the role of gender and masculinity in the formation of subject-subject consciousness. I have no argument with the value of the impulse toward equality in same-sex relationships. My disagreement with Hay stems from his assumptions about what subject-subject consciousness was reacting against, specifically the objectification that was the ascendant trend in gay sexual culture during the 1970s. It seems clear that Hay saw urban gay sexual cultures as "heteroimitative" in that it seemed to be premised on exploitive sexual relationships between a dominant (subject) and submissive (object) partner.[15] This was the period after Stonewall and gay liberation but before the advent of the AIDS pandemic, when many gay men were experimenting sexually. While railing against the incursion of subject-object relations in gay urban cultures, Hay fails to recognize that a kind of equality in same-sex relationships was informing this culture. It may well be that, as Hay seems to presume, an unequal subject-object dynamic was not at work; rather, gay men during what Martin Levine (1998) has dubbed the "clone" period were actively involved (at least in terms of their sexual connections) in constructing *object-object* relationships.[16]

What I mean to suggest here is that while clear distinctions between dominant and submissive roles existed, both were being actively objectified in gay urban enclaves during this period. As Gregg Blachford (1979) suggests, many men found the sexual world of equal-opportunity objectification enormously satisfying. Blachford argues that there is nothing oppressive about sexual objectification per se, but rather it is objectification in the context of unequal power arrangements that is oppressive. Where power is distributed more evenly, the experience of objectification (both being objectified and objectifying others) can actually generate a great deal of pleasure, a point to which many gay men can testify. Several of the erotic practices in gay leather culture, as we shall see, are premised on a sharp distinction between dominant and submissive roles and would have undoubtedly confounded Hay and his simplified notion of objectification.

However, I emphatically do not mean to suggest that this pattern of mutual objectification was the only sexual pattern available to gay men at the time, simply that it was the culturally ascendant form, and the one with which Hay seems to be taking issue. Furthermore, my argument suggests that egalitarian relationships between gay men were already thriving in urban settings, well in advance of Hay's work on subject-subject consciousness in the late 1970s. My argument also raises doubts about the inherent inequality of sexual relationships that include objectification. A posting on an online Faerie e-mail discussion board tacitly acknowledges this: "Anyone think that it's maybe time to give the mind thing a rest and drop the subject-subject ideal for awhile in favor of some object-object consciousness? What I'm saying is maybe its time to get together for a good old group JO [jack-off] party."

By putting the question of objectification on the table, something Hay seems unwilling to do, it becomes possible to see that the emergence of subject-subject consciousness may be informed by a masculinist logic rather than Faerie essence. For Hay, the primary concern becomes how to structure relationships between men once objectification is rejected. His emphasis on rejecting objectification obscures the fundamentally gendered problem that he is dealing with. Perhaps subject-object relations are unsustainable not so much because they are ethically or philosophically problematic but because they are impractical when applied to relations between men. Most, if not all, of the gay men of Hay's generation were raised in families that expected and actively inculcated conventional masculinity and garden-variety heterosexuality. The end result of this socialization is that such men will in most cases not assent to real domination in sexual and interpersonal relationships (although they may joyfully surrender themselves in a controlled arena like a leather play party). To the extent that both male partners in such a relationship have been raised to expect to be the purveyor of the male gaze—the active subject who does the objectifying—a pragmatic move toward equality becomes necessary. In this context, object-object relationships serve just as well as subject-subject relationships. However, by rejecting objectification, the only viable alternative left open to Hay is subject-subject relations. Considered from this perspective, Hay's notion of subject-subject consciousness can be seen as responding to norms of hegemonic masculinity, even as it attempts to subvert them.

Circle of Authority: Challenging Hegemonic Power

In a Faerie circle, who is at the head and who is at the foot? . . . Confronted with the loving-sharing Consensus of subject-SUBJECT relationships all Authoritarianism must vanish.
—HARRY HAY, "TOWARD THE NEW FRONTIER OF FAIRY VISION"

In certain respects, Faerie culture can be read in a Weberian light—as a "re-enchantment strategy" and deliberate attempt to revive and nurture a magical community of meaning in the wake of late capitalism's increasing rationalization. Although few would be likely to articulate their behavior in Weberian terms, in their day-to-day activities Faeries actively challenge the means/ends thinking that is a critical component of Weber's (1964) concept of instrumental rationality. For the most part, Faeries exhibit a kind of cheerful resignation, even pride, in their community's inefficiency. Ostensibly eschewing any overtly hierarchical governing arrangements, Radical Faeries are dedicated to consensus decision making and volunteer labor. When something needs to be discussed, Faeries gather in a circle and pass a talisman along from speaker to speaker. A Faerie may hold the talisman and speak for as long as he or she wishes, and discussion continues until consensus is reached. The circle perfectly analogizes the Faerie philosophy regarding power; it is a physical arrangement of bodies designed to present a strong challenge to the hierarchical arrangements that are central to the logic of hegemonic masculinity (Connell 1987, 1995). As a result, during my time in the field, dinners often took many hours to prepare and were frequently served after 9 p.m. The Faeries featured in this study have had a construction project in the works for close to ten years, but it has not yet passed the discussion phase because no consensus has been reached as to how the building should be used or where it should be located. It is considered bad Faerie form to single someone out and ask him or her directly to wash the dishes, help repair the dock, or chop wood. Faeries who have been around for awhile recognize that newcomers to the community have a tendency to volunteer a lot more than the established Faeries. "After awhile, you realize that no one's going to make you do anything you don't want to do" (Petunia). While I noted many instances of grumbling over the problems this approach caused, there also seemed to be a general feeling that such minor vexations were a small price to pay for eradicating exploitive power relationships from the community. Thus a cursory glance at the community indicates that Faeries have explicitly rejected the kind of hierarchical distinctions and patterns of domination that buttress hegemonic masculinity.

But again my research reveals some interesting gaps between ideological commitment and practice. I touch on just a few examples of these, beginning with an interesting historical example. Less than a year after the first Faerie gathering in Arizona, signs of a classic power struggle within the founding triad of Harry Hay, Don Kilhefner, and Mitch Walker were becoming apparent. At the second gathering held in August 1980 near Boulder, Colorado, Walker (twenty-seven years old at the time) began a carefully choreographed plot to "dethrone" the sixty-eight-year-old Hay. Hay's overbearing personality had been noticed even in his early Mattachine days. One of his cohorts during that time spoke of Hay's tendency to practice "democracy by exhaustion" and observed that he had a distinct tendency to wear down any dissension in the group through a "ceaseless stream of gray logic" (Timmons 1990, 153). Whether it was this domineering tendency that bothered Walker or Hay's status as the spiritual patriarch of the movement that Walker coveted is unclear. What is clear is that Kilhefner and Walker thought Hay was "power-tripping" (282), and the ensuing struggle brought out some very "un-Faerie-like" behavior in both men. Walker instituted a whisper campaign against Hay and even enlisted a group of followers to his cause that he called the "Faerie Fascist Police Force." Said Walker, "I decided that if this was the revolution and Harry was being Stalin, I would be, as second in command, his minister of a secret, CIA-style police force" (275). The bitter dispute that followed led to the complete disintegration of the triad, with Walker referring to Hay as "a cancer on the gay movement" and Hay later recalling that Walker "demanded that I pass on the torch to him, that I was a burned-out cinder and that he was to lead now" (283). The attempted coup that followed led to Hay's temporary displacement from the Faeries, and eventually Walker and Kilhefner left to form a group of their own, where they fought for control between themselves (284).

It is obvious from this example that from the very beginning contradictions were present within Faerie culture with respect to power issues. It should be noted, however, that while all this heated political maneuvering was taking place, the Faeries themselves—the Faerie rank and file, so to speak—went about expanding the movement largely unaware of the struggle. This seems to indicate that despite occasional "backsliding" into dominance disputes by individual members, Faeries as a community remain firmly committed to counterhegemonic values.

My fieldwork revealed many of the same kinds of tensions between an allegiance to egalitarianism and consensus on the one hand and an acknowledgment that some Faeries had "control issues" on the other. Community members sometimes acted less like fae spirits and more like the products of hegemonically masculine socialization—although no one expressed it in those terms. One man I met during the gathering said he had returned that year after taking a couple years off from the Faeries. "When you get that many control queens in one place," he said, "it's too much." Another of my interview subjects put it this way: "I just think it's . . . well, and it's all about control. You know, and this is an organization that talks about the lack of control and the lack of organization, and the anarchy model kind of stuff—and it's all about control." This particular subject mentioned one person by name—TigerLily. TigerLily is one of the more active, long-term members of the Faeries and has earned the honorific title of "granny." Grannies serve as something like tribal elders, but "elder" is misleading, since most grannies are men in their thirties and forties.[17] However, the term "elder" is employed in association with grannies, and those designated as such enjoy an elevated status in the group. One becomes a granny after spending a number of years caring for the land and taking an active role in the community. Like naming, the designation is more organic than official—eventually if you are around long enough, other Faeries simply begin referring to you as a granny.

I had an opportunity to interview TigerLily, one of the most respected and dedicated members of the community, and he acknowledged his controlling tendencies without prompting. The subject came up unexpectedly after I asked him to tell me how he found his Faerie name:

TigerLily: I was just looking for a flower name, you know. Something that would be fun and maybe, in some way fit me. And of course, in a lot of ways it did because of my motherly, controlling, white-bitch kind of energy that I can sometimes, especially back in those days—you're not seeing it, you're not seeing it like it was. I mean I've changed a lot, my role, my role in the community has changed a lot.

Peter: How so?

TigerLily: Well, I was much more in the thick of the inner process of deciding what was going to happen and who was doing what and the, the, you know, who's cooking what and where's everything gonna be located in the kitchen and how is this gonna work and how is that gonna work, and what are we gonna be doing this fall and this spring and next summer, and all of that. Now do you see me as being in the thick of all that these days?

In order to flesh out the picture a bit more, I talked to MoonGaze. Moon-Gaze is the most prominent and beloved of the few female Faeries who attend gatherings. I asked her about an occasion I had witnessed where TigerLily seemed to be ridiculing her when she referred to herself as an "almost granny." She defended TigerLily, saying that I had misinterpreted the scene:

And so as [TigerLily] is stepping back, he is saying that grannies have to teach the other people about [the sanctuary] in order to lead the way, and he has made it clear overtly and covertly that he is pulling back because he has taken such a lead role that he's been dissed for being a control queen, and you know, he is a control queen sometimes because he's so smart . . . so I think that might have been him kind of, you know, looking at the circle going "grannies, get going" and you know I'm so connected with TigerLily I know when he's nudging people.

What I find interesting here is that TigerLily has obviously retreated from a more overtly recognizable leadership role due to negative perceptions from others, yet he has not completely relinquished his controlling tendencies. From behind the scenes he continues to nudge people. My impression of TigerLily is that he cares deeply about the Faerie community and has made many valuable contributions to it. The same affection for the community that motivates his controlling behavior also obligates him to pull back to the sidelines in deference to Faerie egalitarianism.

It's Magick! Faeries Refashioning the Sexual

We've had two, maybe two sex magick rituals, and one of them I only participated in the heart circle . . . And the heart circle about sex was great. I mean, just the kind of thing of who isn't interested in talking or hearing what people have to say about that, but also it's just so illuminating, you know, because you find out so much more about a person when they talk about their sexual being, and sometimes I think it's just interesting because we're all sexual beings, and it takes up such a big part of who

we are, but like about our time in our life, it's of course the minority of our existence
. . . In that heart circle it was just so interesting to see the mix of that in people's realities about where their expectations met their practice, and you see that. There's some
people who have really kinky wild kind of sex lives, some people who don't seem to
have one at all, and yet, of course, they're still hugely sexual beings, and just so that to
see where people were falling in that myriad of existence . . . You know because when
people talk about what they like about sex, I mean it's really interesting, you know,
how vastly different people's needs and desires are, other than I'd say, you know,
everybody has the basic desire to have an affirmation that they're desirable and a valuable partner, but other than that the gamut was pretty big. And for me at the time I
just found that my inner struggle as a heterosexual woman in the Faerie community
was this very different thing that so many of the Faeries had, of having sex with their
friends . . . And I can participate in a sex heart circle and kind of try and figure this stuff
out and figure out how do you reconcile having sex with your friends and your primary
relationship and how does that work and trying to figure out just logistically how you
cope with that between your head and your heart. You know, because intellectually
I've always gotten it, and then heartwise, it's like, "Oh I'm not really sure how I would
cope" . . . So I always wondered about it and tried to kind of reconcile it and then I
ended up, you know, trying to [*pause, laughs*]. Anyway, my boyfriend isn't a Faerie,
let's just say that! (MoonGaze)

During my time with the Faeries I heard several intriguing mentions
of "sex magick," along with references to sex magick rituals, heart circles, and workshops. It was not until I saw it in print that I realized that
this form of "magick," with the addition of the terminal "k," referenced
a specific set of meanings beyond those associated with top hats, doves,
and wands. Not surprisingly, the term is interpreted in a number of different ways among Faeries. It speaks to some degree of cultural overlap
between Faeries and earth-based religions like Wicca and other pagan
traditions. Within those communities magick takes on a number of specific meanings, around which there is broad-based consensus. My sense
is that in Faerie communities, when the term is applied to sexuality,
it is applied in a more diffuse way. It reflects a positive regard for sex
in general, as well as an admonition to approach sex with conscious
subject-subject intentionality and a loving regard for one's partner(s).
Faerie culture sees magickal potential in sex in that it celebrates a wide
variety of sexual practices as a path toward personal and spiritual transformation and fulfillment. As a heterosexual woman, MoonGaze holds a
unique perspective on these magickal proceedings, promulgated largely
by men with same-sex interests. The preceding remarks indicate that to
some extent this has alienated her from her Faerie fellows. She later told

me about her experience with a sex magick workshop, which involved partnering with another Faerie for physical, sensual, and possibly sexual contact. "I opted out of it, and I think that if, I don't know, like if I were gay and if I were a man and not, like would I have gone to the sex magick workshop if I had been a man in the community? I don't know, 'cause I can't crawl outside of my skin in order to really figure that out. But it was never, I never thought for a moment that I would go."

Perhaps it is not surprising that MoonGaze chose not to attend. It would be unfair to expect a complete eradication of gender and gendered barriers to sexual participation in even the most zealous intentional community, given continuing contacts with mainstream cultures and traditional gender norms. Even so, I found several peculiar blind spots with respect to gendered sexuality among the Faeries. In 1991 the keynote address for the Second Gay Spirit Visions Conference was reprinted in *RFD* magazine. In it, poet and activist James Broughton counsels his fellow Faeries to "concentrate on your phallic glory. The penis is the exposed tip of the heart. The penis is a wand of the soul . . . praise it. Give thanks for its awesome powers . . . in the holy balls in your scrotum the treasure of your semen is kept" (Broughton 1991, 44). This passage is particularly instructive in that it clearly references a heteronormative and masculinist symbolic cosmology, involving not only an homage to phallic power but also (surprising from the perspective of gay male relationships) a direct association with fertility. This also suggests (somewhat unexpectedly to my mind) a sexual culture bereft of "gender trouble," as one of Butler's (1990) central theoretical objectives is to decenter phallocentrism and compulsory heterosexuality. In the next section I examine the transgressive limits of parodic gender practices like drag. Here I merely suggest that such practices, and the intentional focus on gender in communities like the Faeries, may not be sufficient to significantly disrupt hegemonic understandings of sexuality.

One of the outcomes that surprised me in the interviews was the range of responses I received to a question that I had included in my interview schedule as perfunctory. When I asked, "Do you think of the Faeries as a sexually liberated community?" I assumed the answer would be yes, and that we could then proceed to discuss the various innovations Faeries had introduced to ways of thinking about, experiencing, and doing sex. I was surprised by the ambivalent and occasionally negative responses I received: "It just seems very repressive. I have felt sexually repressed up there" (Wanda Sue); "Yeah, we talk about sex very freely, but it doesn't happen very freely" (PopTart); "Yes and no . . . my sense is that everyone else brings whatever issues they have about sex into this space" (Zinnia);

and perhaps, most telling of all, from an interview subject whose "whole life revolves around being a Faerie," "We do seem to be competitive in that realm too sometimes. We are men after all!" (Frankie).

Another surprise I recorded in my field notes was the tacit discouragement of public sex during the gathering. While I did not expect a nonstop public orgy, I did expect to see some tolerance for public sexual activity. In fact, I overheard part of a rather heated discussion on the topic, wherein one Faerie was arguing against public sex by linking it with issues of respect. In this argument public sex was interpreted as a sign of disrespect for the land and for the Faerie community. As I had reason to believe that some discrete episodes of sex in the open had taken place during past gatherings, I asked Wanda Sue about this issue:

If I walk up to someone and they're engaged in sexual activity, my first reaction isn't "Oh my god!" My first reaction, first of all, that's cool, second of all, you know, when I was single my second question was, "I wonder if they want company? I wonder if I can join in?" And you know, what's the big deal? I don't get it. The year before that, such a thing happened, and I don't know where he was from and it doesn't matter, but he was just going off because he ran across two guys and they were having sex and "oh I just think that's so disrespectful," and on and on and on, and I'm just going, "Why?" and I didn't feel comfortable enough to ask the question, but "Why? Why was this such an issue?" You know, is it because you weren't asked, or because you weren't, you know, a part of that . . . I don't get it.

Several of my interview subjects cautioned me against making generalizations based on this particular band of Faeries, intimating that Faeries in other parts of the country nurtured far more adventurous sexual cultures. TigerLily told me that "[our] community is definitely the most conservative, slow-moving of the bunch [of Faerie communities]." My interview subjects offered a certain sense of sexual "propriety" informing the larger regional culture as another explanatory variable. However, my historical research suggests that part of the explanation may come from within the community itself, given the rather prohibitive tone that some invocations of subject-subject consciousness take on when applied to Faerie sexuality: "Without subject-SUBJECT perception, the exhortation to engage in "sacred sex" could very well become an excuse for ritual rape, or indiscriminate self-gratification. Only by engaging in sex in a non-objectifying and mutually subjective manner, does sex become 'sacred'" (Rodgers 1993, 26).

However, I also found evidence for another explanation. Two of my interview subjects explicitly linked the discouragement of public sex to the existence of a sexual pecking order. The existence of this pecking order was understood by both of these subjects as problematic, because if it were to be acknowledged publicly, it would present a powerful challenge to the Faeries' emphasis on egalitarianism and sharing. Zinnia explained it this way:

I think sex is most problematic in our community when it comes to those who get it versus those who don't. So, and since no one can know with total certainty who that is at any given moment, the dynamics are constantly shifting. And, but we all certainly have our, I mean, I know what I get and don't get . . . So my sense is that, that there is a, that there's a fundamental inequality at any given moment around sex. Because some are getting it, and some are not.

PopTart, another of my interview subjects, was even more explicit about how normative understandings of desire and attraction structure Faerie sexual culture, while strongly implying that an open acknowledgment of these patterns would work to undermine the notion that gatherings represent a space where love and acceptance are extended to all:

Part of those people, or some of those people that happen to go to a gathering to be accepted that aren't accepted in the regular world, part of the reason that they're not accepted in the regular world is not only because they're gay but because [*pause*] they're not attractive—in the regular world. So, therefore there are a lot of people that go to the gathering that aren't attracted to one another because in the regular world they're unattractive. So how do you facilitate more sex at the gathering? Have really attractive people there, which isn't going to happen. And that's OK, and I'm glad there's unattractive people there.

I found PopTart's obvious interest in maintaining a loving community not centered solely on sexual interaction particularly inspiring given his rather amazing personal history, one that has exposed him to an extremely broad spectrum of attitudes toward sex and sexuality. After some initial experimentation with gay sex, PopTart experienced a religious conversion and toured for a year with an evangelical stage production that was part of Jerry Falwell's conservative Christian ministry. During this time he came to know Falwell personally, and he told me that during the shows, "Jerry often referred to someone that he knew, someone who is with us right now who used to live a lifestyle of corruption and blah, blah, blah, blah, blah. And he's turned his life over to God and he travels with the group today."

Subsequently, PopTart fell away from the fold and into the world of gay porn in California. There he enjoyed a brief but successful career, winning the Best New Rising Star award one year at the porn industry's version of the Academy Awards. Among the Faeries, PopTart is perceived as sexually adventurous, and his status as an ex–porn star confers a fairly high degree of prestige that makes him a sought-after partner. When I asked him to compare porn and Faerie cultures, he first told me that there was no comparison. When I asked him to elaborate, I was surprised to hear him articulate the differences in economic terms: "The porn culture is full of people that are trying to make a buck, and Faeries don't ever try to make a buck." However, when I addressed the topic of sexual objectification, he acknowledged that, at least for him, a certain degree of continuity exists between the two worlds. With reference to sexual objectification among the Faeries, he told me:

I wish I could say honestly that I don't think it does happen, but I can't say honestly that it doesn't because, I don't know whether it's because I've been in the porn culture. I just know that I do it. I can't deny the fact that it's a very, if I'm looking to have sex with somebody, there's a reason. I mean, and 90 percent of the time it's based on looks or endowment, parts that are objectified the most in the porn culture, so . . .

Faerie Drag

If one comes into discursive life through being called or hailed in injurious terms, how might one occupy the interpellation by which one is already occupied to direct the possibilities of resignification against the aims of the violation?
—JUDITH BUTLER, *BODIES THAT MATTER*

Before I began my fieldwork for this chapter, I conducted a study of urban drag performances, wherein I encountered an intriguing, though not uncommon, scene. I include it here because it captures the transgressive possibilities of drag and the way it *may* contribute to gender trouble. These notes were recorded after a visit to a local lounge that offered a very polished drag show popular with heterosexual couples. This passage does not describe a Faerie event—these are professional drag queens, performing for a predominantly straight audience.[18] I offer the following description from my field notes of February 13, 1999, as a point of *contrast* with the way drag operates in Faerie culture:

Obviously part of the appeal of the show is that the illusion of feminine self-presentation is very successful. A common refrain throughout the crowd at these shows is "That's a *man*? Are you *sure*?" What I wonder about is the men who decide to accept a kiss from the performers—how many of them identify as straight, and what's going through their minds?

In sharp contrast, very little of the drag that I observed at the Faerie sanctuary placed a premium on illusion. In fact, quite the opposite was the case. The most sought-after effects seemed to be shock value and humor, usually from mixing already recognizable elements of femininity and masculinity in novel and outrageous ways. Most (but not all) of the Faeries in drag look very much like men in dresses, including, for example, a bearded man with a hairy chest wearing a leather biker cap and a prom dress; a middle-aged man with hairy arms and a conventional haircut wearing a 1960s-style party dress with a large turban hat, replete with oversized flowers; a powerfully built man in his thirties wearing taffeta; and a man in a miniskirt that does not quite cover his genitals.[19] These examples describe the dominant pattern, one that is clearly parodic.

But there was more. Another pattern I observed seemed to indicate a much more serious investment in drag. I found this less common pattern to be distinctive in at least two ways. First, this style featured a unity of presentation that eschewed the stark juxtaposition of masculine and feminine elements. This is not to say that these elements were not combined, only that the level of contrast was lower. For example, in this second style you would not see leather culture and prom dresses referenced in the same presentation. A continuity is seen in the clothing and adornments that blends "gendered shades of gray," if you will, rather than the incongruous "black and white" elements characteristic of the parodic style. Second, in achieving this unity of presentation, proponents of this second mode began with items that placed less emphasis on exaggeration (bright colors, hoop skirts, large hats). Rather than the aggressive celebration of difference exhibited in the parodic style, the overall effect of this second mode of drag was much more understated.

For these practitioners drag seemed to represent much more than play; it was linked to a lived history of interior struggle with gender identity, something that was not indicated by those who deployed drag as a form of playful parody. Over the course of my fieldwork, I observed two Faeries who favored this second type of drag—a use that I found much more difficult to visually analyze in binary terms. My subjective conclusion was that this style was deployed with the intention of signaling something that at least looked like a third gender, rather than simply juxtaposing masculine and feminine elements.

Moreover, data from my field research indicate that at least two distinct accounts are offered by Faeries themselves to explain what they are doing when they do drag. One account sees drag as playful and parodic; Zinnia provides a good example of this perspective:

So drag in the woods is like, you know, it breaks the rules about gender identity, it breaks the rules about creativity for me . . . For me, it's the ultimate camp because it is, I mean, camp is making fun of oneself and norms, and in the woods it's almost like we're both thumbing our nose at that, and the need to do it. The very need to thumb our nose at it. We're in the middle of the friggin' woods! Who's watching? [Laughs.] It's, um, you know, who needs fashion in the woods? It's about survival, man. So it's a real, it's the ultimate play. Performing for the squirrels, you know.

Calliope was one of the two Faeries whose drag seemed to signal a deeper engagement. Calliope has long, beautiful hair that cascades down his back; he uses it to great dramatic effect when he tosses his head back in conversation. He also sports a neatly groomed van dyke beard and moustache and wears simple madras skirts, perhaps a smart vest, and assorted pieces of junk jewelry that he somehow manages to wear quite tastefully. Regal in his bearing, Calliope speaks in well-organized paragraphs. He was by far the most articulate of my Faerie interview subjects. He confirmed my suspicions that drag holds a deeper meaning for him when he spoke of his alienation from the "mainstream" drag community in the city (the professional drag queens mentioned above): "I was no longer willing to let them interfere with my comfort with drag. So I just found different ways to present myself and different images to show to people where I could remain relaxed and comfortable."

The articulation of these two perspectives on drag—the playful, parodic, and performative view indicated by Zinnia versus the more serious engagement signaled by Calliope's words—raises an important question: which of these perspectives is more likely to produce a politically engaged subject, one that is effective in disrupting the heterosexual matrix through gender trouble? If by "gender trouble" we mean an embodied challenge to gendered dichotomies, and if by "politically engaged subject" we mean one that carries an embodied commitment toward transcending the gender binary (rather than playfully juxtaposing expressions of its two terms), then the evidence I have presented here suggests that it is Calliope's deployment of drag that should be the more politically potent form—but this is contrary to Butler's (1990) focus on performativity and her dismissal of the interiority of the subject doing the drag. I do not mean to say that Faerie drag, regardless of its manifestation, is not resistant—surely it is. But this does raise questions about the usefulness of performativity as a strategy for producing gender trouble.[20]

Even in the case of Calliope, the prospects for gender trouble are constrained. Calliope is doubly marginalized. As he was on the fringe of not one but two subversive communities (i.e., the drag and Faerie communities), I was eager to hear his thoughts on the possibilities for gender trouble among the Faeries. I was quite surprised by the following:

> We are men, and no matter how you slice it, we're men. And no matter how pretty you can make yourself and no matter what you can do to yourself, you're still a boy in a dress. And that is the bottom line, and you can make yourself look wonderful, and you can adopt all of the movements and the attitudes and, to whatever degree you feel comfortable with, or able to do, and it doesn't change. You are still a boy in a dress. And the difficulty that I see is that so many of them refuse to see that.

What is interesting here is that while Calliope readily acknowledges the performative nature of gender, he ends up returning to a surprisingly conventional and essentialist perspective that puts formidable restrictions on the possibilities for gender trouble.

My field notes record a curious development on my third day at the Faerie gathering. It was on the third day that I began, quite unselfconsciously, to refer to two of the Faeries as "she." One was Calliope, and the other was a Faerie who also fit the "serious drag" profile. Using feminine pronouns to refer to gay men (even drag queens) is not something I normally do, or have ever done. Thus the realization that I was doing so involved "catching myself in the act." When I reflected upon this later, I realized that I had taken my cue from other Faeries in the community who were also using feminine pronouns, and in reference to the same two people. What I am suggesting here is that those Faeries like Calliope who signal a more serious perspective on drag tend to be feminized by the community itself, while those whose perspective on drag is playful and parodic are not. I have no doubt that this is intended (if it is consciously intended at all) as a compliment, or more likely an homage. Thus, it may very well be that within the group this more serious deployment of drag may confer higher status. But what interests me here are the repercussions of this designation *outside* of Faerie space. Expanding the Faerie vision beyond the confines of the sanctuary will at some point entail political interaction with the outside world, where hegemonic logic will work to undermine the feminized political subject. For me, the most important implication of this process is that by feminizing the more politically potent deployment of Faerie drag (to my mind, Calliope's mode), Faerie culture may itself be unwittingly undermining its potential.

I conclude this section with two speculative thoughts. First, a competitive element is at play that goes along with Faerie drag, which is in some respects surprising, given the community's devotion to egalitarian values. Frankie captures this idea beautifully:

You remember the whole thing about the $300 broach, and why that $3 one is more fabulous? Well, to me it's like, some of that was such bullshit, it's like, the reason the $3 one is more fabulous is because we're competitive and we value the skill it takes to find a $3 broach more than the skills it takes to have $300 extra dollars in your bank account to buy a broach . . . It's so, you know, some of that is reactionary, and then a lot of it is competition [*laughs*] you know. You know there aren't, the Faeries aren't particularly competitive in, in the way that the mainstream society might, you know, sports, or like who can make the most money or whatever. But, you know, having the worst-looking dress or, you know, whatever, it's the same sort of activity [*laughs*]. It's a little more lighthearted, but yeah. I mean showing up at some event in a killer dress is not just about 'isn't this a great dress?' it's also a little, you know, there's a competitive edge.

Might this emphasis on competition be a subtle link to the competitive ideology of hegemonic masculinity? Obviously, whatever level of competition exists is lighthearted, and may itself be a form of parody. Furthermore, many women are competitive, especially regarding clothing and jewelry. Still, I am left wondering why the celebration of drag takes this particular turn. Why *competition*? Why not, for example, a more collaborative send-up like the "gauche jewelry exchange," or perhaps "the god-awful dress collective?"

Second, Faerie culture is reflexively self-mocking, and drag figures as a central part of this strategy:

I saw this horrible dress that, I mean it really looked like it was made from a shower curtain, and it was like plasticized and kind of fake reptile and pearl eyes. I mean it was so god-awful. And it certainly doesn't express any aesthetic, you know, belief system that I have or I didn't find it pretty or it was just so god-awful that someone had to wear it. Something, and it was like a rainy day so it was like the perfect dress because it was like completely waterproof. (Frankie)

This suggests the possibility that Faerie drag serves a kind of defensive purpose, a way of heading off any form of ridicule from heteronormative culture, and from straight men in particular, by getting there first and doing it better. After all, who makes more fun of Faeries than a Faerie? As Zinnia puts it, "camp is making fun of oneself and norms, and in the woods it's almost like we're both thumbing our nose at that, and the need to do it." In many conventional drag show "lounge" performances like the one cited earlier, the drag queen's skill in responding to hecklers in the audience by "one-upping" their insults extemporaneously becomes a lively part of the show. This leads me to speculate that perhaps there are protective and competitive aspects of Faerie drag that add to its enjoyment while simultaneously providing a buffer between the community and the broader heteronormative culture.

Still Here, Still Queer: Faerie Culture as Abeyance Structure

What we see here with respect to the use of drag among the Faeries echoes what we have seen happening around issues like sex and identity. Faeries are committed to subversion and resistance, which is only partially realized in practice. This is perhaps unsurprising, given the cultural forces arrayed against these gentle gender warriors. Still, the resistance is real. To my mind, the institutionalization of reflexivity through group discussions and consensus-building efforts and the emphasis on consciousness raising are the community's strongest points. As I look back on my experiences in the field, these features continue to engage my interest. They also make the community's future all but impossible to predict.

I am reminded of Taylor's (1989) work on social movement abeyance structures. Here Taylor argues that to ensure social movement continuity, contentious social movements retreat into abeyance structures during hostile or nonreceptive political periods. She uses the women's movement during the period between first- and second-wave feminism as her empirical example, and I am struck by the connections between her case and that of the Faeries. The most obvious prompt here is the Faeries' preference for sanctuary, reflecting the fact that many of those first attracted to Faerie communities in the early 1980s were explicitly seeking a place to recover from the exhaustion they felt after years of political activism. Furthermore, the first Faerie gathering coincides neatly with the Reagan-era return to social conservatism in the United States.

The ethnographic data from this study introduce a degree of caution in assessing actions that are assumed to be transgressive in theory. In fairness to Butler, it is important to acknowledge that she has attempted to clarify her position on the transgressive possibilities for performative acts like drag on several occasions. She has conceded that there is nothing inherently subversive about drag. In this chapter I have gone beyond Butler's position to raise questions, grounded in my empirical data, about the usefulness of performativity itself as a strategy for subverting gender.

In presuming to test Butler's poststructural theory empirically I have focused on an interiority in my Faerie subjects that Butler clearly wants to discount. I have presented evidence that points to the pragmatic value of bringing the subject back into the discussion about transgression and subversion. But this subject must be brought in on an "as if" basis—

deemphasizing the question of whether subjectivity is "really" only the effect of sedimented discursive and institutionalized practices, and with a renewed appreciation for how people understand themselves. Even if they are mistaken, if the autonomous subject is fictive, the members of communities like the Faeries go about their lives as if they were autonomous. The data here suggest that ignoring this disposition may lead to an overestimation of the possibilities for transgression through parodic forms like drag.

Faerie culture represents a cultural response to the "effeminacy effect," one that is both ironic and amusing. By actively embracing and mercilessly parodying the stereotype, Faeries do in fact achieve a kind of limited agency with respect to gender. However, the space opened by the Faerie community is largely apolitical, or at least it seems to have become so in recent years. The transformations that Faerie culture enable are at the individual level and are typically therapeutic. There is little in the way of an organized challenge to the larger system of gendered meanings beyond these aspects of Faerie culture at present. The impulse toward introspection and retreat from the larger culture seems now to be something that Faeries take for granted, as is the need for the sanctuary that the Faerie community provides. But again, the strong emphasis on reflexivity and consciousness raising within Faerie culture suggests the possibility that Faeries could easily become more politically engaged at some point in the future. If this happens, Faeries may indeed, as the quote at the beginning of this chapter portends, cause "curious disasters which are harbingers of new beauty."[21]

––––––

Whereas the pretty dresses donned by Faeries in their woodland retreat signal a commitment to gender trouble that is only partially realized, the more conventionally masculine self-presentation promoted by the members of my next case study community may be masking a more fundamentally troubling (and perhaps unintended) challenge to the heteronormative assumptions of hegemonic masculinity. I venture now to another part of the forest, in search of Bears.

FOUR

Bear Bodies, Bear Masculinity: Recuperation, Resistance, or Retreat?

We are a community woven together by an appreciation of masculinity and genuineness in a man. This is what really makes a Bear. The most important of Bear traits is masculinity, a trait for which we are obviously known. The emergence of a true Bear actually takes years, a culmination of experiences, attitudes and self-discovery.

—SCOTT HILL, "AROUSED FROM HIBERNATION"

Shortly after I arrive at my first Bear Camp I notice a group of husky, hirsute men huddled around a digital camera. Two of the Bear campers had just come off the hiking trail, where they had seen *real* bears—two cubs playing in the woods. They paused to snap some photos and were now showing off the images. During the ensuing excitement, much joking was made about the cubs, but not a word about the danger the hikers had so obviously placed themselves in. As any experienced camper knows, female bears in defense of their cubs are ferocious. But perhaps the testosterone-laden air made it easy to forget about mama bear. The next morning I enjoy my first breakfast at Bear Camp, the menu fit for a man-sized appetite: French toast stuffed with cream cheese, pecans and cinnamon, cinnamon rolls, caramel rolls, potatoes fried in butter, bacon, mini-muffins, and a tasteful assortment of fresh fruit. At breakfast I meet Franklin, Jim, Tom, and Steve. I spend most of my time talking to Franklin, and I am fascinated to learn that,despite the fact that he is an older man, he has only recently come out. He tells me of his recent divorce, he complains about his ex-wife, then we discuss books for awhile. But eventually his exuberance gets the best of him, and he steers the conversation toward some recent sexual experiences. Having just left the closet, he seems eager to share his adventures with me. One encounter he tells me about was with an eighteen-year-old man. Franklin smiles and tells me how impressed he was by the hardness of the young man's erection, remarking that it "slapped against his stomach." He mentions another encounter, during which he lost his erection. "I'm sixty-three years old, and I knew it wasn't coming back. So I asked the guy if he minded not coming. He said no, not at all." As he recounted this episode, Franklin seemed genuinely moved, perhaps surprised, by the generous response.

One of the most intriguing features to appear on the queer cultural landscape in the last fifteen years is the Bear subculture. During that time, many gay men seeking to resist the stereotypical association of homosexuality with effeminacy have found the hirsute, masculine image of the Bear enormously attractive. For a significant cohort of men who came out in the late 1970s and spent their youth reveling in the freewheeling post-Stonewall sexual culture, the Bear movement's emphasis on the appeal of the "husky" man provides an enticing antidote to the heartbreak of a slowing metabolism. Consequently, Bear culture has flourished in this country and expanded internationally. At the time of publication, a resource Web site for Bears[1] lists more than sixty active clubs in cities across the United States, four in Canada, eighteen in Europe, one in Central America, and four in New Zealand/Australia. Bear culture has spawned a number of popular books, including *The Bear Book* (Wright 1997a), *The Bear Book II* (Wright 2001), *Tales from the Bear Cult* (Hemry 2001), *Bearotica* (Suresha 2002a), and *The Bear Handbook* (Kampf 2000). The movement has also produced popular periodicals like *Bear* magazine, *American Bear*, and *American Grizzly* and dozens of Bear-related Web sites. Several dozen Bear organizations sponsor social events, "runs" (treks to visit other clubs; see chapter 5, note 1), or camping weekends every year, with the most popular attracting as many as 800 visitors from around the world. Interestingly, although people from a variety of queer communities are likely to know something about Bears or Bear culture, the phenomenon is not widely recognized outside of these communities.

As is the case in Faerie culture, the very undecidability of identity is a prominent subcultural feature of the Bear community. Just what is a Bear? Responses to this question reveal a variety of answers, but almost all reference the Bear body, either in an attempt to describe what the typical Bear looks like or to refute the idea that Bears can be defined *exclusively* by their bodies. As Travis, one of my interview subjects, put it, "You know, physical attributes such as stockiness, height, weight, how much facial fur you have, things along those lines. But other people see it as being 90 percent attitude, 10 percent looks." What constitutes Bear attitude? Responses I encountered ranged from "natural, down to earth, easy going, likes to have fun" (Larry) to "closer to the heterosexual community in their tastes" (Brian) to "a sense of independence" (Burt) to "an easiness with the body" and "the masculinity thing" (Grant).

"The masculinity thing" within Bear culture is complex and inextricably tied to the workings of hegemonic masculinity outside of it. Whereas the Faerie strategy in responding to the "effeminacy effect" involves parody, Bears respond to masculinity by forcefully repudiating effeminacy with a renewed claim to "authentic" masculinity. "I think some of what is really appealing to me about the Bear group is that if you saw these guys on the street, they could just as easily be rednecks as gay guys," says Franklin. This suggests that the Bear image is not only conventionally gendered but includes a specifically classed presentation of self as well.

Bear culture was born of resistance. According to historian and founding figure Les Wright (1997b, 21), in the early 1980s, men frequenting leather bars in San Francisco and other cities began placing a small teddy bear in their shirt or hip pocket as a way of "refuting the clone colored-hanky code," whereby gay leathermen place different colored hankies in their back pockets to signal their interest in a variety of sex practices. Not willing to be objectified and reduced to an interest in one specific sexual activity, these men sported teddy bears to emphasize their interest in a less instrumental sexuality. According to Wright (1990, 54), this was a way of saying, "I'm a human being. I give and receive affection."

Bears reject the self-conscious, exaggerated masculinity of the gay leatherman in favor of a more authentic masculinity. This look includes (but is not limited to) jeans, baseball caps, T-shirts, flannel shirts, and beards. To the uninitiated, Bears seem above all to be striving for "regular guy" status. "The Bear look is all-natural, rural, even woodsy," note Silverstein and Picano (1992, 128–30), "full beards are common, as are bushy moustaches . . . They're just regular guys—only they're gay." But are Bears "just regular guys"? Some observers stress the Bears' disruptive potential, arguing that in its attempt to revise and normalize gay masculinity, Bear culture presents a profound challenge to some of the most oppressive features of hegemonic masculinity. Feminist scholars Kelly and Kane (2001, 342) concur, albeit cautiously:

Is there perhaps something radically subversive of orthodox masculinity at work here, despite all the butch trappings? Might not Bears represent the sort of "marginalized men" that Susan Bordo [a feminist philosopher who studies the body and cultural studies] describes as "bearers of the shadow of the phallus, who have been the alchemical agents disturbing the (deceptively) stable elements" of orthodox masculinity in a newly percolating social psyche?

With its emphasis on camaraderie instead of competition, with the rejection of "body fascism" (as evidenced by the acceptance of heavier and older men), and by popularizing "cuddling" and "the Bear hug," Bear culture provides ample evidence that this is not the type of masculinity that predominates in other gay cultures. As Wright (1997c, 10) remarks, "Competition with other gay men for sex partners and the depersonalizing effects of a steady stream of sexually consumed bodies is balanced by the humanizing effort to . . . establish contact with the person inside of each of those bodies." But at the same time, one finds signs of a recuperative current, a rejection of the insights of feminism, even outright hostility. As Lucie-Smith (1991, 8) notes, "There is a challenge to aggressive feminism, which not only seeks female equality, but often tries to subject men to the tastes and standards imposed by women. To be a 'Bear' is to assert a homosexual masculinism which rejects this. One can even say that the male child here continues to revel in his own playful liberty. No, he will not come indoors at once and wash behind his ears. Nor wash any other part of himself, for that matter."

Thus, in staking their claim to gay masculinity, Bears challenge hegemonic assumptions about male sexuality by introducing what feminists have identified as an "ethic of care" (Gilligan 1982) into an objectified sexual culture perceived as alienating. On the other hand, insofar as their rejection of effeminacy signals a broader devaluation of the feminine, Bear masculinity recuperates gendered hierarchies central to the logic of hegemonic masculinity. Furthermore, the pastoral fantasy encoded in Bear semiotics can be linked with earlier movements aimed at revitalizing an "essential" masculinity under assault from the feminizing effects of civilization by retreating to the wilderness, if only symbolically. How then, from a feminist perspective, is one to adjudicate these simultaneously resistant and recuperative features of Bear culture? In this chapter I draw on ethnographic and historical evidence as I attempt to make sense of these conflicting currents, with a special emphasis on the way that Bear masculinity is embodied and the effect this has on Bear sexual culture.

As Bear organizations go,[2] the Friendly Bears are somewhat atypical in that they do not hold regular meetings, do not charge membership fees, and operate with a relatively informal administrative structure. Like other Bear clubs, the Friendly Bears have a board of directors and a slate of officers, but their work is very low profile. The vitality of the club is maintained through monthly social events, all organized on a pay-as-you-go basis by volunteers, and various fund-raising events for local charities. Most other clubs have regular meetings and membership dues, and the executive officers of those clubs tend to be much more visible. However, a great deal of communication and interaction takes place between Bear clubs. Some of this happens via Internet communication between individual members of different clubs via Bear chat rooms and message boards, and some of it occurs through a series of regularly scheduled weekend events sponsored by clubs across the United States. These events, billed primarily as social opportunities, are often closely affiliated with local charities and typically draw men from a wide geographical area. In addition to the half-dozen such events that may attract as many as 800 participants from all over the world, numerous other events are sponsored by clubs in mid-sized cities. These draw anywhere from 100 to 200 out-of-town guests. Thus, despite the peculiarities of my particular case study community, the extraordinary level of interaction between groups suggests a certain degree of national homogeneity across clubs in the United States.

My ethnographic data are drawn from approximately 300 cumulative hours of participant observation at various Friendly Bear sites during 2001 and 2002. As a gay man in my early forties, I had lived in "Friendlytown" for more than ten years before beginning this research. Thus, I had already developed a number of informal relationships with Friendly Bears, greatly facilitated by my own expanding middle-aged frame and natural hirsuteness. My response to these interactions was overwhelmingly positive, following along two distinct dimensions. In the beginning the hedonic appeal of having my aging body recast in a significantly sexier social frame, through the approving glances of the Friendly Bears, provided the overwhelming appeal. But as time went on I found myself engaging intellectually. What does the rapid growth of Bear culture mean, and how is it that these men managed to collectively reinterpret and eroticize the very physical attributes stigmatized by the greater gay community (extra weight, body hair)?

As a result of my situation, I found that gaining access to appropriate research sites was relatively easy. In addition to attending a number of semi-private functions, I attended two Bear summer camping trips (each with more than a hundred men attending), a smaller camping trip in the fall of 2001 (approximately 30 attendees), numerous "Bear bar nights" (typically hosting more than 150 men), and many casual face-to-face encounters. Observation sites also included "play parties" where sex happened, but this was never the sole purpose of the gathering.[3] The men I observed were overwhelmingly white (approximately 96 percent), and while a range of social classes was represented, the majority of the Friendly Bears would best be classified as middle class (see below).

Interview subject selection was guided by a theoretical sampling logic. I made an effort to recruit men who presented a more or less "typical" Bear image in terms of body size and appearance, but I also sought out subjects who decidedly did not fit this profile (i.e., smooth-skinned, thinner men who nevertheless considered themselves members of the Bear community). I also attempted to sample a range of sexual attitudes and styles among my interview subjects. At one end of this spectrum, my youngest subject spoke proudly of his sexual conservatism and devotion to monogamy. At the other end was a man of substantial experience who genially spoke of his desire to "have sex with as many men as possible." Finally, I tried to take account of subjects' activity profile within the group. While I interviewed several Friendly Bears who had served as officers of the club, I also included men who were less active.

A Brief History of Bears

In addition to its appeal as a hedge against effeminacy and its eroticization of the heavier body, the Bear phenomenon features at least two additional factors contributing to its emergence during the 1980s. One was, unquestionably, the AIDS pandemic and the effect of AIDS-related wasting syndrome on the erotic imagination of gay men. In an era when thinness could be linked with disease and death, the fleshier body was reinterpreted as an indicator of health, vigor, strength, and virility. The second contributing factor was the Bear movement's ability to co-opt an existing subculture that had been operating on an informal basis for decades prior to the Bears' arrival on the scene. In 1976, a national network of "chubbies" (big men) and "chasers" (men who were sexually attracted to chubbies) emerged as a new national organization called Girth and Mirth. A dozen years later, as the Bears became a recognizable subculture within the gay community, an uneasy relationship developed between the two groups as significant numbers of men left Girth and Mirth chapters to join Bear clubs (Suresha 2002b). One reason for the out-migration from Girth and Mirth may be the more appealing imagery employed by the Bears. The iconic figure of the bear was enormously successful in linking the bigger body with nature, the wilderness, and more conventional notions of masculinity.

Indeed, to fully appreciate the Bear phenomenon one must acknowledge its place in the broader spectrum of "return to nature" masculinity movements dating back at least two centuries. American history reveals richly sedimented associations between the wilderness and escape from the perceived feminizing forces of civilization. In the early decades of the nineteenth century, popular biographies of pioneers and backwoodsmen offered accessible literary escapes. By the 1840s and 1850s Kit Carson, Daniel Boone, and Davy Crockett "all became mythic heroes . . . when their biographies were rewritten as primitivist narratives of innate, instinctual manhood" (Kimmel 1996, 63). Of course, those men who were not satisfied with mere fantasies could escape in reality to the vast American frontier. Immediately after the closing of the frontier in the latter half of the nineteenth century, an enthusiastic nostalgia developed that seemed to serve the same purpose. Rodeos, Wild West shows, cowboy lore, and wilderness adventure novels were all extremely popular during this time. Like the image of the bear, "A cowboy on a bronco symbolizes the rugged individuality of the Western man and beast . . . a true taste of the wild and woolly" (A. M. Bond, cited in Kimmel 1996, 176). More recently, the mythopoetic men's movement has stressed the importance of rediscovering various masculine archetypes, a process that is apparently greatly facilitated by drumming rituals in remote forested areas. The Radical Faeries can in many ways be seen as echoing this impulse, in that most Faerie gatherings are held in remote, rural areas.

But the Bear phenomenon is remarkable in that, despite its reprisal of the time-honored masculine "call of the wild" and its lush backwoods imagery, it has been nurtured and sustained almost exclusively in urban settings. For example, several of the sources I consulted mentioned the 1950s gladiator movies of the actor Steve Reeves as a formative cultural influence on Bear culture (Wright 1997b, 24; Suresha 2002b, 81). One source even specified that it was the films in which Reeves appeared bearded that really provided the impetus for the eroticization of the hairy male body (Lucie-Smith 1991, 6). Another example is the oft-noted predilection of Bears for computer technology and Internet communication.[4] Michael Bronski (quoted in Suresha 2002b, 40, 41) links this to the inauthenticity of the "natural" that informs Bear imaginings:

Bear culture is paradoxical. Anyone really brought up in the wild knows that it is not half as romantic as Bear images try to make it. It is an urban fantasy about what a world in the wild would look like . . . the artificiality of the so-called natural. I think that is why so many Bears are in love with cyberspace. The Bear idyll has always taken place in a cyberspace, which is nostalgia for something that never was.

The most complete history of the movement's emergence in the United States is Wright's (1997b) "A Concise History of Self-Identifying Bears."[5] In a letter to a fellow Bear aficionado, Wright (1997b, n. 3, 38–39) cites the first use of the term "Bear" to signal something approximating its contemporary meaning in the newsletter of a gay Los Angeles motorcycle club called the Satyrs in 1966, which "make notes (sic) of the fact that the Bear Club in San Francisco is having their first open meeting" in February of that year. A club called The Koalas (possibly the same club) "put out a newsletter called *The Bear Facts*. They were into leather and rode buddy on motorcycles and carried tiny teddy bears in their hip pockets." Wright also cites evidence of a group of self-identifying Bears in the Dallas area as early as the early 1970s.

Wright's account continues with an anecdote regarding an association of "bearlike" men centered around the Miami bar scene in the 1970s. According to one initiate:

A dozen or so men with beards, most of them husky, were piling out of the bar door as I was walking in. Two of them grabbed me by each arm . . . I thought I was headed for my first orgy (gay or straight), but it turned out to be a real party . . . Real men having a hell of a good time without a woman in sight. Imagine!! We watched the second half of the Dolphins game, played some cards, then sat outside under the moonlight, slowly pairing off and disappearing back indoors or off into tropical hiding places beyond the patio . . . It was too early in Beardom, I guess, to have a Bears club or organization of any kind. Nobody thought of it. There were spontaneous parties arranged by word of mouth, picnics, beach volleyball. We even loaded three vans full of bears and invaded Key West. (Wright 1997b, 24–25)

In a 1979 *Advocate* magazine article entitled "Who's Who in the Zoo: A Glossary of Gay Animals," the author provides the first mass-market description of Bears as "hunky, chunky types," with "larger chests and bellies than average" and "tangled beards" who will "stay and cuddle all night even if nothing else happens" (Mazzei 1979, 42). Most notable is how this description gained a certain legitimacy almost as soon as the author perceived it. Wright notes that a friend of the author related that the category "Bear" came up spontaneously in a public setting while he and the author were at a gay bar:

[We] were standing in Griffs', a Los Angeles leather bar, one evening discussing the types of men we were and those to whom were attracted. We decided we were Bears and continued on to formulate what we thought constitutes a Bear. Once we had described Bears it was an easy step to look around the bar and create the rest of the article. (Wright 1997b, 26)

Thus began the social construction of the Bear, a process that would quickly become commodified and dispersed across the country. When Lucie-Smith explains why the Bear image struck such a responsive chord with so many gay men, I almost get the feeling he is identifying a niche market, one previously overlooked in the post-Stonewall rush to accessorize gay culture:

Anyone who recognized homosexuality as an integral part of himself also knew it was too late to retire into the closet and slam the door. Many of these homosexuals had never been happy with the still very constricted range of role models offered to them—by the outside world, by their own kind, and above all by the gay press. Many had tastes and interests which had little to do with the accepted variants of the supposedly gay life-style. They were not necessarily young, nor in any stretch of the imagination pretty. Sexual attraction in their view was often a version of the daddy/son or buddy/buddy relationships. Quite a few could probably be described as good ole boys who liked other good ole boys, not just for company but for sex as well. It followed from this that they made little distinction between their sexual and their social selves; what you saw was what you got. (Lucie-Smith 1991, 7)

The emphasis here is clearly on normalization, but the implications are not immediately apparent. Does political complacency go along with the Bear image as well? Or is there perhaps, as Kelly and Kane (2001) suggest, something deeply subversive about the idea of a normalized gay masculinity? If the latter is the case, political consciousness raising was not a priority among those who shaped Bear culture in its early days:

Part of the genesis of Bear identity—or at least of Bear commercialization that became "Bear Disney"—centers on the alliance of two Bears with ambitious Bear-based businesses in San Francisco in the late 1980s: Rick Redewill, the original owner of the Bear bar Lone Star Saloon, and Richard Bulger, the publisher and cofounder (with photographer Chris Nelson doing business as Brahma Studios) of *Bear* magazine. (Suresha 2002b, 97)

Rick Redewill opened the Lone Star Saloon in San Francisco in 1989. Suresha (2002b, 98) notes that, "Following the closure of all gay San Francisco baths—the Lone Star functioned as a kind of Bear community center." But it is clear that from the outset, the Lone Star was primarily understood by its owner as a commercial venture. Bob Vafiades, one of the original Lone Star bartenders, recalls:

Rick was really getting into the whole idea of "tourist product sales" of Lone Star items like T-shirts and belts and posters at that point. I remember his eyes widening with excitement as he described how much merchandising profit *Bear* magazine was making—and he wanted to carve out a piece of that for himself. I think he realized then that there was a real promotional opportunity, and I think he was also encouraged at that point by Richard Bulger. (Suresha 2002b, 107)

Redewill's preference for cash over community is apparent in what happened after the Loma Prieta earthquake of 1989 severely damaged the building that housed the original Lone Star. When Redewill was forced to relocate he held a fund-raiser to help finance the move. Vafiades comments that "They were making it out to be like some sort of charity!" (Suresha 2002b, 108). Furthermore, once the bar reopened, its identity as a Bear bar was solidified, thanks to a lucrative friendship with the publisher of *Bear* magazine:

The new bar got a national reputation due to its exposure in *Bear* magazine . . . The reopening of the bar seemed very connected with the Bear thing, I guess, because *Bear* magazine was the main source of news about it . . . If they hadn't been friends or even friendly, I doubt the Lone Star could have hitched its wagon to the magazine's star. (Suresha 2002b, 109)

Vafiades adds that Redewill's dream to "develop the retail thing" has now been fully realized: "They have a full Lone Star merchandise store upstairs and go all over the country to different Bear events to sell their merchandise" (Suresha 2002b, 113).

While the Lone Star provided a physical space to nurture Bear culture, it is *Bear* magazine that is frequently credited with shaping Bear consciousness, particularly with respect to the idealization and eroticization of the Bear body. Wright (1997c, 9) notes that "the promulgation of idealizing Bears in the gay mass media, for better or worse, is the single most powerful force in the current construction of 'Bears,' The magazine featured short articles, fiction, and perhaps most important, lots of photographs of naked Bears. "*Bear* started life in 1987 as a pocket-format desk-top publication. With a run of only a few hundred copies. It soon grew to quarto size and achieved a circulation of many thousands" (Lucie-Smith 1991, 7). Furthermore, the photography represented a fully deliberate attempt to tease out and foster an erotic interest in larger, hairier men: "It was these [photographs], inevitably, even more than the text, which defined the new image . . . The photographer's concern has been to give what he sees [as] an added dimension, a certain aura which explains the attraction of the cult, and tells us why these men have been selected as desirable (Lucie-Smith 1991, 7–8)." Publisher Richard Bulger, along with photographer Chris Nelson, emphasized the "natural" appeal of these men from the beginning, as distinguished from the professional models used by other gay men's magazines: "Most of the men seen here had never done a photo-session before." However, this construction of the natural Bear was somewhat circular, in that some of the men photographed "were already known to the photographer. Others came into contact with him by different routes; for example, because they were readers of *Bear*" (Lucie-Smith 1991, 8). In any event, the photographs made a strong visual statement that clearly appealed to many gay men in the Bay Area, and this appeal was quickly amplified through *Bear* magazine and expanded across the country through the magazine's rapidly expanding circulation.

But it is also clear that aside from combating body fascism in the gay community, *Bear* magazine was launched first and foremost as a money-making enterprise (Suresha 1997, 45). Gay fiction writer and contributor to *Bear* magazine Jack Fritscher takes an accommodating view:

Richard Bulger was trying to find a niche and fill it, get laid, and make some money. So, Richard, finding a slice of the pie, chose Bears. He could just as easily have chosen husky men, as someone else did with *Husky* magazine . . . [6]

Richard made it appeal to a wider audience, an underserved demographic niche, so that he could sell magazines. Nothing wrong with that. *Bear* magazine is a marketing phenom appropriate to the sunny capitalism of gay lib. *Bear* and *American Bear* [another Bear magazine] have become a wonderful business that makes a lot of people happy, and that's a wonderful thing because most gay magazines don't make people happy. (Suresha 2002b, 87)

For others, the rapacious commodification of Bear culture takes on a more sinister tone. Ron Suresha, a Bear writer and editor of a recent book on Bears, laments:

Now within the context of the Bear community this means something like, "you have value as a person as long as I want something from you." In other words, "Buy my stuff, give me sex, validate me and, if I like you, I'll say nice things about you too." . . . So, there is that multidimensional consumer dynamic that people tend to be very blind to. (Suresha 2002b, 117)[7]

But while commercial enterprises enthusiastically exploited the emerging niche market in Bears and "Bearaphernalia" (Marks Ridinger, 1997, 83) and undoubtedly shaped many of its cultural features, it did not create the community out of whole cloth. "The magazines put in what people will buy. So you can't blame the magazine publishers for promoting their idealized Bears—After all, that is what people are willing to spend money on" (Suresha 2002b, 117). "In actuality, *Bear* magazine emerged from a Bearness that had already existed for at least 15 years before the magazine" (Suresha 2002b, 89). How then do we explain this sudden explosion of interest in all things ursine? What existing cultural strands had these entrepreneurs managed to bring together?

Like the Radical Faerie community, the Bear movement can be seen in part as a response to the hypermasculine clone phenomenon of the 1970s. However, in this case the reaction is significantly more complicated. Bear was a reaction not against the clone's masculinity per se but against *hyper*masculinity, and the particular way that the clone deployed the body to signal masculinity—hard, lean, muscled, toned, and smooth.

If this is true it would seem to indicate that Bears were interested not so much in revising conventional masculinity but in resignifying it. Wright (1997c, 6) concedes as much when he acknowledges that "Bears are fully engaged with hegemonic masculinity, seeking an alternative answer, both accepting some of the trappings while rejecting others."

In an intriguing argument, Suresha (1997) acknowledges the influence of two other communities that assisted Bears in their attempts to resignify the masculine body. He first credits the Radical Faeries, identifying them as the "foremost cultural influence" on the Bears and crediting them with creating a contemporary iconography of the hairy "natural man."[8] Suresha (1997, 43) sees an important connection between the photography in the 1970s editions of *RFD* and that which appeared later in *Bear* magazine— "unposed photos of nude and semiclad bearded, hairy men . . . a unique medium in which the 'alternative' male body could be romanticized and adored." Suresha even speculates that Faeries may have trumped Bears in their claims to the natural:

One may well postulate that, because of the Faeries' existence prior to the Bears, and based on the cultural evolutionary concept that the natural precedes the artificial, that the Bear culture took the ideal of the "natural man" from the Faeries, applied an urban spin to it, and produced a cult that espouses a so-called natural-man ideal while in actuality embodies its opposite. (Suresha 1997, 44)

Suresha makes another surprising statement when he acknowledges radical lesbianism as a source of encouragement for Bears. He clearly admires lesbians' efforts to "reclaim their own bodies from the dominant straight white patriarchy and redefine their own sense of self from the inside out . . . "Among these were radical, Rubenesque lesbians who, like Bears, were disparaged and fed up with the stereotypes and offensive role-playing presented for common consumption by the traditional heterosexist mainstream" (Suresha 1997, 45).

Both of these strands signal an embodied response, one that was elaborated even further through the influence of a third community. For decades prior to the Bears arrival on the scene the informal national network of chubbies and chasers existed. In the mid-1970s these contacts were extensive enough so that an informal list could be drawn up and circulated throughout the United States. In 1976 this list was used to develop the Girth and Mirth organization. The original clarion call, appearing in the *Berkeley Barb,* was entitled "Chubbies and Chasers, Unite!":

And clarion it was. It was like, "Telephone, tell a friend, tell any chubby chaser and chubby that you know!" This was a Saturday or Sunday morning, and people were still home in their robes and slippers, drinking coffee and reading the morning paper when they got the call. It was like electricity went through everyone, thinking, *Finally! It's happened!* (Suresha 2002b, 69)

Because of the preexisting network, news of the organization "spread like wildfire," and soon Girth and Mirth chapters were established across the country. Reed Wilgoren, one of the founding members of the original Girth and Mirth group in the Bay Area, captures some of the excitement the group generated and the deep meaning it held for many men as a means of raising their status in the greater gay community. Wilgoren describes the group's participation in the first Gay Day parade in San Francisco and his acute apprehension about how the new group would be received:

I did not know what to expect, but when we pulled into the mainstream of the parade onto Market Street, it seemed like, for that moment in my life, the whole world was gay, and we were an incredibly significant part of it all. We had no idea how it was going to change all of our lives as big men and eventually as Bears. It was truly amazing how well we were accepted and encouraged to be there at that moment! We were in tears, and we were smiling, we were laughing, crying, all through the whole parade. It was a very moving experience—and still feels so, even to talk about it at this moment. (Suresha 2002b, 71)

Shortly after the Bears became a recognizable subculture within the gay community, tension developed between the two groups. Wilgoren records his continuing attraction to and misgivings about the Bear community:

When the group started, if you sat a big man up next to a Bear, you'd see a difference—in size and age and mindset. Now, of course, it's changed a lot over the years . . . Still, in the early day they were very typecast . . . I found it kind of difficult to cross over into that group, to be honest with you. Coming from my own personal life experience and being very well accepted socially and sexually as a big man, then going into Bear groups was definitely quite a different experience for me. I felt, and still do feel sometimes, that age and size are definitely a discriminatory factor with Bears. It's lessening though: Those attitudes in general have improved greatly. (Suresha 2002b, 75)

In the early years, some Bears resented the incursion of "the Girth and Mirth crowd" into the Bear community, fearing that fleshiness could be too easily read as feminine, that the "softness" of the Girth and Mirth body was exactly the kind of representation they were trying to avoid.[9] Nevertheless, a great deal of overlap occurred between the two communities. Interestingly, in many cities Girth and Mirth chapters went into decline just as Bear organizations were cropping up.[10] This shift in membership had a profound effect on Bear culture and self-image:

At some point in the early San Francisco Bear years—around 1990, when the first Girth-and-Mirth groups appeared to infiltrate the Lone Star Saloon crowd and to intermingle with the Bear Hug sex groups—there was a noticeable shift in the way that the local community defined Bears, and in the way Bears defined themselves. It was only later that the basic defining characteristic of a Bear as having abundant facial or body hair changed to an equal if not greater emphasis on body weight. (Suresha 1997, 48)

The fact that such an incursion was accomplished despite formidable resistance speaks to another formative influence on Bear culture and the Bear body: AIDS. Kelly and Kane, who describe themselves irreverently as "a couple of fat dykes," observe that "Many relate the popularity of Bears to AIDS and the fear of the emaciated bodies as signifying illness" (Kelly and Kane 2001, 333).[11] In his introduction to *The Bear Cult*, Lucie-Smith (1991, 7–8) makes the connection explicit: "In Africa, India and the Pacific Islands a certain amount of extra weight has traditionally been regarded as a sign of power and potency. With the advent of AIDS, similar attitudes may yet take root in the developed countries. In Africa itself, the colloquial name for the disease is 'slim.'"

All of these elements, then, contributed to the enormous popularity and growth of Bear culture nationwide during the late 1980s and early 1990s and its expansion internationally in the years thereafter. Detailed published accounts chronicle the formation of local Bear organizations in Colorado (Floyd 1997); Minnesota (Gan 2001); the East Coast (Goecke 2001); Iowa (Toothman 2001); Houston (Froelich 2001); and Rochester, New York (Noble 2001). Accounts of Bear culture abroad can be found in

Australia (Hay 1997; Sharman 2001; Hyslop 2001), New Zealand (Webster 1997), Europe (McCann 1997), France (Mey 1997), and even Turkey (Sahin 2001).

What Is a Bear?

As is the case with Faerie identity, a certain tension between fluidity and fixity is reflected in the identity narratives generated in Bear cultures. Wright (1997b, 21) asserts that "Since the term 'Bear' is applied in a self-defining manner, it is vaguely defined, sometimes in self-contradicting ways, and is interpreted variously." But it seems that these definitions of "Bear" vary within a fairly well-defined field, one that is heavily influenced by gender. It has never been, as Wright suggests below, a matter of Bear identity as a kind of *tabula rasa*, upon which each Bear man inscribes his own particular meanings:

The underlying theoretical starting point is the notion of "a bear": As Saussurian or Barthian empty signifier. Each self-identifying Bear, over the last ten years, has filled in his own definition and meaning. From the experiential base of gay male subjectivities the gay mass media has taken over, selling to the Bears consumable, standardized images of "real" Bears and broadcasting these images and attendant values to society at large. The political shift has been from anarchic to authoritarian. (Wright 1997c, 2)

It seems that the very anarchism that Wright nostalgically invokes here is itself gendered. It brings to mind Lucie-Smith's (1991) comment about the Bear's refusal to "come indoors at once and wash behind his ears" and resonates with the long history of masculinist anxieties regarding the feminizing effects of civilization outlined in the previous section. Elsewhere Wright (1997c, 7) acknowledges the central role of masculinity in Bear identity when he offers his own definition of a Bear as "a gay man who is as comfortable being a man as he is being gay, and who has a good heart." Jack Fritscher exhibits this same tendency toward defining "Bear" as an indeterminate identity that is nevertheless profoundly structured by gender: "Bear is a concept so receptively blank that as a label it welcomes and absorbs all *masculine* fantasies, fetishes, identities, and body types. 'Bear' is all-inclusive" (Suresha 2002b, 80; emphasis added).

For some of my interview subjects, questions of definition devolved to intuition. As Don says, "You know it's a little, gosh, it's one of those things you have to just experience, I guess, and understand." Burt concurs when he says, "I don't think that there's a, there's a real definition." Yet this fluid, ineffable quality of Bearness is in sharp contrast with some of the definitions I gleaned from other subjects, who had little trouble with definition:

"A Bear to me is somebody who, quote unquote, has a potbelly." (Don)

"I would say, physically I would say at least facial hair—beard, moustache. And personality-wise—natural, down to earth." (Larry)

"I would say stockier, definitely hairy—either facial hair, hairy chest, probably a little bit older." (Grant)

"This is my personal opinion, the majority of people base what a Bear is based on, I think, more physical looks than anything else, obviously." (Travis)

Another prominent feature of Bear culture is the proliferation and fetishization of typologies deployed to capture various aspects of Bear identity. There is, first of all, a general typology that divides Bear men into various categories by elaborating the bear analogy and even extending it to other animals: Bears (the default category, but sometimes used in a more specific sense to indicate sexual dominance and a more independent attitude), Cubs (used to indicate a playfulness and youthful attitude that is not necessarily tied to age but may be associated with a smaller body frame; "cubbishness" usually signals sexual submissiveness), Daddy Bears (the dominant partner of a Cub), Grizzlies (more mature and demanding Bears), Polar Bears (older Bears with white or grey hair), Otters (thin framed and smooth), and Wolves (thin framed and hairy). While I found that these categories are widely recognized within Bear communities, I also heard a variety of definitions for each from my interview subjects. There seemed to be general agreement as to the physical characteristics corresponding to each category, but less agreement on the attitudinal correlates of each.

In addition to this detailed typology, there is a second, very popular method of categorizing Bears, known as the "Bear code." Similar in some respects to computer code, the use of the Bear code reflects both an instrumental attitude toward self-description and the culture's close association with computer technology and Internet communication. Here Bears assess themselves along a variety of dimensions and assign a quantitative measure (ranging from + + to – –) in reference to their various physical and personality characteristics, including beard type, fur (body hair), height (included as the "tallness" factor), weight, cubbishness, daddy tendencies, the "grope" factor (how much one likes to be "pawed"), the "kinky" factor ("for those who dare"), degree of monogamy practiced in relationships, amount of muscle mass, endowment (penis size), the "behr" factor (specifically for those men who do not have beards, to indicate what other forms of facial hair they may have), and the "rugged/outdoor" factor. Nontraditional Bears may also include two additional designations in their self-descriptions: the "p" factor (for peculiar—if you have "some idiosyncrasies") and the un-designated "q" factor (judging from its description, the "q" is most likely understood as designating "queer"—"Stereotypes be damned, get out the chiffon"). Crosscutting all of these categories are a series of qualifiers: "v" if the trait indicated is not very rigid, "?" if the designation is based on insufficient information, ":" for traits that are observed but ambiguous, "!" when the trait is "as close to the prototype as possible, or an exemplary case of a specific trait," and "( )" to indicate crossovers or ranges on a specific dimension that may change in different situations (Donahue and Stoner 1997, 149–56). Thus, using this complex coding system, a Bear seeking social or sexual contacts can convey a great deal of very specific information about himself with a single line of code. For example, the Bear who describes himself as "B0f+t+w+ccdg+s+e+h" has little or no beard (B0), has above-average fur (f+), is taller than average (t+), is a "big boned" bear (w+), identifies as a Cub with Daddy tendencies (ccd), likes to be touched most of the time (g+), will form relationships that are generally open ended (s+), is above average in terms of penis size (e+), and has a moustache without a beard (h). Although the use of the Bear code seems to have declined somewhat in recent years, the fact that it was ever taken seriously is somewhat ironic, as authors Donahue and Stoner claim to have developed the Bear code as a joke.

Furthermore, while in the field I observed a wide degree of variance in identity investment. A minority of those who attend Bear events probably do not identify as Bears at all; a larger segment self-identify as Bears, but beyond cultivating the traditional Bear "look," it is not an important part of their self-presentation. But for another large segment of the community, more deliberate signaling seems to indicate a deeper investment in Bear identity. For example, while at Bear Camp I saw a number of vanity license plates with Bear themes: "CUB," "LIL CUB," "WOOFY,"[12] and "BEAR CKR" (for "Bear seeker"). T-shirts included slogans such as "Motor City Bears," "Bear Patrol," "I Have the Body of a God (Unfortunately, it's Buddha)," "Got Fur?" (advertising the Lone Star Saloon), "Bear Pride 2001" (from the annual Memorial Day celebration in Chicago), a cartoon of an anthropomorphized bear on another gay pride T-shirt, and several hats with various Bear images on them. Bear paw tattoos are popular with some, especially younger Bears. I asked Travis, in his early twenties, about his new tattoo:

I got my bear paw tattoo in September. It's almost, I always wanted to get one, specifically also because I saw a lot of other guys that had them. And you know I'm normally somebody who doesn't like to do what everybody else does, but when it came to the bear paw I think to some people it almost is considered, I don't want to say rite of passage but it almost, it all seems that way, that getting your bear paw tattoo almost makes it, in some way, quote unquote official.

When I asked Don if he had any Bearaphernalia in his apartment, he laughed and told me of his extensive collection, which includes the head of a real bear, stuffed and mounted: "I mean it's one of those—yeah, they can't help but notice, I mean there's a big huge polar bear head right in front of the door when you walk in. Actually, you know I put it on the patio to scare the squirrels away for a bit. Um, it's just a big old polar bear head" (laughs). He also told me of his hopes for expanding the collection:

Yeah, I go out there and buy certain objects with bears, I mean I'll be honest, there's a, there's a, there's a Baccarat bear sitting in [a nearby shop], you know, I walk by when I go to Starbucks and it's like, "I want that," and it's just, you know, just really a[n] ice-crystal polar bear, so . . . Who has $300 to buy a crystal polar bear? So . . . [laughs].

Brian introduces an essentialist element when I asked him about such extensive collections, attributing the impulse to an innate bear-loving spirit:

I think it's funny because you coincidentally will hear people talk about, there are lots of guys in the Bear group who sort of collected bears and teddy bears and stuff like that, long before they knew. You know, long before they would have even known or before the Bear group even started anywhere.

The varying degrees of investment in Bear identity correspond roughly to Brekhus's (2003) concept of identity density. But here we encounter an interesting paradox. Brekhus's research on gay men's identity construction is based on their status as a "marked" (or recognizably different) social group. Here we have a group of gay men who have forged a community wherein they collaborate to "unmark" themselves in the eyes of the larger public; they're just regular guys. But in doing so, they create a new kind of marking for themselves within the gay community. Brekhus (2003, 74) describes (non-Bear) gay men who pursue normalization by living in the suburbs and downplaying any distinct attributes arising from their sexual orientation as "integrators." Yet his description of integrators does not quite capture the way Bears, in pursuing normalization, actually make themselves more distinct. Most gay men recognize "Bear" as a marked subcultural formation, and most can describe a typical Bear. This identity pickle may partially explain why Bears have yet to register as a distinct social type among heterosexuals. The idea of erasing difference is, after all, central to the Bear project. But how then does one evaluate Bears in terms of their identity density, if it is defined as "the degree to which identity is packaged and presented in a concentrated or diluted form" (Brekhus 2003, 28)? Bears are actively concentrating on diluting their identities.[13]

With respect to social class, Wright (1997c, 11) observes that "Bears' 'naturalness' registers in the key of 'blue collar.'" Bears present an image of working-class masculinity, yet many, if not most, are middle class. Rofes (1997, 89–90) ponders this as he asks, as a middle-class academic, "When I put on my Harley cap and walk into the Lone Star, exactly who am I and what am I doing there?" As he looks around the bar he observes the distinctively working-class self-presentation of his friends (jeans, baseball caps, black boots, flannel shirts). "My mind suddenly switches to another channel . . . One man's father was a classmate of my dad's at Harvard. Another is a self-employed computer techno trainer. The fourth works as an aerospace engineer and another is an attorney."

Because of their purported impatience with abstractions and their daily trials with the harsh realities of material life, working-class men have often been understood as more authentically masculine than their middle-class counterparts. As Connell (1995, 36) observes, "Hard labor in factories and mines literally uses up the workers' bodies; and that destruction, a proof of the toughness of the work and the worker, can be a method of demonstrating masculinity." Furthermore, working-class bodies have long held an erotic fascination for the middle class, as Wray (1994, 1) suggests: "Any cursory reading of popular representations of lower-class whites suggests that the middle classes seem obsessed with what lower-class whites do or threaten to do with their sexual bodies." Finally, working-class masculinity is validated through homosocial networks; as Chauncey (1994, 79–80) describes the conviviality of an early twentieth-century working-class saloon in New York City, he does so in terms similar to Rofes':

The solidarity [that the working-class bachelor subculture of 1900] celebrated was expressed in the everyday ties built at work on the waterfront or in construction; it was symbolized by the rituals of saloon conviviality that expressed mutual regard and reciprocity . . . A man's "manliness" was signaled in part by his participation in such rituals . . . but it was demonstrated as well by . . . evidence of his relative virility compared to other men's; manliness in this world was confirmed by other men and in relation to other men, not by women.

For all these reasons it is perhaps not surprising that middle-class Bears, as they sought to construct a normalized gay masculinity, would find working-class images appealing. What *is* surprising is the silence surrounding these issues, not only the unexamined, underproblematized acceptance of the equation of masculinity with working-class men but also the lack of reflection as to what it means when middle-class men do working-class drag. In this context, Rofes' (1997) awareness of class contradiction is exceptional, as is Brian's insightful commentary:

I will never forget going to a, in fact I was a judge at International Bear Rendezvous in San Francisco in—when was that?—'97. And um, you'd see these guys and they were all dressed like, you know, in the Bear drag, bubba drag, you know, the uh, flannel shirt and the ripped jeans, ripped flannel shirts, working boots and all this sort of stuff, and they were all like—systems analysts at Sun Microsystems !! [*Laughs loudly.*] I mean they were all like these, they were all like computer geeks. Not one of them was—you know, like I was saying—a bricklayer, a plumber, a fireman, a policeman.

Bear culture advertises itself as racially inclusive but remains overwhelmingly white. For example, my field notes indicate that on a typical Friendly Bear bar night, with well over a hundred men attending, I saw two African American and two Asian American men. Similarly, at Bear Camp 2001, with an enrollment of nearly 120, one African American man and one Latino man attended. Fall Bear Camp attracted fifty-four white Bears and one African American Bear. My sense is that this is not simply a local problem. According to most of the printed discourse, the Bear body has nothing to do with white skin. To their credit, most Bear organizations actively seek to diversify their ranks, and racially inclusive language can be found on many Bear Web sites. Yet several writers mention the conspicuous absence of Bears of color in their communities. In two separate content analyses of Bear erotic magazines, both Locke (1997) and McCann (2001) comment on the predominance of white bodies. Kelly and Kane (2001, 344) ask why Bears "feel the need to adopt a rhetoric of racial inclusivity when the iconography of the texts before us is so overwhelmingly white?" More than one commentator on Bear culture has acknowledged the tacit encoding of the Bear as white. Grant, one of my interview subjects, works cautiously with a tacit equation of the "naturally white" Bear body:

I don't think there's a lot of hairy Asians [*laughs*]. Just their body type I don't think, you know I think there has to be, I don't know, certainly Chinese, but I think there are some hairy Japanese. I think there's some cross there. You know, same thing with Latinos. Latin men, you know, tend to more times be smoother. But then you get your Mediterranean men—oooh! [*Laughs.*]

Like the Faeries, the whiteness of Bear culture is probably due at least in part to the foundational image of the community—the bear itself—and how this image is perceived across racial lines. For most white men who join the Bear community, the appeal of the bear image is based on its association with masculinity and strength while at the same time signaling a capacity for tenderness and conviviality. But when, in the early 1980s, the forerunners of the Bear movement sought to humanize the impersonality of the leather community by wearing teddy bears in their pockets, they were unwittingly drawing on a raced cultural history of *white* American masculinity. As Bederman (1995, 44) demonstrates, the inspiration for the teddy bear, Teddy Roosevelt, possessed a "talent for embodying two contradictory models of manhood simultaneously—civilized manliness and primitive masculinity." Civilized manliness, she explains, was a character model that "comprised all the worthy, moral attributes which the Victorian middle class admired in a man" (18). As such, manliness was intimately linked with whiteness. By contrast, masculinity was understood in essentialist terms, referring to "any characteristics, good or bad, that all men had" (18). But here again, this "primal" masculinity was understood to be threatened by the feminizing effects of civilization. On Rotundo's (1993, 228) reading, white masculinist anxieties were further fueled by fears of domination by the more authentic masculinity of the tribesmen of "Darkest Africa," the "savage" Indian. Such descriptions of the recuperative back-to-nature narratives of the period reveal their racialized character.

Consequently, as the heirs of a raced cultural dynamic that equates the return to nature with whiteness, Bears may be unintentionally reproducing the raced appeal of the bear image. Exacerbating these effects is the racialized history of identification with animals. While many white men revel in their identification with the bear, men of color may be much less eager to do so in light of historically racist comparisons between animals and people of color (Plous and Williams 1995; Becker 1973). But the unintended racialized effects of Bear iconography are complicated by the deliberate appeal to men of color in this primarily white community's rhetoric. Here it seems that Bears are at least trying to challenge the hierarchical ranking of raced masculinities that is a prominent feature of hegemonic masculinity (Connnell 1995, 80), but they do so from within a symbolic cosmology heavily structured by race. In the final analysis this remains a heartfelt and conciliatory gesture extended to men of color to participate in what is still fundamentally a white fantasy. Can efforts to diversify the Bear community succeed under these conditions? Perhaps, but such success will entail further consideration of Almaguer's (1991, 86) observation that men of color "do not negotiate the acceptance of gay identity in exactly the same way white American men do." Any success in this effort will also mark an interesting cultural reversal insofar as men of color will be adopting the symbol of the bear and ascribing to it a new set of resistant and racially inclusive meanings.

Given the context established here, what possibilities might Bear culture open up and close off in terms of gender resistance, and how are the particular inflections of Bear masculinity exhibited in the community's sexual culture? In what follows I explore these questions through various theoretical lenses, beginning with Bourdieu.

"A Bear of a Man": Reimagining Bear Bodies

I used to visit prisoners . . . We were chosen to have a story done on us by the local press . . . the article describes, "And in walks a bear of a man" and then described me physically, you know, how I dressed and such, and identified me as Burt. And I read that, that was really actually my first key, and my first inclination was to be offended. Because the other thing that a bear carries is some weight, which is not thought of very well by our society . . . And, at first I was offended because this was a recognition that I had put on that weight—which I now see as healthy—but when I came back to the article and began reading it over and over again, the more I read it the more I really saw that this really was a very warm image, the image of a man who walked tall, strong and yet had a gentle approach to life. And I like that. I think there are a lot of men who do. (Burt)

Bourdieu (1977) proposes "habitus,"[14] the deeply interiorized and embodied set of mental and physical dispositions that guide social action, as relatively durable, but not impervious to change. He allows that individual experience, or, on a societal level, "times of crisis, in which the routine adjustment of subjective and objective structures is brutally disrupted" (Bourdieu 1977, 45), may indeed affect the habitus in profound ways. I argue that men who come to understand themselves as Bears experience just such a time of crisis. However, I first examine several of Bourdieu's more specific concepts as they relate to the embodiment of Bear masculinity. In *Masculine Domination* (Bourdieu 2001), he uses his fieldwork on the Kabyle in northern Algeria to abstract the processes governing the embodiment of gender and specifically the way these processes come to be understood as natural, thereby obscuring their arbitrary nature and the gender politics they reflect.

Bourdieu (1997, 194) calls the first principle that serves to naturalize embodied masculinity "necessitation through systematicity." Here he acknowledges the influence of structuralism on his work and the primacy of gender as a "master binary": "The limit *par excellence*, that between the sexes, will not brook transgression" (1990, 211); "[the] binary opposition between male and female appears founded in the nature of things because it is echoed virtually everywhere" (1997, 194). Thus the arbitrary "nature" of gender is obscured by virtue of its richly homologous relationship with other already gendered binaries: hot (masculine)/cold (feminine), hard (masculine)/soft (feminine), outside (masculine)/inside (feminine) (2001, 13–18). By this method the "arbitrary of the social *nomos*" is transmuted into "a necessity of nature" (2001, 13). The critical point here is that masculinity is defined relationally, *against* the feminine. In Bear culture this pattern is reproduced when Bears define their masculinity not only against the feminine but more specifically against the feminized, hairless, and gym-toned body of the dominant ideal of gay masculinity—"the twink," as he is dismissively known in Bear culture. Wright (1997c, 9) suggests that "When a Bear makes such a counter-statement, that he is not a 'woman,' not a 'twink,' not a 'heterosexual,' he is using his body to participate in changing social practice and challenging hegemonic power." I would argue that, with respect to embodied masculinity, this statement obscures the fact that Bear masculinity simultaneously *challenges* and *reproduces* hegemonic masculinity.

Bourdieu's (1977) concept of "hexis" is instructive here. Closely related to habitus, but more specifically focused on deportment (i.e., ways of presenting and moving the body in social situations) as the physical instantiation of objective political and social relationships, hexis represents an embodied "political mythology" (Bourdieu 1997, 93). Thus the embodied hexis of Kabyle women includes a somewhat stooped posture, with the gaze directed downward. A Kabyle man, on the other hand, gazes directly at others, and his dominance is "asserted in movements upwards, outwards, toward other men" (94). Likewise, when Bears refuse to "do submission" or "do effeminacy" with their bodies, they in fact exercise a kind of limited agency insofar as the Bear body is perceived by heterosexual men as both "not heterosexual" and "not effeminate." Moreover, this is an agentic deployment of the Bear body that may act to radically destabilize the effeminacy effect. However, this possibility is significantly complicated by the way that Bear masculinity operates within gay culture and how it is deployed against other homosexual men. I strongly suspect that of the three defining functions of the masculinized Bear body as neither woman, heterosexual, nor twink, it is the twink that provides the real oppositional anchor for most Bears. In their virulent rejection of the effeminate stereotype and female drag, Bears wish to convey that they are not women, but in practice this is accomplished indirectly, through an attack on the feminized, narcissistic body of the twink. Furthermore, while Bears may proudly acknowledge that they are not heterosexual, this should not be read as a rejection of heterosexual masculinity. On the contrary, it seems that most Bear discourse seeks to *minimize* the difference between Bear and heterosexual masculinity. On this reading, the Bears' challenge to hegemonic power is negligible, and the power relations reflected in the embodied hexis of Bear masculinity reproduce the hierarchical assumptions of hegemonic masculinity. Both assign lower status to bodies perceived as feminized.

Furthermore, despite their use of the twink as oppositional anchor, the "natural confirmation" (Bourdieu 1997, 194) that is the desired consequence of this systematicity remains problematic within Bear culture. This is because, in contrast with heterosexual masculinities, no "rich homology" of binaries exists to obscure the arbitrary features of gay masculinities. Thus Bear masculinity must be developed and sustained intersubjectively, within the community itself, an interactive process that is greatly facilitated by the symbol of the bear. The bear operates to link this new form of gay masculinity to the natural; it provides an opportunity for rich elaboration (through the designation of various types of Bear men as sexually submissive Cubs, sexually dominant Grizzlies, gray or white-haired Polar Bears, etc.), and, most importantly, through the nostalgic wilderness imagery it evokes, it links Bear masculinity with heteronormative masculinity.

But this construction remains unstable and its arbitrary nature easily revealed, as in this scathing assessment by Harris (1997, 106):

Its hirsute ideal of rugged masculinity is ultimately as contrived as the aesthetic designer queen. While Bears pretend to oppose the "unnatural" look of urban gay men, nothing could be more unnatural, urban, and middle class than the pastoral fantasy of the smelly mountaineer in long johns, a costume drama that many homosexuals are now acting out as self-consciously as Marie Antoinette and her entourage dressed up as shepherds and shepherdesses.

My time in the field leads me to speculate that this fragility probably works to increase, rather than undermine, group solidarity among Bears.

Bourdieu (1997, 195) identifies the other critical process that naturalizes embodied masculinity as "gendered socialization and the somatization of domination." This process describes the various practices that inculcate a gendered habitus during childhood, and Bourdieu further divides it into four subcomponents.[15] Here I apply three of these subcomponents to the *revision* of a gendered habitus in adult gay men and apply his ideas to the reconstruction of masculinity in Bear culture. The first practice is identified as "rites of institutions." These rites, such as ritual circumcision in many cultures, serve to underscore the difference between those who participate—men—and those who do not—women (Bourdieu 1997, 195). Participation, of course, is determined directly by the characteristics of the body. Local Bear organizations like the Friendly Bears serve the same institutional purpose, and the Bear body becomes the point of reference for those who participate in Bear clubs, organizational planning, and activities. It is worth noting here that membership in these clubs is not strictly limited to men who self-identify as Bears. Most clubs welcome "Bears and their admirers." The inclusive description serves at least two purposes. First, it expands the possible membership beyond those who exhibit the typical Bear physical traits. Second, even as it expands the membership it underscores the centrality of the Bear body and its existence as an object of desire. Slim men, hairless men, younger men—all are welcome, *provided they identify as Bear admirers*. I observed one such admirer at numerous Friendly Bear events. He was a relatively young, tautly muscled, smooth-skinned ex-gymnast. While he fit the physical description of a twink, his enthusiastic sexual interest in older Daddy Bear types meant that he greatly reinforced, rather than undermined, the intersubjectively sustained erotic of Bear sexual culture. As such he was warmly welcomed in the club, and his interest in larger men was enlisted as supporting evidence of the natural appeal of Bears. Thus the inclusive membership policy contributes significantly to a key agentic function of the Bear clubs—the embodied reassignment of the fleshier, hairier frame from stigmatized to desired object.

The next important process is the "symbolic remaking of anatomical differences." Here Bourdieu (1997, 195) explains that "the socially constructed body serves as an ideological foundation for the arbitrary opposition through which it was itself constructed." Bourdieu uses the example of the interpretation of "swelling" and all its various analogies as based on a taken-for-granted association with the male erection and phallic swelling (Bourdieu 2001, 13). In the case of the Bears, the association (again) cannot be taken for granted; it must be actively constructed in community and applied to the swelling of the Bear's phallic body. On this reading the Bear's generous frame, contrasted with the more compact frame of the twink, becomes a kind of homage to phallic power and masculinity.

The third process I extend is that which Bourdieu (1997, 198) identifies as "differential usages of the body and rites effecting the virilization of boys and the feminization of girls." Here he cites several practices among the Kabyle to virilize boys, such as the cutting of the boy's hair and the father's assistance in dressing him for his first trip to the exclusively masculine world of the public market. Analogous practices for Bears are instructed not by a single patriarch but by the normative structure of the entire group. The self-conscious attempt to dress and groom oneself like a "real" man approaches but never quite registers consciously as drag in the typical Bear consciousness. Nevertheless, appearance is an ongoing project among Bears, one requiring active construction and constant vigilance. This vigilance is perhaps best indicated by those attempts that are perceived as falling short of the prescribed mark. Fritscher (2002) complains, "There's nothing worse than seeing a big brute doing all this standing and posing at a Bear convention or in a Bear bar, only to then watch him pirouette out the door." Two of my Friendly Bear subjects made similar observations:

[Gil is a] very handsome man with a very nice beard . . . you walk up to Gil and you think, "Boy, this is a guy who just fits the image," and then he'll open up his mouth, and flowers come out! [That] kind of subtracts a little Bearishness somewhere along the line. (Burt)

I think, honestly, that you need to, you know, your mannerisms, how you talk has to fit how you look. And that's kind of a problem sometimes. You know, I know guys who can be, who look extremely butch, you know lumberjack types who open their mouth and the chiffon flies out! [*Laughs.*] (Travis)

Returning to the concept of hexis, it would seem that these discordant displays of improperly masculinized "corporeal dispositions" are upsetting precisely because they reveal the constructed nature of what Bourdieu (1997, 195) refers to as "the doxic experience of masculine domination as inscribed in the nature of things, invisible, unquestioned."

Don's case is particularly interesting with respect to the social construction of the Bear body. Don grew up on a farm and attended high school in a small town, which I quickly surmised was a painful experience for him. He told me, "I came out to myself back when I was nine, ten—I knew I liked what I liked." In high school, Don weighed more than 350 pounds and was ridiculed for being heavy. During his senior year, his situation got uglier when he was outed by his classmates in a particularly public way. "They were chasing me down the hall with a video camera, because they were putting together like this news footage and . . . they just outed me and the next thing you know I was the gay guy in school."

After graduation, Don wasted little time, waiting only three weeks before moving to the nearest big city. He also managed to drop a considerable amount of weight, and while he was still big, for the first time in his life he began to feel good about his body:

I had a forty-five-year-old woman stop me on [Metro] Mall when I was about twenty and said that if she were twenty years younger she'd make me her husband. I was just having my lunch! A chicken salad sandwich, and she came up storming, and she wasn't nuts. I mean she was a business-professional type woman, and it was like, she just said that I was an attractive young man. And I went, "Well thank you," and then it dawned on me that, well fine—I must be attractive.

But even as this encounter bolstered Don's self-confidence, it also highlighted his same-sex interests. As revealing as this encounter was for Don, it was not something he could pursue. His sexual self-confidence did not really blossom until he found the Friendly Bears, at which time he felt he had "found family." "I mean I'm big and hairy, it's obvious . . . I found my niche, where I was welcome to be who I was and don't have to hide anything."

But Don makes it clear that finding the Friendly Bears was not just about finding interested sex partners. "I never really had a hard time finding sex," he tells me. "When I found the Bears I found a lot more of what I liked in a man, within that culture. I sort of like knocked out the nellyisms . . . I knocked out the, you know, the flaming drag queens." Upon discovering the club, Don was able to quickly parlay his good looks, stocky build, and tall stature into Bear social capital. He is currently very active in the group, both socially and sexually, and often makes a gregarious show of his affection for the community. At the campfire, from my Bear Camp field notes, I observed that "[Don] seems to be running the show, making various bad jokes and, interestingly, using a variety of voices that incorporate growls and grunts into his speech. He is, I realize, talking like a bear."[16] His association with the Friendly Bears has allowed him to come to terms with his traumatic high school experiences, albeit in a way that is obviously informed by hegemonic masculinity. Don says, "I still, I see five or six classmates that I went to high school with down at the bar now. So it's sort of like . . . I was sorta like, "Uh, what was this—I'm the gay one and you're not? ON YOUR KNEES!" (laughter).

Don's complex and contradictory journey is perhaps best summarized by again returning to Bourdieu's concept of hexis. Don's acceptance within the Bear community is reflected in a new understanding of his body and the way it can be deployed in social and sexual situations. The ridicule he suffered as a youth left him with deep-seated feelings of shame and inadequacy. From the Bears he has learned to adjust his gait, posture, and gaze in a way that now signals strength, dominance, and virility. These traits are in turn read by other members of the community as evidence of a positive attitude toward his newly discovered "Bear" self. Perhaps this is why, despite the obvious prominence of a specific body type among Bears, many members (e.g., Larry, quoted earlier) continue to insist that what distinguishes a Bear is "90 percent attitude."

In his appendix to *Masculine Domination* entitled "Some Questions on the Gay and Lesbian Movement," Bourdieu (2001, 19) observes that "Bearing witness to the universality of the recognition granted to the androcentric mythology, gays themselves very often apply the dominant principles to themselves."[17] The chapter up to this point provides strong support for this idea. But it is also true that the Bear culture's acceptance of dominant modes of masculinity can be seen as deeply subversive in that it is linked explicitly with same-sex desire. From this perspective Bears come closer to fulfilling the promise Bourdieu (2001, 118) sees in the gay/lesbian movement as a whole when he opines that "This movement . . . very profoundly calls into question the prevailing symbolic order and poses in an entirely radical way the question of the foundation of that order and the conditions for a successful mobilization with a view to subverting it."

Doing What Comes Naturally: Bear Sexual Culture

A distinctive Bear sexual culture emerged in the late 1980s, primarily through the efforts of four Bay Area men who wanted to provide a "safe, social and sexual meeting ground for men who are Bears or who like Bears." The men planned a series of small parties.

The name came from a time in mid-1987 when "Bear" was just beginning to assume its current meaning. The early Bear Hug meetings were called "Bear Hug/Bare Hug." We wanted to encourage an erotic feeling and safe sex practices. Remember, the mid-eighties were a time of fear and paranoia about AIDS. The "playgrounds" were being forced to close. We wanted to provide private places for fun . . . Those of us who founded the group either were Bears or liked Bears. (Wright 1997d, 201)

The invitation list for these Bear Hug parties quickly grew to more than a hundred names. Within two years the list exceeded 300 names and the parties had to be moved to a large nonresidential space on 14th Street in San Francisco. "They were uninhibited and erotic," reports founding member Sam Ganczarurk, "since we were building a sense of community, and there was a sense of novelty. There wasn't any of the "been there, done that" feeling" (Wright 1997a, 203). By 1990 these parties attracted curious Bears from all over the country, many of whom returned to their respective communities to sponsor their own Bear play parties.

Given its paradoxical relationship to hegemonic masculinity, how distinctive is Bear sexual culture? What separates the erotic imagination of Bears from other gay men? I was able to locate two empirical studies that partially address these questions through comparative content analysis of "mainstream" gay and Bear erotic magazines (Locke 1997; McCann 2001). Both studies comment on the predominance of white bodies, many of the images signaling the working-class status of the model, either through dress or setting. Not surprisingly, both studies reveal that Bear magazines favor men who are heavier, hairier, and older than gay magazines targeted for other audiences. Locke (1997, 132) notes an interesting paradox, that the magazines he analyzed were all established to foster acceptance and appreciation for the "nonconventional" Bear body, yet he found a pronounced tendency toward the production of "superbear" images, which may reinstate the alienating effect of an unattainable beauty ideal. Kelly and Kane (2001, 341) looked at Bear erotic fiction and noted the refreshing emphasis on support, nurturance, and playfulness included in the descriptions of sex that they analyzed, albeit with some caution:

I'm wondering whether this discourse of nurturance has to be presented through a discourse of sex in order to make it OK for men to participate? Or is it a way of reclaiming the whole body for eroticism and thereby dephallicizing the cock? And besides the nurturance, what about the playfulness? I think that really mitigates my discomfort with the wild man myth's seeming to reproduce old time sexism.

In this section I take a look at what is really "new" about Bear sexual culture, the role that gender and masculinity play in this culture, and the extent to which that role challenges and/or reproduces an emphasis on penetrative, genital sexuality and phallic eroticism.[18]

Although my fieldwork included attending several Bear play parties, which included sexual activity, I observed a marked contrast in the sexual temperature of Bear Camp versus Leather Camp (see chapter 5). Unlike Leather Camp, no designated spaces were set aside for sexual activity at Bear Camp. This is not to say that there was no sex at Bear Camp; quite the contrary. At summer Bear Camp I observed an orgy in progress as I passed by one of the larger cabins, and my field notes record the following during a mealtime conversation in the mess hall: "One of the guys at my table says, 'Amazing, when a breeze blows in you can actually *smell* sex.' Apparently, there has been a lot more going on than I have been privy to, or at least this man thinks there is." There was, however, much more discretion here than at Leather Camp in terms of how this sexual activity was organized. I came to understand that unlike the "open admissions" policy at Leather Camp, much of the sex that happens at Bear Camp is filtered through various social networks. If you happen to be out of the loop and are interested in participating in a group scene, you have to go "hunting" for it. This finally became clear to me at fall Bear Camp, after my attempt at an afternoon nap was interrupted twice by men stopping in my cabin "just to check things out." As I describe in my field notes:

These two incidents help me to understand how sex is organized on these weekends. I'm convinced that both of these guys wandered into the cabin hoping to find an orgy in progress or some other sexual opportunity. Unlike Leather Camp, there is no general announcement of where (or when) sex is going to take place. There were some whisperings about a spontaneous orgy in the shower on Saturday morning, but since I didn't hear much about this, I suspect it was either an intimate affair (three or four Bears) or that it never happened . . . One has to keep one's ear to the ground; some people know, some people don't. I wonder if this is connected to a heightened sense of vulnerability, which in turn is connected to the perceived risk of having the heavy body rejected, thus one has to be selective about who one invites to the orgy.

My read on the situation was corroborated when I subsequently ran into Michael, one of the Bears who had attended summer Bear Camp:

Michael remarked that he didn't get much of a chance to play at Bear Camp this year. He had attended last year and said that the sex was much more prominent that year. However, he indicated that he hadn't even realized until the end of the weekend how much sex was happening in the camp. A friend clued him in to the fact that the group sex scenes just kind of "happened" in cabins and that you just had to invite yourself in . . . This requires a great deal of confidence on the part of the newcomer; it's no wonder Michael didn't know it was happening. Perhaps this norm functions in an informal way of screening out newcomers. If you're well connected in the group, you can figure out where the sex is happening and you know how to get involved. If you are not sufficiently integrated, you're out of luck.

The "orgies" are not as open as I might have expected—why? I think this may relate to the fragility of the desire generated in this community. Even here it's probably very important that no one is admitted who might remind orgy participants of this, by laughing or making a fat joke.

As I mentioned earlier, Don is thoroughly integrated into this community; everyone knows Don, and my impression was that just about everyone likes him. He provides a good example of the relationship between social integration and availability of sex in that he reports having no trouble getting as much sex as he wants at Bear Camp. Don describes himself as "just a man out there who has a huge sex drive who tends to like to fuck." Don is aggressive without being threatening. In fact, his come-ons seem to be appreciated as compliments. His physique puts him very close to the "ideal" bear, and he has won at least one national Bear "beauty contest." On the first evening of fall Bear Camp he tells me, "The way I figure it, you've got thirty-six hours once you get here. You might as well try to get all the sex you can." There is a certain reserve and shyness with many Bears, but aggressive men like Don who are known to the community can find plenty of sex.

The same is not necessarily true for some of the less established members. On a rainy Saturday at fall Bear Camp, Stuart talks incessantly about how horny he is and the dearth of sexual opportunities. I listen for awhile, along with two other Bears. I'm surprised when after an hour or so of complaining, he actually suggests we try doing something about it, as I chronicle in my field notes:

And so the great Saturday sexpedition begins. It starts with Stuart, myself, Bill, and Aaron. We make our way into the first cabin, tentatively at first, but then Stuart simply sticks his head in the door. "Any sex in there? Is anybody having sex in this cabin?" There is no response; the cabin is empty. At the next cabin there are a few people relaxing, but no sex. The next cabin is mine; it's also empty. At the next cabin we encounter a few more people, but no one is interested in our hunt. The routine is varied a bit at each cabin. "Sex police—if you're not having sex, we want to know why," etc. Eventually we pick up George, Eddy, and Sal. We are now a band of seven horny Bears looking for sex. I suggest we might stop looking and get something going with each other. There is a momentary pause. But it is clear that this option will not be pursued. The hunt continues. Stuart walks into the next cabin, bolder than ever. "Any sex in here? Anyone having sex in this cabin?" Alas, our objective is never realized, and George and Eddy begin talking about taking a hike up to Eagle Point.

I must reluctantly admit the remote possibility that my suggestion was rejected because one or two in our merry band were deemed unappealing. I even more reluctantly admit the possibility that *I* may have been one of these. But for obvious reasons I prefer a less traumatizing explanation. I think our collective effort was fundamentally social rather than sexual in nature. The Saturday sexpedition strikes me as more of a lighthearted protest at the way sexual activity was integrated with social networking. As social outsiders we were demanding more visible, convenient sexual outlets or, failing that, immediate social acceptance that would give us access to the discreet sex that was already happening at Bear Camp. Either of these would have obviated the need for our unseemly little spectacle. In any event, I think this incident speaks to the way Bears have stepped back from a purely instrumental approach to sex and have to some extent established an ethic of care within Bear sexual culture.

Kelly and Kane's concept of "dephallicizing the cock" is not a new one, and speaks to the process Bourdieu (1997, 197) refers to as the "symbolic coding of the sexual act." Among gay intellectuals, perhaps the best known proponent of a symbolic "recoding" of sex between men is Hocquenghem (1996),[19] who called gay men to a "revolution of desire." Drawing on his critiques of Freud, Deleuze, and Guattari, Hocquenghem advocated moving beyond what one commentator referred to as the "phallus and receptacle" paradigm (Moon 1993, 20). In his preface to Hocquenghem's *Homosexual Desire*, Weeks explains:

Practicing homosexuals are those who have failed their sublimation, who therefore can and must conceive their relationships in different ways. So when homosexuals as a group publicly reject their labels, they are in fact rejecting Oedipus, rejecting the artificial entrapment of desire, rejecting sexuality focused on the Phallus. (Weeks 1996, 39)

Thus Hocquenghem (1996, 35) holds that "homosexuality expresses an aspect of desire which is fundamentally polymorphous and undefined" and that gay men should reject the oedipal entrapment and its privileging of the phallus, with its attendant emphasis on penetrative intercourse. He calls on gay men to collectively transform themselves into "desiring machines" and disperse sexual pleasures across the body.

To what extent does Bear masculinity enable this recoding of penetrative intercourse? In the last section I introduced the idea that Bears practice limited agency insofar as the embodiment of Bear masculinity simultaneously resists and complies with hegemonic masculinity. In this section I discuss the implications of this paradox for Bear sexual culture, as I present evidence that Bear masculinity both challenges and reproduces an emphasis on genital sexuality.

"Sexuality among Bears is sensuality first," Burt tells me. I've seen enough in the field to appreciate what he's talking about. There is a great deal of emphasis on physical touch, both affectionate and sexual, between

Bears. On this reading, institutionalized practices like the Bear hug provide strong evidence of sexual innovation among Bears. My field notes from Bear Camp include an especially vivid example of this. I observed a spontaneous group Bear hug in the middle of the mess hall, wherein six men alternately engaged in kissing, fondling, and massaging each other. After several minutes, another man joined the group:

I am surprised to hear him introducing himself to one of the other men kissing him, rubbing his body and nuzzling his beard. I can't help but notice how "bearlike" the men's movements are, especially the rubbing and nuzzling of the face. This goes on for some time. Throughout the "hugging" people come in and out of the mess hall and take very little notice of the activity. The hug group is momentarily interrupted as new arrivals come in wondering if they can still get some supper. The guy in orange doesn't miss a beat; he takes them back into the kitchen, the younger guy who had been giving him a backrub stands back from the group looking a bit bereft, but then he starts working on another guy and is drawn into a "group hug" with the remaining four.

What impressed me here was the absence of any sharp division between the sexual/sensual activity and the practical activity in this scene. This strikes me as a way of claiming space, of sexualizing and sensualizing the everyday—an almost territorial ritual that seems to say, "This is Bear space now." For a variety of reasons, this sexualizing of space is not possible for these men in the outside world. I am also struck by the fact that, other than a brief episode of genital fondling that I see initially, this activity does not seem to be very genitally centered, but this may be because it is public. All members of the group seemed to know the Bear hug "script," as evidenced by the easy accommodation of the newcomer and the casual introductions during the hug. There is also clearly something going on here beyond instrumental sexual "scoring." Franklin told me that this kind of contact has a very special meaning for him. "There was one bar night where about eight guys were all just kind of glumped together . . . like a litter of puppies—some feeling each other up, some hugging, just feeling good to be alive that way."

Burt observes that the emphasis on sensuality helps to foster a more responsible attitude toward safer sex practices. As a longtime member of the community, he has observed this among HIV-positive Bears. "Think of all the varieties of sexual practices that we have to draw on. And we can enter in the 'not so safe' with a few men, but we don't have to. I mean we can still pleasure total strangers if we want to, without ever getting into the unsafe category, or even close to it." This is significant because it demonstrates that, at least for some Bears, fostering a sexual culture that decenters penetrative intercourse is a conscious and deliberate choice.

Burt clearly articulates this in his critique of what he calls "dick oriented" sex. "You will find that the language amongst a lot of straight men that indicates subservience surrounds a quick sexual encounter. To fuck you is really meant to say, 'I'm gonna get my rocks off you and leave,' or 'She's a whore.'" When I ask Burt whether Bears would be more or less likely than other gay men to emphasize the importance of fucking in their sex lives, his initial response is equivocal. Eventually he settles the matter by telling me that "only in the Bear group will you get the, the idea that there are other parts of the body that really bring the intense pleasure. And you can do it in many different ways." He smiles warmly and concludes, "I think we're damn good at sex, to be perfectly honest."[20]

Beyond this assessment, however, my time in the field yielded little that distinguished Bear sexual culture from others in terms of specific sex practices. When I ask Larry about this, he relates the question directly to the Bear body. "I'd say there's some things I only do with a guy who's hairy . . . like nuzzling chest hair—I can do that for a long time—I love it." Given the obvious emphasis on sensuality and increased attention to touch among Bears, I was surprised when several of my subjects explicitly *rejected* the idea of distinctive sexual practices:

Sex is sex—one form, shape, or another. (Don)

I think in some respects when it comes down to it, the sex is sex . . . when it comes down to the basic sexual practices, it's all the same. (Travis)

Men are men. (Grant)

Clearly, not all Bears understand their sexual activity in Burt's more expansive terms. At a Bear play party, I witnessed a scene suggesting that some Bears understand sex in fairly narrow terms, centered on penetrative intercourse. My field notes describe "a brief but enthusiastic fuck session" involving a Bear visiting from out of state. Afterward, the visitor proudly proclaims to the small group of men watching the scene, "*That's* the way we do it in Texas!" After a brief pause I hear another onlooker wryly reply, "That's the way we do it here, too."

When I ask Brian how he regards intercourse, he smiles and admits, "Honestly . . . everything else is an appetizer (laughs) you know?" On the other hand, Larry seems to concur with Burt, while once again directly referencing the Bear body. "I just base it on more the enthusiasm, the enjoyment of the touching, the feeling, the nipple play, the kissing." Don tells me that intercourse itself is not important to him, but because of his large frame and aggressive personality, and because it is important for *other* men, he finds that he is often asked to play the top (insertive partner). He responds to these requests with a confident mixture of care and machismo, "if they want it they'll get it. They'll get it good." Finally, Travis responds to my question about the importance of intercourse in a way that equates it with "real" sex, a definition shared by all "real" men. "You know guys are guys. They're gonna have sex, you know, whether you're, whether you're in the Bear community or if you're in the gay community in general."

I also wanted to know how important sexual roles (top/bottom) were in Bear sexual culture and whether those roles were understood as stable aspects of identity or fluid preferences. I first asked whether these roles were understood as more or less important for Bears, as compared with other gay men:

I'd say it's about the same. About the same. (Larry)

I don't think that we would be much different than the larger community. (Grant)

Gosh, I would say that it's a lot less than, it definitely is a lot less than the leather community. (Brian)

Brian went on to tell me that most of the Bears he's known have described themselves as "versatile," meaning they can enjoy either the active or passive role in sex. Grant, on the other hand, understands his preference as a stable aspect of his identity: "As a bottom, I want and need to get fucked occasionally." One evening around the campfire Ray enthusiastically rejected the whole dichotomy because he said it doesn't reflect his primary interest in oral sex. "I hate that whole top/bottom thing—it leaves out all the orals." Another camper responds with a big smile, "Oh no, orals are always, always welcome!" After the laughter died down, Ray went on to discuss how he gives different "grades" of blow jobs, telling the group that he is only very rarely moved to give an A+. He talks about the pleasure he receives from choosing precisely which grade of blow job he's about to give. This struck me as an interesting (and to my mind bizarrely precise) control fantasy that centers on oral sex rather than intercourse.

I detected a certain generational tension within the community, in that older Bears often expected younger Bears to be sexually submissive. Members of the Younger Bears, an organization for Bears in their late teens and twenties, encounter this problem fairly frequently. Bill, the coordinator of the local chapter, told me that when older Bears learn of his affiliation with the Younger Bears they typically observe, "Oh you're rounding up the Cubs for us!" Bill tells me he resents the implication that all Younger Bears are sexually submissive (bottoms); "That's totally not the case." But his observation underscores the fact that, at least for some Bears, doing Bear masculinity may also entail doing dominance (West and Zimmerman 1987, 146). This tension carries strong associations with the traditional definition of patriarchy ("rule by the fathers") and suggests another aspect of Bear masculinity that is in compliance with hegemonic masculinity.[21]

We're Here, We're Gay: Assessing Bear Normalization

It seems clear that Bear sexual culture has been heavily influenced by hegemonic masculinity and, to a lesser extent, heteronormativity. But evidence of resistance and sexual innovation within this subculture is also ample. Institutionalized practices like the Bear hug, the nuzzling of fur, and the easygoing sensuality of these men do indeed signal a partial reclamation of the body for eros, along with a corresponding and equally partial decentering of phallic sex. But Bear culture is not quite as Hocquenghem (1996) would have it; no out-and-out rejection of the phallus is seen, nor has this community entirely transcended the "phallus and receptacle" view of sex. Moreover, these men surely do not understand themselves as the undisciplined "desiring machines" of Hocquenghem's imagining. On the other hand, they have clearly come to understand their sexual relationships in novel and evolving ways. Perhaps the most accurate way to conclude my observations with respect to Bear sexual culture would be to say that the practices that disperse pleasure across the body coexist with, rather than displace, the phallic emphasis on insertive intercourse.

Do Bears make gender trouble (Butler 1990)? What does it mean when Silverstein and Picano (1992, 128) observe of Bears that "They're just regular guys—only they're gay"? Clearly Bears have exhibited a move toward normalization,[22] as well as an identification with heterosexual men, a move that may, ironically, turn out to be profoundly disruptive of hegemonic masculinity. When Franklin remarks that "Some of what is really appealing to me about the Bear group is that if you saw these guys on the street, they could just as easily be rednecks as gay guys," he speaks for many men who identify as Bears. Herein lies the *possibility* of subversion, as Bears have been largely successful in divorcing effeminacy from same-sex desire and creating a culture that looks like a bunch of regular guys. The subversive implications, however, have everything to do with reorganizing sexuality and very little to do with challenging gendered assumptions. Most of these men would like nothing more than to have their masculinity accepted as normative, an acceptance that is largely accomplished within the group but remains problematic outside of it.

This is the particularly intriguing aspect of Bear culture with respect to the future. What will happen, for example, if Bear masculinity meets with increasing acceptance in the larger culture, if Bears as a group come to be elevated to the status of "model homosexuals" and the positive assessments of their traditionally masculine demeanor proceed in a disciplinary direction, deployed against less compliant queers who persist in acting, well, *queer*? It is tempting to think that at such a point, the tension between the masculinity conceded to these men and their sexual orientation would serve as a potent means of disrupting the heteronormative assumptions of hegemonic masculinity. But is the limited agency fostered in Bear culture enough to succeed in such a challenge? My conclusion is that although the Bear community has nurtured resistant experience and understandings through the valorization of the Bear body, in the absence of a commitment to consciousness raising and serious discussion of some of the more compliant aspects of Bear masculinity identified here, their resistant "window of opportunity" will soon close.

How is it that Bears come to understand their particular brand of masculinity as "natural"? It seems clear that this is accomplished deliberately, through the appropriation of back-to-nature masculinity narratives that are sustained intersubjectively, as group members reinforce these meanings and associations through their day-to-day interactions. Thus Bear culture seems currently disposed toward renaturalizing rather than denaturalizing gender relations. It seems far more likely, then, that increasing acceptance of Bear masculinity will encourage greater investment in a heteronormative sexual culture, less experimentation with new pleasures, less dispersal of pleasure across the body, and a renewed appreciation for insertive intercourse as "doing what comes naturally."

Why is it that the Bear body plays such a formative role in the construction of Bear culture? I think Don's story goes a long way toward answering this question, as it represents a compelling case of double marginality, experienced by way of a body that is nonnormative, even in the marginalized gay/queer community. Don's case is analogous to somatic effeminacy (see chapter 2) in that certain characteristics of the body signal one's membership in an already constructed category. The historically constructed effeminacy effect *finds* a particular type of body and labels it as not only effeminate but also gay. Once Bear identity has been established and reified, a body like Don's can, in a similar way, be "found." It becomes possible to realize one's true Bear nature, just as prior social formations and the reification of the identity category "gay" allowed people to discover their true sexual orientation. In this sense Scott Hill is entirely correct when he says in the quote at the beginning of this chapter that Bear identity is "a culmination of experiences, attitudes and self-discovery."

As Connell (1995, 156) reminds us, "The choice of a man as a sexual object is not just the choice of a-body-with-a-penis, it is the choice of embodied-masculinity. The cultural meanings of masculinity are, generally, part of the package. Most gays are in this sense 'very straight.'" I can certainly see this logic operating among Bears. Like the Faeries, the Bears are essentially apolitical, albeit for very different reasons. Faeries stake a claim to radical difference that makes their public activities, political or otherwise, problematic; hence the need for sanctuary. Bears, on the other hand, are staking a claim to radical *similarity*, both to heterosexual men and to conventional masculinity. But to pursue this claim politically is to undermine its natural, self-evident character. Thus a kind of political acquiescence reveals itself. An aggressive political profile, it seems, would work to undermine the regular-guy status that so many Bears seek to establish. For this reason, I think we are unlikely to see any direct political challenges coming from the Bear community in the near future. It may well be that as these men gain confidence in their own constructions of masculinity, they will find that their sexual orientation becomes increasingly irrelevant in the larger social world. But if this is true, it seems clear from the material I have presented here that it will involve Bear men pledging their unwavering allegiance to the flag of hegemonic masculinity. Bourdieu (2001, 121) puts it this way:

To accomplish a durable change in representations, [acts of symbolic subversion] must perform and impose a durable transformation of the internalized categories (schemes of thought) which, through upbringing and education, confer the status of self-evident, necessary, undisputed natural reality, within the scope of their validity, on the social categories that they produce . . . for everything takes place as if the homosexuals who have had to fight to move from invisibility to visibility, to cease to be excluded and made invisible, sought to become invisible again, and in a sense neutered and neutralized by submission to the dominant norm.

Thus Bears seem trapped in political acquiescence and vulnerable to the recuperative currents discussed above. But again, a significant degree of agency and resistance is exercised here. Perhaps what we are seeing is only a temporary retreat from the political arena—a period not of social movement abeyance but of political hibernation. Everyone knows that in the wild, bears emerge from hibernation with a ferocious hunger. Perhaps one day the Bears featured here will demonstrate the same ferocious hunger for change in the gender politics governing resistant masculinities.

———

Depending upon one's perspective, Bears can be read as either compliant with hegemonic masculinity (in that they cultivate a "normal" masculinity) or as disruptive to it (precisely because this move is accompanied by a refusal to hide their desire for other men). But before making a final assessment, there is another group of men I would like you to meet, a group of anything but regular guys. Some ways off, in yet another part of the forest, is the last stop on our wilderness odyssey. Follow me now to Leather Camp.

FIVE

Feeling a Bit under the Leather: Hypermasculinity, Performativity, and the Specter of Starched Chiffon

Pain, my young friend, is the Master's gift. Tie a man up, make his body ache with pleasure, and you've given him a gift. Stretch him, bind him, and love him and he'll come after you with his tail wagging like a grateful pup. Give him pain, deep in his body and deep in his mind and then break him completely and he will be your slave forever.

—ADVICE TO AN ASPIRING LEATHER MASTER (CIRCA 1950)

Don't let that leather fool you, honey—it's only starched chiffon.

—ADVICE TO THE AUTHOR (CIRCA 1982)

At this writing the Sentinels, the oldest gay leather club in Friendlytown, are celebrating their thirtieth year. Every summer the group sponsors a leather camp at a state park not far from Friendlytown.[1] On my maiden voyage to Leather Camp I entered the site with some trepidation. Although I knew several members of the group and had attended many of this group's functions (including several dinners and parties) I was traveling alone and had no idea what to expect from this experience. As it turned out, I had some reason for concern. My first few moments at Leather Camp were inhospitable, to say the least. I parked my car in the designated lot and made my way cautiously toward the camp (a series of cabins that had served as a German prisoner of war camp in World War II). As I approached I noticed a small group of men in their fifties, all of them strangers to me, hanging out in front of the main mess hall. The first person I spoke with seemed to be the leader of the group. The man, whose name I later found out was Billy, appeared a bit rough around the edges. His graying beard unkempt, he wore a pair of faded jeans, an old T-shirt, and a leather vest. Attempting a playful tone I demanded, "OK guys, who's in charge here?" An uncomfortable silence followed, then Billy muttered curtly, "No one's in charge until 7 p.m." More silence. I explained that I just needed to know if there was a check-in procedure, and which cabin I had been assigned to. Billy's eyes flared. He snapped angrily, "*Excuse me*?! You haven't been to Leather Camp before, have you?!" Not exactly the most cordial welcome, I thought. Around this time, Graham introduced himself. To my great relief he was civil; he even managed a smile. I mustered the courage to ask Billy if I should just choose a cabin to bunk in. He grunted in assent, "Any cabin but five . . . cabin five is the sex cabin." Ah, cabin five. Little did I know what curiosities, pleasures, passions, torments, and transformations awaited me there. Despite such an inauspicious beginning I managed to find my way into the heart of this community, and it was far from the heart of darkness that popular stereotype might have led me to expect.

The Sentinels are one of several dozen gay leather organizations across the United States. The first of these groups were closely associated with motorcycles and riding during the 1950s and 1960s, but that association has attenuated considerably over time. Since the mid-1950s, these groups have fostered a hypermasculine image and, through a carefully managed self-presentation that includes various articles of leather clothing (e.g., vests, chaps, caps, pants), a strong association with rough sex, bondage, discipline, and a variety of sadomasochistic practices. As exemplars of gay hypermasculinity, leathermen are uniquely positioned to appreciate the radically constructed nature of gender. As Rick, one of my interview subjects, put it, "If you really knew what was under this leather, you wouldn't be intimidated at all." But are leathermen really more acutely aware of the performative aspects of gender? If so, how does this awareness exhibit itself? How does the paradoxical position of the gay leatherman, located as he is at the crossroads of the hypermasculine and the effeminate, affect leather sexual culture? In this chapter I explore these questions, with special attention paid to leather as a form of drag (albeit not in its classic form) and to how leather sexuality is embodied.

Any examination of gay male leather culture has to acknowledge several ambiguities. The first is the relationship between leather and a number of other practices, notably sadomasochism (S/M), bondage and discipline (sometimes abbreviated with S/M as BDSM), and a range of more exotic practices commonly referred to as "kink."[2] According to at least one experienced leatherman, as recently as the early 1980s the gay leather culture in the United States could be characterized as "leather, leather everywhere, but hardly any S/M in sight" (Stein 2001, 144).[3] The second ambiguity is the relationship between S/M practices in a heterosexual context[4] as distinguished from gay S/M, the relationship between gay male and lesbian/bisexual S/M communities, and the emergence of a "pansexual" S/M community organized around specific practices and techniques that strives to minimize distinctions based on gender and sexual orientation. While these enormously complex relationships would make for a fascinating study, my focus here remains on how these various intersections and distinctions reflect historically sedimented tensions around gay masculinities and the enduring power of the "effeminacy effect" and its ability to shape leathermen's cultural, social, and sexual lives. For these reasons I have focused most of my attention here on the more extreme segment of the diverse leather community. Most (but not all) of what follows goes beyond simple leather fetish to embrace intersections of leather with BDSM and kink.

A Brief History of Gay Leathermen

The literature on this community reveals a general consensus that gay leather culture first emerged as a recognizable part of the queer cultural landscape in the United States in the decades following World War II. A fair degree of consensus has also been reached in terms of the explanations offered for the emergence of gay leather S/M communities during this period. Steward (2001), for example, provides evidence of the effeminacy effect when he explains gay leather S/M as a reaction to the loss of, and search for, heroes. "Maleness was vanishing," he argues, attributing the destruction of the masculine hero to three forces that reached a crisis point in the United States during the 1950s: matriarchy, automation, and science. "The increasing domination of women in all fields except the production of spermatozoa" marks what Steward sees as "the speed-up toward the matriarchy" (Steward 2001, 84). Citing Philip Wylie's 1946 diatribe, *Generation of Vipers*, he sees "Momism" (the dominance of the mother in the family and the resulting feminization of boys) as the "cult" that "displaced that of the Hero" (Wylie 1996, 84). The claims behind this attribution would be laughable if they did not appear so consistently in the literature; American anxieties about insufficiently virilized boys go back to at least the turn of the twentieth century (Kimmel 1996, 157). Science played an important role in the hero's decline as well; Steward specifically cites the emasculating effect of the Copernican revolution: "Look, little man, you are a dweller on a minor planet scudding around a dying cinder of a sun!" The subjugation of the hero culminates in the explosion of the first atomic bomb, "For what can a man, a male, do against the little killing sun of Hiroshima?" (Steward 2001, 85).

A far more robust explanation sees the roots of leather S/M in a biker culture that was itself an homage to automation and industrialization. As Harris (1997, 200) explains, part of the reason that the outlaw biker image carried so much weight is that he encoded "the consummate expression of the Western worldview, a cult that revolved around technology, a machine."

In the early gay biker clubs, studded leather jackets were the ceremonial vestments of a vehicular religion whose central totem was an unlikely god, a mode of transportation, a device manufactured by a highly industrialized culture. The leather fetish in its earliest forms was rooted in the body of iconography that grew up around heavy equipment and the internal combustion engine, a symbol of industrial power. (Harris 1997, 200)

From a gendered perspective, this fetishization of the machine during the early 1950s is ironic in that it was precisely the incursion of industrial machines into the American labor force during the latter half of the nineteenth century that was typically associated with a *loss* of virility. As Kimmel (1996, 82) states, "Workers increasingly seemed to lose control of their labor and the production process, which was transferred upwards to a new class of managers and supervisors." Further, "Rapid industrialization, technological transformation, capital concentration, urbanization, and immigration—all of these created a new sense of an oppressively crowded, depersonalized, and often emasculated life" (Kimmel 1996, 83). Part of this paradox can be explained by the fact that the new machines— motorcycles—enabled many men to revive the powerful masculinist narratives of the untamed frontier and the lure of the open road. Whatever the case, it is clear that for gay men, a prominent erotic component was involved in the fetishization of this particular machine:

One of the enticements of leather for many men was its connection with an ultimate heterosexual symbol of masculinity—the straight man on a bike was one of the earliest and strongest images of straight trade . . . It wasn't just that those men represented the fantasized outlaw; they were also an unquestionably sexual male image. Part of the attraction of the motorcycle was the power and vibration of the big engine between a man's legs. (Preston 2000, 27–28)

But such an appreciation would be impossible without a dissident sexual community to nurture it. The impact of World War II on the emergence of a homosexual consciousness is attributed to a number of factors. First, the war disrupted stable social patterns both within the military and on the home front. For the young men who served in the military, the war provided a period of freedom from parental supervision and, for many, freedom from the restrictive social norms of the small towns and communities in which they grew up. For some enlisted personnel, the war years represented a unique period of experimentation between adolescence and marriage; for others it was a transformative experience with same-sex relations (D'Emilio and Freedman, 1988, 289; D'Emilio 1983, 38–39). Second, the psychological pressures of war encouraged sexual experimentation and made it easier for some to act on homosexual desires. Third, the reaction of the military to homosexuals within their ranks helped consolidate a feeling (albeit negative) of belonging to a distinct minority, but one that was nevertheless formidable enough to evoke a strong reaction at the institutional level. In 1943–1944 the military revised its policy on discharging homosexuals in a way that may have indicated to some an increase in social tolerance. At that time the service personnel who were suspected of being homosexuals were issued a special "blue" discharge, which was neither honorable nor dishonorable. This replaced the "yellow" discharge that had been used previously and indicated that the discharged person was "undesirable." Nevertheless, the new blue discharges often included an indication of the person's homosexuality, a fact that became particularly important for the postwar social organization of gay men discharged at the port of San Francisco (Bérubé 1989, 388). Of course, in true Foucauldian fashion these official certificates of perversion may have also abetted the formation of resistant communities, as they provided a material rallying point for a discourse reversing the narrative of pathology. Finally, the American media's postwar effort to reassemble the nuclear family ignored the transformative experience that many gay men had during the war and further defined a sense of difference. Commenting on this situation, Allan Bérubé (1989, 392) remarks that "lesbians and gay men, many of them unable or unwilling to conform to this narrow family ideal, stood out more and more as 'queers' and 'sex deviates' who endangered the fragile security of the postwar American family."

But for a certain segment of gay men returning to postwar America, this sense of alienation ran much deeper. For these men their combat experiences had so traumatized them, had so altered their lives and personalities, that they found it necessary to seek out the company of others like themselves, to organize a furtive "alternative" culture rather than return to the mainstream. This "wounded masculinity" is described by Thom Magister (2001, 93), an acknowledged leather master, who recalls his early encounters with such men during the early 1950s:

Hitchhiking back to Hollywood from downtown L.A., one afternoon I was picked up by an ex-Marine who had joined the many others who became the core of what we later called outlaw bikers. These men, both gay and straight, had been damaged by the war and felt that they could "never go home again." Tortured and tormented often beyond anyone's comprehension, they drifted together in a mutual loss of innocence. They had been mere boys when they left home to serve Uncle Sam in his great war against the Axis nations. Six years later they came home broken men with nowhere to go and no reason to go there.

Magister (2001, 93) later relates how his new friend had been tortured and castrated while a prisoner of war in Japan. When Magister met him, he "hung out at a biker bar with his war buddies and their partners." (93)[5]

The postwar conservative consensus and the rebel culture it spawned became a powerful cultural narrative of threat, rebellion, and masculinity that was exploited by gay men reacting to the effeminacy effect. This narrative was articulated repeatedly throughout my research with reference to the 1954 Marlon Brando film *The Wild One*. The film was mentioned explicitly by two of my interview subjects as a formative influence on early gay leather culture, and references to the film popped up repeatedly in other research sources. The film was based on a 1953 *Harper's Magazine* story, "The Cyclists' Raid," by Frank Rooney, which was a fictionalized account of an actual incident that occurred in Hollister, California, over the July 4 weekend in 1947. More than 4,000 motorcycles converged on this small town, and the bikers proceeded to stage a forty-hour riot that left the residents of the small town terrified. Nearly a hundred bikers were jailed as the police tried to quell the unrest. In the film, Brando is cast as Johnny, the leader of the Black Rebels Motorcycle Club. The film was extremely controversial and banned in England until 1968 because of its perceived antisocial message. More important in terms of this history, the film provided gay men with an available script and image with which they could refute the charge of homosexual effeminacy. Whereas in Bear culture the feminized gay other is designated as "the twink," here it is "the fluff," against which the gay leatherman sought to distinguish himself. In this rendering he is recognized by his penchant for "fluffy" sweaters:

Leather was a welcome way out of the closet for masculine men who in larger numbers than anyone ever suspected thanked the gods that the New Leather Culture allowed them to do their Father's Act rather than their Mother's Act, and in doing their Father's Act to excel beyond the father. The sign on the ceiling of The Tool Box [a gay leather bar] said, "No Tennis Shoes," which nixed limp wrists, fluffy sweaters, and the passé code slang of the Friends of Dorothy. (Fritscher 2000, 11–12)

[Leathermen] took off the sneakers and the angora sweaters of the swish and stepped in to the rugged dungarees and leather jackets of Marlon Brando. (Harris 1997, 183)

Thus a process of what Connell (1987) calls *cathexis* began with respect to leather, in that gay men began to invest leather with a certain erotic power intimately tied to the way it signaled masculinity. This appeal sprang first and foremost through the powerful appeal of the unassailably masculine rebel cyclist, for whom leather was a practical necessity. Perhaps because adopting this image helped some gay men resolve an intimate identity issue (to the extent that it successfully divorced their self-image from the stigma of effeminacy), their attitude toward leather was erotic rather than practical.

One of my interview subjects described the advent of leather this way:

And this subculture sprang up, and it was about, you know, there was a certain militaristic, masculine ethos about it. Motorcycles fit into that very well, and the black leather that you wore for motorcycling, you know, for riding motorcycles, the protection, that fit very well too. It was just a nice masculine look, it was practical for riding motorcycles. But that's, that's where that came out of, and then Marlon Brando and *The Wild One* . . . (Eric)

This impulse was greatly facilitated by the formation of gay motorcycle clubs, the first of which, the Satyrs, held their first meeting in Los Angeles in July 1954. Four years later, the Oedipus Motorcycle Club was founded, also in Los Angeles. By the late 1950s, bars catering specifically to gay leather cyclists began to appear, most notably the Gold Coast in Chicago (1958), Kellers in New York City (1959), and the Why Not in San Francisco (1960).[6] The formation of leather clubs and bars greatly accelerated in the late 1960s and early 1970s, so that by the mid-1970s almost every major metropolitan area had some sort of leather bar or club.

But it was not only the image of the biker that lent an erotic masculine charge to leather. Leather was also richly suggestive of cowboys, the frontier, and a life on the open range, far from the feminizing effects of civilization. As Lance, one of my interview subjects put it:

I think here, my particular instance is part of a general pattern. And that is that leather has a certain attraction. Part of it is historical and cultural—the biker and his leathers. For me, growing up in Montana, it was also the cowboy and his chaps and hat. And there's an extent to which out West there still is very much a cowboy worship. With the guy out there on his horse, you know, herding the cattle and herding them in and getting them safely home through fire, storm, and flood and stampede and rustlers. And very much a cultural myth out there, of the cowboy. And what he wears is very much a part of that. How he lives is a part of that. You know there's a bunch of guys just there, we're here together, we're out on the range, and you know, we've got this job to do and we're going to do it. And a certain nobility has become attached to that.

But whether it was the image of the nomadic cowboy or the outlaw biker that leather suggested, the important point is that leather allowed gay men to understand themselves as "real men." As one writer put it, "Leather is a sock-to-the-jaw statement that, contrary to the straight stereotype, gay men are not faux females driven to dresses" (Fritscher 2000, 11–12). Harris (1997, 183) acknowledges the same point when he writes, "it was about gay liberation, about creating an alternative image of the subculture. For most of the early participants in the leather phenomenon, rough, unsentimental S/M sex was less a means of erotic fulfillment than a political affectation."[7] Harris writes disparagingly of the decline of leather kink culture in recent years and chronicles what he sees as the devolution of leather culture in terms of five discrete historical phases, each of which he associates with what he calls an "implied dungeon" (183). In what follows I borrow Harris's convention to frame some additional historical material while critiquing some of his interpretations.

The first of these historical phases is the "dungeon as dressing room," where feminized gay men discovered leather drag as a masculinization strategy and an effective response to the effeminacy effect. Thanks to *The Wild One* and the sudden ubiquity of the menacing biker image, many pre-Stonewall gays found that simply changing their clothes allowed them to change their self-image. However, on Harris's (1997) reading, an important point is obscured: his conflation of gay leather culture and S/M masks the fact that a fair degree of separation remains between the two. As John Preston, the author of a gay leather S/M novel entitled *Mr. Benson*, writes, "Thousands, then tens of thousands of gay men adopted a carefully studied Tom of Finland look, but the sexual flavor of choice for the vast majority, once out of their clothes, was still plain vanilla"[8] (Stein 2001, 148). Once the uniforms have been distributed, the dungeon transforms itself from dressing room to clubhouse. Here Harris (1997, 83) makes a point substantiated by several of my interview subjects, the idea that for many men, the attraction of leather culture was (at least initially) social rather than erotic. "The vibrant social dimension of the leather world . . . is not a by-product of the S/M fetish, but one of its primary incentives." On this reading, it is initiation into a homosocial community, rather than the attraction of leather per se, that explains the appeal that leather clubs held for alienated gay men (Hopcke 2001, 73). The social appeal of these groups was corroborated by several of my interview subjects, including Cal and Lance:

The Sentinels are more of a social club . . . allowing the people who have like minds to associate with each other real freely. (Cal)

A great deal of it, or even the majority of it, is your interaction with other club members and [*pause*] to some extent your organizational skills and your organizational aptitudes, how you work with other members of the club and work either on a project or organize a project or an activity and, um, in a sense so where you can get along with each other. (Lance)

The social aspect is significant because it suggests that for some men, the social attraction and solidarity *precedes* an erotic interest in leather and leather sex. Thus if the attraction of leather groups as *social* groups is being obscured, then so too may be the process of the social construction (or amplification) of certain kinds of desire generated within these solidary groups. Harris (1997, 184) captures this sense of the social construction of desire when he remarks that "leather is a *social* fetish" (emphasis in original).[9]

But while motorcycle clubs and leather organizations may have provided certain benefits for the gay men who joined them, they also created a significant backlash. In 1976, two busloads of riot police were dispatched in Los Angeles to raid a "slave auction" organized by a local leather club as a charity fund-raiser. Two helicopters with searchlights and sixty-five commandos stormed the hall and "freed" the slaves, arresting several of the guests. The conservative *Orange County* (Calif.) *Register*'s headline read, "Police Free Gay Slaves" (*Drummer* 1976, 12). Harris (1997, 185–86) remarks that while "the leather fetish helped some homosexuals solve the problem of effeminacy, it nevertheless created a new difficulty . . . In an effort to achieve a new kind of legitimacy as a macho clan of menacing hoodlums, gay men only succeeded in reinforcing the prevailing belief in the homosexual's unsavory status." The backlash, both from conservative gays within the community and feminists[10] outside of the community, profoundly shaped developments in leather culture, leading into what Harris calls the "dungeon as therapist's office":

Writers refuted accusations of depravity not only by denying the abnormality of S/M sex but by holding up erotic experimentation as a surface method for promoting a preeminently *healthy* lifestyle, one of its practitioners advertised it as a kind of miracle cure, an anomalous form of therapy that accelerated the process of "personal growth" and "self-discovery" . . . Rather than accepting their illicitness and welcoming their reputation as a subversive fringe element that skirted the margins of respectable society, leathermen engaged in a self-betraying act of bad faith. (Harris 1997, 186–87)

John Preston expresses similar misgivings and notes the same change:

I listened to the speakers who interrupted the parade of handsome men on stage. They were talking about the "leather brotherhood." They talked about teaching people about the "good" aspects of the "leather life-style." They wanted acknowledgment from the general society that they were constructive members who were simply finding an "alternative way to love." And I thought: *Give me a break!* (Preston 2001, 211)

Harris (1997, 192) complains that this move marked a feminization of leather; a kind of "feel good" mentality invades the classic flogging scene whereby "every stroke [is] an act of love" that left the dominant top "warm with the feeling of having created this ecstasy in another man's life" (Mains 1984, 48). This new concentration on how bondage and domination *feel* as opposed to what they mean (Harris 1997, 195) led leathermen inexorably toward Harris's fourth dungeon, that of the "laboratory of pure sensations." Here the focus is on the body itself and how it functions as a kind of sensation-producing machine.

I found ample evidence of this perspective, in both my interviews and my secondary research sources. For example, Owen, an interview subject, talks about the altered state of consciousness facilitated by S/M in biologistic terms: "It's a major endorphin rush. It's like a flogging scene where, you know, you work up very slowly but by the end you've got so many endorphins going off in your body that you don't even notice that you're back's being turned basically into hamburger." Endorphins are the most commonly mentioned physical agents responsible for the S/M "high" or altered state of consciousness in the secondary literature as well (Truscott 2001, 21; Bean 2001, 262); mention is also made of "alpha brain waves," and "adrenaline" (Bean 2001, 262) as well as "body chemistry" and "opiates" (Mains 2001a, 40).[11] One of the amazing aspects of leather culture is the fact that this thoroughly medicalized discourse is produced by the same communities that produce robust narratives of spiritual sexuality and mystical transcendence through pleasure/pain. Later in this chapter I elaborate on how the technical vocabulary relates to the rationalization of sex and the production of sexual pleasure.

With the fifth and final implied dungeon, the "dungeon as temple," Harris argues that leather S/M culture has mutated into the exact opposite of its original form. With its emphasis on the spiritual aspects of leather sexuality, of pain and power play as gateways to mystical enlightenment, "what began as a satanic movement has become an angelic one" (Harris 1997, 199). Here the concept of leather shamanism comes into play, and as one such shaman (whom Harris refers to as a proponent of "asshole consciousness") puts it, "for me a day without cosmic erotic ecstasy is like a day without sunshine" (Thompson 2001, 293). Along these same lines, Rubin (2001) subtitles her sentimental tribute to a famous S/M venue in 1980s San Francisco "A Temple of the Butthole."[12]

What Is a Leatherman?

Generally speaking, the most prominent identity feature I observed in leather culture was the foregrounding of gender, specifically masculinity. The vast majority of leathermen I encountered identify themselves first and foremost *as men* and, in some cases, men who understand themselves as actually *more masculine* than heterosexual men.[13] A virulent rejection of effeminacy runs throughout the culture, and this is reflected in my research sources as well as my fieldwork. Same-sex orientation for many of these men, far from marking them as effeminate, is understood as a more authentic embrace of masculinity than heterosexuality.[14] Unlike straight men, leathermen make no artificial distinctions between the homosocial and the homosexual. Whether bottoms or tops, leathermen amplify their sense of masculinity through their ability to "take it like a man" or to "deliver the goods." When I asked Cal what he thinks draws most men into the leather community, he responded that it is "actually the idea that they are meeting with other men . . . it's the attraction that it's another man that you're dealing with and no questions that that's what you're dealing with." It seems safe to assume that Cal is not referring here to the possibility of running into a woman in drag passing as a man, but rather the uncertainties surrounding an encounter with a man who may look like a man but is really effeminate. Leo Bersani (1987) illustrates this idea as he describes the "classic" case of the pickup that begins with "the butch number swaggering into a bar in a leather get-up" and ends when he takes you home. The first thing you notice is his "complete works of Jane Austen"; later he "gets you into bed and—well you know the rest." The point Bersani is making here is that the policing of real masculinity takes place almost entirely among gay men themselves, informed throughout by "the dark suspicion that you may not be getting the *real* thing" (Bersani 1987, 208; emphasis added).

Adam, an interview subject, echoes these sentiments bluntly in an unqualified condemnation of effeminate men as "fags":

You know I, being gay isn't—like being a fag is a poor choice of words. You know there are some fags, I think they're like in their twenties and they hang out at Lola's [a local coffee shop] and they have high-pitched—they're pretty effeminate, I'd call that a fag. But, that's not the man I have, I play with. You know? And there's nothing wrong with them being that way, in that part of their culture. But you're not coming in my house, and if you do I'm gonna get the duct tape out! [*Laughter.*]

What I find interesting here is that Adam, who identifies himself as "a dominant bottom," objects to the "fags" who hang out at Lola's on grounds that differ significantly from the complaint Bersani recounts. Bersani's objection may be summarized by a slang aphorism borrowed from lesbian culture: "butch on the street, femme in the sheets." Adam, on the other hand, has effectively masculinized his sexually submissive role and objects, not to a preference for bottoming and submission in sex but to what he sees as an effeminate presentation of self.

Lance sees the cultivation of hypermasculinity within leather culture in more broadly political terms, as a logical consequence of the greater freedom gay men have enjoyed since Stonewall, which has allowed them to escape from the oppressive stereotypes of effeminacy:

To the worship of the masculine. Switching it over. You know, eight hundred to nine hundred thousand years of being forced to be effeminate, being told that if you're gay you're effeminate, if you're effeminate you're gay, um, we've reached a point where people can no longer, you know, round us up on the street and burn us at the stake. We can live our lives openly. I love men, I don't want to love a woman in disguise so I want a manly man for my lover. I want to be a manly man. And we're just making a fetish of the masculine image.

The emancipatory emphasis here at least partially obscures Lance's taken-for-granted assumption that gay effeminacy is a historical perversion of a presumed "natural" and "authentic" gay masculinity, which leather culture allows gay men to recover. Interestingly, Lance seems to be fully cognizant of the fact that masculinity is artificially exaggerated in leather culture, yet this is not seen as a perversion of natural masculinity, but rather as an homage to it.

The leatherman's masculine identity is constructed and maintained socially, primarily through the kind of microsocial interactions facilitated by leather clubs and bars. My interactions with Jack at Leather Camp illustrate this point exquisitely and are worth quoting at length:

> One of the first things [Jack] said to me is that "I ride bulls." He told me about his extensive experience riding bulls in presumably straight rodeos and how "all these guys want their cocks sucked." When I asked him what he did for a living, he told me that he was a high school teacher and that he did the rodeo stuff during his off time . . . After getting acquainted with Victor and Adam we were back at the picnic tables for a bit. Here Jack showed us his scars: one recent one on the side of his head (a raised bruise) and one long scar down his belly, which he said was the result of being gored by a bull. He said he lost his spleen in the accident . . . Throughout this period, Jack keeps up the heavy cruising pressure on me. I find this both exciting and challenging. I am very attracted to Jack, but I am not entirely certain I can pull off the role I am being asked to play. He tells me about a play session during which "it took six guys to get me in the sling." I surprise myself when I respond, "That's very impressive, but what I want to know is how it felt once they got you in the sling." His smile lets me know that I have figured him out. He likes being dominated, but only after an all-out struggle. I make a mental note to myself to expect him to challenge me physically . . . It is also during this time that Jack begins to bait me a bit, making semibelligerent remarks and basically acting like a punk. He tells me he can easily pin me and that I won't be able to subdue him alone. I realize this is part of a game Jack plays. I give him a defiant look and say only, "I guess we'll see."

During the course of our interactions, both Jack and I were carefully managing our gendered identities. Although I knew absolutely nothing about rodeos, I realized that his introduction of the topic was a form of negotiation designed to build his masculine appeal and raise the sexual temperature between us. It was fairly obvious that he was asking me to play a game that obligated me to respond to this information in a narrowly prescribed way. I had to give some indication that I thought his rodeo experience was interesting while at the same time taking it in stride (e.g., under the circumstances I was *not* free to shriek, "Oh how icky—your spleen?!"). Conversely, despite the fact that I had briefly mentioned to Jack that I was also a teacher, it was clear that following that line of conversation would not be part of the game. The fact that I doubted much of what Jack was telling me (can a person live without a spleen?) was entirely beside the point. The game was about constructing sexual tension through a particular way of doing gender.

But dyadic interaction patterns like the one described above are not the only way that masculine self-presentation is reinforced. The open sexual culture indicated by my introduction to the Sentinel's Leather Camp ("cabin five is the sex cabin") means that a public aspect of sexual activity is involved, and thus "orgy etiquette" can become a highly effective means of organizing effeminacy out of leather culture. For example, my field notes record the following, which occurred during an intense sexual "play session" on the first night of camp:

[Our] enjoyment is interrupted by the sound of high-pitched, flutelike laughter coming from across the room. Adam and Jack notice it as well and pause momentarily. Then we are back in the scene, then the same sound again, this time more insistent. We all look around and realize that the sound is coming from the front sling. The incongruous nature of the laughter is too much—it is so out of place in this intense leather man-sex scene. Someone begins to chuckle; this quickly erupts into hearty laughter as everyone stops what they are doing momentarily to see what's going on. Someone (I think Larry) says sarcastically, "I didn't realize we were holding opera auditions tonight!" It turns out that it is Owen in the front sling, very vocal in his enjoyment of something, I'm not sure what . . . The remarkable thing about this incident is how it led to a rapid decline in the sexual temperature in the play cabin. While everyone seems to appreciate the comic relief, it takes a while to recover the energy, and several people take this opportunity to exit the cabin for a break.

As Owen is a full member of the Sentinels and well liked, no one thought to scold him for this inappropriate gender performance. Furthermore, the consensus seemed to be that the incident was genuinely funny. But the net effect of Owen's decidedly nonmasculine behavior was that it represented a break in the action, an unusual sequence in the chain of events, an interruption. Consequently, the sexual activity declined rapidly. I have no doubt that if this behavior continued on a regular basis, some informal method of remedying the situation would be attempted (e.g., one of Owen's friends might speak to him about it, arrangements might be made for him to play with his partner in a separate area, etc.). However, this would probably prove unnecessary, as I suspect Owen may have intuited the situation and adjusted his behavior accordingly.

Finally, with respect to the social construction of gendered sexuality, I comment on the following passage from my field notes:

A note on sexual euphoria: In thinking about this experience of pleasure, I keep returning to the concept of rest. It seems that on a good night, all the role playing, mind play, and sensory stimulation build to a place where your acceptance is total—for a man in a society that so closely links masculinity and sex, this may be experienced as a time when your masculine identity (or your connection to masculinity through the homage of submission to masculinity) seems overdetermined, there is an excess of attention paid to you, that which is normally unstable (the experience of the "eternal masculine") is experienced (at least for a time) as fixed. I experience this as "rest," an interval wherein I don't have to try to "be" masculine, or do anything else to appear sexually attractive. Another fitting metaphor is the breath of fresh air—it's like the moment when you emerge from a dank, stuffy room to the fresh air outside; it's a refreshing experience of revitalizing clarity.

As I reread this passage, what strikes me is **how much of the "rest" I experience is tied directly to gender and masculine performance.** That this is experienced as rest is paradoxical, given the strictly prescribed behaviors that this community promotes. Is this euphoria a kind of reward for proper gender performance—like the dieter who takes delight in a fattening dessert after losing ten pounds? Like the happy dieter, a leatherman is allowed to let down his guard, to disregard the disciplinary rules that allowed him to get to this point in the first place. But this seems an inappropriate metaphor—no sense of shame comes from a leatherman having "fallen off the wagon," no awareness of paradox or contradiction. There is only respite, a deep and calming spiritual sigh. This reaction touches on some of the central paradoxes of masculinity that I mentioned in chapter 2: masculinity is understood as an essential and natural consequence of biological sex, yet real men must remain ever vigilant against the feminine. Effort must be made, and a substantial amount of energy expended, to ensure that one's actions are in line with what one has so carefully learned about masculinity. Why, if the leatherman's dilemma is simply a matter of being misperceived as effeminate by the larger culture, if he truly *knows* that he possesses an innate masculine essence, does it take such an intensely collaborative social experience to achieve this sense of stability in masculinity, this moment of rest? Then again, this quandary is not unique to leather masculinity. Indeed, my point here is that what I have described above differs only in degree from the very similar efforts of men who identify as heterosexual in an attempt to stabilize their sense of themselves as heteronormatively masculine. The men of the Sentinels do not differ significantly from straight men in this respect. For both, an enormous amount of gender work takes place in the company of other men.

Although it is by no means common, I found it very interesting that several members of the Sentinels display precisely the kind of "wounded" profile described by Magister (2001) in an earlier section of this chapter. For some, this damage is directly attributable to combat action; for others, it has to do with a history of personal abuse. Billy (who was the first to greet me upon my arrival at Leather Camp) and Wayne fit into the former category, as shown from my field notes:

Along with Billy, Wayne made a point of identifying himself as a Vietnam vet, but Wayne obviously survived with far less psychological damage. On Saturday night I heard [Wayne] speak of his racist upbringing in rural Iowa and how a close friendship with a black soldier in Vietnam "shot all the bullshit my old man tried to tell me all to hell."

Billy, I found out, was considered dangerous by many of my fellow leather campers. Brett told me that Billy had been thrown out of the play cabin by the dungeon master at last year's "run" (see note 1) because he was abusing the bottom he was playing with. Brett intimated that Billy's idea of S/M is to simply "beat the hell out of a guy" and that the motto "safe, sane, and consensual" means nothing to him. Despite the fact that Wayne was obviously in better physical and mental shape than Billy, it was apparent that a strong bond existed between the two men:

Shortly after this, I witnessed one of the most peculiar incidents of the entire weekend. Billy was naked, leaning back in one of the cabin chairs. Wayne was crouched before him and seemed to be rather tentatively giving Billy some head. Tentatively, I think, because Billy was babbling nonstop about some Vietnam experience.

I thought this was extraordinary, one of the most arresting images I witnessed during my time in the field. In its own humble way it speaks to the presence of an ethic of healing within leather culture, something much less easily dismissed than Harris's dungeon as therapist's office. Here and elsewhere I sensed a generosity and sensitivity toward psychological pain and a willingness to attend to it through sexual and erotic contact. Eric underscored this point when he spoke of his attraction to the leather scene as an abuse survivor. He shared a candid account of his long-term relationship with an extremely manipulative boyfriend who strictly controlled Eric's social life and was prone to physical abuse:

Eric: Yeah. See he used, he used to taunt me with fire.

Peter: Really?

Eric: Yeah. He, once upon a time I was taking a shower and he pulled back the shower curtain and turned a blowtorch on me.

149

Peter: What a charming guy . . . it must have been your birthday!

Eric: No, no, he was, he was laying some floor tile and he was, you know, heating up the back of the tile with his blowtorch, and he just thought it would be a fun thing to do to . . . He thought it would be funny! That's, that's, I mean and, and he, I don't think he ever knew why I was, why I went so crazy. And he didn't understand what he was doing at all. But anyway, so after having lived through that, to see fire play where people are doing the same thing but there's no coercion involved, there's no threat, everyone is enjoying himself and having fun, and it's all consensual. To me that's healing. So that's, you know, yeah, that very much resonates with me.

But the vast majority of contemporary leathermen, and the majority of the Sentinels, have no such connection with past trauma. For these men, the attraction to S/M is understood either in essentialist terms (as a practice they are attracted to naturally and that captures the more authentic aspects of erotic exchange) or as a method of exploration that expands and heightens the pleasures already inherent in sex. As Adam tells me, "It's about experiencing a new level of trust and control and exploring your limits . . . adrenaline does a lot." Owen reminds me that "it's a major endorphin rush."

In recent years a small but growing community of leather BDSM enthusiasts of all genders has emerged to celebrate the "pansexual." Here the premium placed on training and technique, as well as the specific sensations and emotions aroused by particular S/M practices, has advanced to supersede the gendered aspects of leather play. This environment is attracting a significant minority of men who initially came to S/M through gay leather communities. Cal explains the appeal:

And then the pansexual is that they're more interested in, in some of the experiences and whatnot, it doesn't make any difference the gender that it's, you know, the play is more important, whereas I think in some of the, the gay men's clubs and whatnot it's more that you're, you're actually, you want to participate with another man more so than just another person.

The gay men I spoke with who play in pansexual environments made a sharp distinction between the erotic and the sexual. I became aware of the pansexual community at the end of my research period, and my sense is that it is an emerging and a very controversial sexual culture, even among some leathermen.[15] Pansexual clubs exhibit a fascinating postmodern collapse of almost every sex and gender distinction imaginable. Curt and his partner Eddie are gay men who belong to one such club. Curt describes his first pansexual play party for me:

Then I went into another room and there was a woman flogging a tranny [transsexual] boy. And they were obviously way into the scene and really enjoying each other. I went into another room, and there was a man tying up a woman in, in really elaborate bondage, really elaborate bondage. I mean when they were done the woman was completely trussed up and she was almost all full of rope [*laughs*], you know? Almost mummified. And so I saw all of these different things going on, and none of them were gay male oriented. None of them. None of the activities I saw were gay male oriented. And I thought, "Wow—there's this much energy going on, and there's no fuckin', there's no suckin', there's no sex, it's all S/M play. And it's all different kinds of people, and, and that was like—this is great, this is great. And so that's what it was.

When I first became aware of the overlap between gay leather and pansexual communities I was truly mystified by the paradox. How do men so heavily invested in their masculinity come to disregard gender? How does an "ungendered" eros come to supplant the elaborately gendered sexuality of the hypermasculine gay leatherman? My subsequent experiences suggested that this is perhaps not so surprising, given the hints I obtained that hypermasculinity may in some cases operate as a way of transcending gendered aspects of sexuality among at least some gay leathermen (e.g., the rest period I experienced). It seems to me that these men have found a way to effectively exorcise the specter of starched chiffon.

Memories: Tradition and Change in Leather Culture

As I suggest in the anecdote of my experience at Leather Camp that introduces this chapter, one of the aspects that struck me immediately about the leather community was the openness of its sexual culture. While at first blush this may seem to indicate a more liberal, emancipated community in terms of sex and sexuality, the more public aspects of sexual activity facilitate certain panoptic disciplinary pressures (Foucault 1995) not possible in more discreet sexual cultures, which I concentrate on in this section.

Performing leather and S/M sex for others apparently has a long history. In an article originally published in 1991, Sam Steward recalls performing various S/M scenes for Alfred Kinsey in May 1949 in Bloomington, Indiana. During this time he and a partner (a submissive leatherman unknown to Steward and also recruited by Kinsey) performed scenes for Kinsey's research. Steward reports that at the time, both he and his partner were aware of the need "to present the comparatively newly revived sport of sadomasochism in a light good enough to make it acceptable and politically correct for coming generations into the next century." He even adds, rather dramatically, that "A sense of history was on us both" (Steward 2001, 87). In his detailed account of his training as a leather top in the early 1950s, Magister (2001, 102) recalls that running his first public scene was witnessed by "easily over two hundred leathermen." This came after a long apprenticeship of attending similar group sex scenes wherein "The host, a bottom would invite his crowd and select a number of Masters to work their wonders on his body for his pleasure and the delight of the assembled faithful" (101). Magister indicates the importance of his debut and the pressure he felt from the assembled crowd of leathermen watching him: "My time had come. Like a student pilot, I was about to fly solo. Jason shook my hand, patted me on the ass, winked one green eye, and sat down in the front row. I was alone now—on my own" (102).

Likewise, in a fictionalized reminiscence of his experiences as a bottom in the S/M leather world, Mains (2001b, 236) makes the appeal of the public aspects of his sexual performances explicit:

Part of what feels good about this is that I am being fisted publicly . . . The men at the door can see my pleasure, they can watch the crazy dance of my eyes. This is pure performance, this is a statement from two men to others; I can give like a man, I'm as good as any porn star at turning them on. I can be hot, my sexual prowess can excite.

The importance of the fact that it is an audience of *men* witnessing his pleasure is indicated when Mains (2001b, 237) writes that "This is a world, a community. A fraternity. I give freely so my brothers can read my statement."

This emphasis on group sex and semipublic sexual displays is borne out by my field notes. It was indicated not only by the way sex was organized at Leather Camp (I recorded hearing about exactly one case of a private coupling, in contrast to the dozens of sexual interactions that I witnessed in group/semipublic settings) but also by my prior experience in the larger culture. Occasionally I would hear a tale recounting some particular "one on one" incident during a session of private leather sex play, but the preponderance of this anecdotal evidence included tales from more public venues like play parties, after-bar orgies, or leather runs. Given this emphasis on public sexuality, it seems a bit strange then that such a venerable figure in the leather world as John Preston (2001, 211) would complain that by the early 1990s, "The world of S/M had been overtaken by the sightseers."

Preston's remark reflects a host of anxieties about changes in leather sexual culture since its inception in the immediate postwar years. He is not alone in bemoaning the decline of leather culture and the increasing elusiveness of "real" leather sex: *The Real Thing?* Was 'the real thing' to be found at all, or was there only dressing up in leather and fuckin' and suckin'?" (Stein 2001, 143). From the literature I reviewed, it seems that these anxieties are centered around four major issues: the decline of the "old guard" who were trained into leather S/M culture in the 1950s, the changing perspective on the nature of sex roles, the decline of the leather top's prestige, and the new emphasis on therapeutic and spiritual aspects of gay S/M leather sexuality. I will deal with each of these briefly in turn, as four discrete "nostalgia narratives."

The old guard/new guard nostalgia narrative revolves around the declining standards for training in S/M methods and the kind of communal accreditation process that (according to this narrative line) was much more demanding in the late 1940s and early 1950s.[16] When Thom Magister (2001, 98) went through his training as a leather top in 1950, he had to train for six months before he was allowed to participate in his first scene with a bottom. During that time he trained four hours a day with various masters who taught him "how to shave a man correctly—how to pierce, flog, bind, and cut a man—correctly" (100). Even then, he had to face the demanding standards of his peers, to publicly display the proof of his expertise and master status in a group scene. Lance, one of my interview subjects, intimated that he learned of the old guard standards firsthand from his travels in the southern United States, where he believes the gay leather S/M culture is more traditional:

It begins with who trains you or what family adopted you, and then after that you begin developing your own name for yourself, and then your status, as it were, within the community can develop accordingly . . . there's a very hierarchical structure and everyone knows their place within that, I mean, like starting off with who trained you and then where your reputation has taken you from that.

"Nowadays," complains an old guard leatherman from San Francisco, "buying a well-fitted pair of chaps and wearing your keys on the left is generally thought to transform a clone into an experienced topman."[17] The new guard, in this narrative, is depicted as far less discerning and far less committed to the overall leather S/M scene than its old guard elders:

Just as hardly anyone today thinks less of someone who switches roles, playing top one night and bottom another, perhaps even with the same partner, so no one puts anyone else down for not being "heavy" enough or versatile enough. It's perfectly all right, for instance, to be into bondage but not pain, or to like flogging but not electricity, or to like a little spanking and tit play but nothing more. No one today expects you to "earn" the right to wear black leather, or a uniform, or anything else you want. Each to his own taste, we say now, and the stance of our organization is: Do whatever you want as long as it's safe, sane and consensual. (Stein 2001, 152–53)

As a corollary to this narrative, much has been written on the decline of the top's prestige in gay leather S/M culture in recent decades. This comprises the second nostalgia narrative. The classic form this narrative takes is that in the world of the old guard, tops were held in high prestige and sought out for their particular areas of expertise by bottoms who enthusiastically submitted to them. In recent years, however, in what is often characterized as a "perverse" role reversal, it is actually the bottom who has come to dominate the sexual culture. In some versions of this narrative, the blame is laid squarely on feminism's doorstep:

The sexual politics of domination and submission have become so complex and so closely scrutinized by the feminist sex police that the inequities of power in the traditional scene have swung in the opposite direction. The top has swapped roles with his bottom, who, in an extraordinary act of manumission, is actually gaining ascendancy over his supposed master. (Harris 1997, 196)

This is a robust narrative of cultural decline, one I encountered in both my research and my fieldwork. Interestingly, the vitality of this narrative remains unaffected by countervailing evidence gleaned directly from men who participated in the leather culture of the 1950s, suggesting that bottoms have *always* exercised control over leather tops:

When tops outnumbered bottoms by ten to one, the way they did in the 1950s, the incentive was greater for tops to spend the time and energy to master esoteric specialties or to reach new heights of ability in the staples. (Stein 2001, 153)

Back in those early days of leather there were so many Masters and so few slaves that the bottom men came to be in charge. (Magister 2001, 97)

But it seems that for members of the old guard some of the most intense anxieties center around changing conceptions of sexual roles. The third nostalgia narrative centers around fixed versus fluid sexual roles. In the old days, bottoms were bottoms and tops were tops, but these days all that was solid has melted into air:

The debonair treatment of roles that were once viewed as basic ontological classifications, like "left" and "right" or "inside" and "out," reveals that the very structure of the S/M scene is finally succumbing to the concept of personal liberty implicit in the human potential movement. (Harris 1997, 197)

What about the duality of role-switching? What does a bottom man feel after he has surrounded and entrusted himself to a man he believed was a Master, only to discover this same man down on his knees kissing another Master's boots? Do I know the answer? No. (Magister 2001, 100)

My field notes reveal a vivid example of just this type of role switching. On one occasion, Victor, whom I had just seen put on a masterful topping performance in a fairly complicated scene on Friday night, had changed markedly by Saturday morning: "At one point Victor came back from the front room and began wrestling with Jack on the bunk directly across from mine. It began to rain; the thunder was occasionally deafening. After a while Victor began teasing Jack. 'C'mon, let me see your cock. I wanna suck it. Come on, please, I just want to be a big old bottom boy today.'" But for others I encountered, it is clear that identities with respect to sex roles are understood as fairly fixed:

Eddie: Yes, as a top, and I am primarily a top.

Curt: No, you're almost *exclusively* a top! [*Laughter.*]

For others, this sense of fixed role identity exists comfortably with a recognition of fluidity. Owen says, "When we play I'm usually top. Um, and I'm fairly versatile. Lance is more bottom all the time, but, yeah, so in some relationships I'd say I'm the more dominant, you know, between the two of us."

The fourth nostalgia narrative centers on the decline in the authenticity of the sexual experiences facilitated by the gay leather S/M community.[18] This narrative proposes that in the old days, the sex was self-validating and needed no ideological, therapeutic, or spiritual justification. In some variations of this narrative, the leather sex of the olden days was better because it explicitly embraced all that the culture currently disowns: domination, rough treatment, humiliation, and an unflinching exploration of the "dark side" of the human psyche. Thus, in the recent turns that emphasize the spiritual and therapeutic benefits of leather S/M, a great deal of the "realness" has been lost: "S/M is no longer about tying people up or crawling worshipfully on one's belly before figures of masculine authority

. . . rather it is about inflicting pain to achieve higher levels of consciousness and to induce a state of ecstatic mysticism" (Harris 1997, 198). What
I found interesting here is that even in some of the narratives promoting
leather S/M as a door to spiritual enlightenment, the same realness imagery remains:

> Leathermen share this use of what have been suppressed or forbidden pain-pleasure
> capacities with many cultural groups. Yet from Dervish to flagellant, and from fire walker
> to Kavandi dancer, leather stands apart in exploring sexual capacities in terms of ecstatic
> experience. To its participants leather sex brings release and revelation. And to the world
> leather becomes at once a symbol and a culture. *A black and animal side of the soul has
> been rediscovered and let out.* (Mains 2001a, 43; emphasis added)

Furthermore, what I find fascinating about each of these narratives of
deterioration (from old guard to new, from fixed to fluid sex roles, from
dominating to dominated top, from "real" sex to spiritual and therapeutic
sex) is how they all subtly encode feminization into their stories of decline.
The old guard, who should rightfully command the contemporary cultural
scene as the experienced leather patriarchs, has been upstaged by what
they no doubt see as a bunch of dizzy new guard leather queens who cannot even seem to decide whether they are tops or bottoms. The fluidity of
sex roles can easily be read here not as an emancipatory cultural innovation that allows for the expansion and multiplication of sexual pleasures
(a la Hocquenghem) but as either a lack of commitment or a fear of some
ontological identity truth on the part of the indecisive youngsters. Either
way, the new guard exhibits a lack of manly virtue. The old guard image
of the virtuoso leather master, who takes charge of a scene with the un-
shakeable confidence that he possesses the talent and expertise to deliver
what his dutifully submissive bottom *needs* (as opposed to what he might
simply *want*) is replaced by an army of emasculated tops tentatively check-
ing in with his partners "to inquire if the scene [is] meeting their needs"
(Harris 1997, 195). The flight to therapy and spirituality likewise betrays
a "softness" at the heart of leather culture, an inability to reckon with the
cold, hard, "real" truth of leather S/M. In each of these narratives it seems
the old guard leatherman detects the lurking specter of feminization, the
fear that his leathers may really be nothing more than starched chiffon
after all.

This being said, the Sentinels and the leather S/M community I studied
were by far the most sexually innovative of my three case study communities. I either observed, heard of, or read about an astonishing array of

sexualized and eroticized practices, including (but not limited to) bondage, discipline, role playing, spanking, flogging, whipping, paddling, nonpermanent piercings (using a series of small needles inserted temporarily under the skin), electricity, edge play (knives, swords, and razors), fire play, tit play, cock and ball torture, water sports (urine), scat (feces), humiliation (various psychological techniques often used in conjunction with some other practice, like bondage or flogging), handballing or fisting (the insertion of the hand and fist into the anus),[19] scarification, branding, hot wax, and play with clothespins and clamps. Clothing fetishes included leather, rubber, latex, and scuba gear.[20] I asked several of my interview subjects how they explained the high degree of innovation within the leather community. Many linked this explicitly to the leatherman's status as "outsider"; for example, Adam says, "But then I think when you start getting more into leather a lot of people say, oh that's kinky. Just the mere mention of leather is kinky . . . And so that's why it's more into leather, but I think it's outside of leather too, it's just those people don't talk about it, is what I'm thinking." Becker's (1997) labeling theory is implicated here to some extent, as the successful labeling of leathermen as "kinky" has apparently worked to amplify the community's propensity for kink:

I think because we're more open about it, probably . . . because we're basically here for sex. Um, you know it's, it's like how the gay community is much more out about information like that than the straight community is, because you know we're judged by what kind of sex we have in the first place. And you know the leather community, you're talking about BDSM, kink, everything. I think maybe it's something to kind of wear on our sleeve. Uh, to, you know there are certain points of, you know, a little bit of bragging rights even. (Owen)

Lance, by far the most articulate of my leatherman interview subjects, attributes the sexual innovation of leather culture to a kind of radical honesty fostered by an acceptance of the role of outsider:

The leather community takes the sort of deep personal honesty and the role of outsider, again takes it more deep than . . . the general gay community. And that's because eroticism and fetish is a taboo, and even within the gay community we still deal with that taboo . . . Sex, sexuality is part of life. Part of my life, the way I want to live my life is to experience this fully and completely. So I'm going to think about it, I'm going to talk about it, I'm going to do it. I'm going to do it without shame. You add the element of fetishism or eroticism with objects and materials—leather, latex, bondage, discipline, S/M. That is another element of stepping more into the role of outsider, stepping more into the areas that are taboo . . . And that's, so part of it is this honesty—this is taboo, I've looked it in the face, I've stepped around it, torn it down. You've accepted the role of outsider—I'm doing things that other people don't approve of, don't want to hear about, don't want to think about, don't want to see. And now I've created a space where I can be me and where I can experience what I want to experience. And that desire is to, um, experience kinky fetish sex. Completely, to do it in a complete whole way. Every culture develops a set of expectations and goals for its members, and we have as well.

Several of my interview subjects indicated a similar response to their initial encounters with the leather community, and in each case, this response emphasizes the social nature of the force behind innovation. Victor describes himself in his preleather days as an "everyday gay man that would go dance and do the vanilla sex, and that was pretty much it." The critical turning point for Victor, the decision that drew him into a social network where S/M and kink were celebrated, was the purchase of his first leather jacket:

Victor: You do find a lot more of, at least that's what I've experienced, I mean I've seen some extreme things that people do to their bodies that you don't find in the mainstream. [*Pause.*] Well I think it's stepping out of the norm, to start with. When you start with, you know wearing your leather stuff and you just kind of carry it and it builds from there. That's what's happened to me at least. I mean, I got my first leather jacket and then it kind of went from there—you know harnesses and this and that and . . .

Peter: So was that a really big step—I mean the idea of putting on a leather jacket and saying, "I'm into leather now"?

Victor: Yeah, yeah—that was a big step.

Peter: And you're saying once you make that transition, other things just kind of fall into place naturally?

Victor: I think with, even with the leather jacket, you know then if you go to a leather bar, you, then you have some people that talk to you, then it just kind of evolves from there. Whereas if you didn't get the leather jacket and you went to the leather bar, maybe less things would happen.

While this kind of subcultural interaction may work to amplify some seemingly exotic impulses in terms of sexual subjectivity, it is clear that this community is intimately informed by a larger world of sexual meanings and orientations.

Hanging a Sling in the Iron Cage: Rationalization and the Production of Erotic Pleasure

The tension between a "masculine" desire for rational control and a "feminine" desire for erotic surrender helps us understand Weber's sociology . . . Eros, ecstasy and emotion represent the threat of losing control: loss of mastery, loss of rationality, loss of manliness.
—ROSLYN WALLACH BOLOGH, *LOVE OR GREATNESS*

When Weber was once asked why he undertook his wide-ranging studies, he replied: "I wish to know how much I can take."
—LEWIS A. COSER, *MASTERS OF SOCIOLOGICAL THOUGHT*

Perhaps it was the vaporous intoxication of all the new mischief I was discovering, but at several points in my fieldwork I could have sworn I caught a wraithlike glimpse of Max Weber, that most ascetic of sociologists, lurking in the corner of cabin five. There he was—now scribbling a note, now stroking his beard thoughtfully, with an occasional arched eyebrow betraying something other than an academic interest in the proceedings. Oh, to know his thoughts! The amazing innovation of this sexual culture, which at first glance suggests a community freed from traditional constraints, exists alongside an ensemble of thoroughly rationalized erotic practices. Pain as a means to pleasure serves as a peculiar metaphor for a variety of technical, rule-bound activities thoroughly informed by means-ends thinking. Here I explore the surprising implications of Lance's observation that "every culture develops a set of expectations and goals for its members." My fieldwork and research left me with a strong sense that in the world of gay leather S/M, erotic practice itself has become an eminently goal-oriented activity. In some respects leather culture merely reflects Weber's (1998) warning about the rise of instrumental rationality in all areas of contemporary life in the industrialized world. It is certainly continuous with the rationalization of sexuality in general, as in the case of the rise of sex manuals and "how to do it" advice (Tyler 2004; Garner, Sterk, and Adams 1998; Jackson and Scott 1997; Seidman 1989), the technical mapping of the eroticized body (Petersen 1998; Winton 1989), Viagra culture and the social construction of erectile dysfunction (Loe 2004; Tiefer 2006; Marshall 2006), and the surgical alteration of sexualized body parts (Braun 2005; Davis 2002).

However, in other respects the rationalized erotic techniques of leather culture can be interpreted as a conscious embrace, amplification, and celebration of rationalization. For leathermen, this means-ends approach to sex is evidenced by an enormous emphasis on technique, training, and the proper equipment required to "get the job done." In this case, the job to be done is pleasure—as intense and prolonged as possible—but the means have been thoroughly mechanized. Stein writes wistfully of the "disenchantment" of leather sex:

There is no denying that a great deal of the mystery has gone out of S/M as it has emerged from the closet and the back rooms into the light of public meetings and open discussions. Being a master of bondage or flagellation these days is like being a minor-league pro athlete; people may respect your skills, but no one looks at you in awe. (Stein 2001,153)

Harris (1997) points to the difference between the first and second editions of Larry Townsend's classic, *The Leatherman's Handbook* (published in 1972 and 1983, respectively), as evidence of the rise of an instrumentally rational attitude toward gay leather S/M: "Townsend strips S/M of its intellectual fictions and concentrates on the sheer physiology of pleasure and pain. He describes the sadist torturing his slave as if he were a surgeon operating on a patient, inducing sharply defined sensations whose effect has been calculated in advance through careful preparation" (Harris 1997, 194). On this reading, just as beginning medical students learn to abstract the human body from its mundane social context and reconceive it as a series of puzzles to be solved or problems to be fixed (Smith and Kleinman, 1998), so the contemporary leather top sees the body of his submissive as a pleasure-producing instrument that must be expertly played by employing the proper techniques to achieve the desired result.

Curt told me of the complex techniques involved in piercing scenes, wherein a series of small colored needles are inserted temporarily under the skin, often in a specific pattern. He cautioned that these scenes should only be run by experts who are familiar with the various gauges of needles, insertion techniques, and requisite safety measures. Simple piercing scenes run approximately half an hour, with several hours required for more complex procedures. Scenes that include fire play and electricity also require extensive training and are likewise governed by a set of complex rules and regulations. Eric discusses a recent fire play workshop he attended:

This fire play workshop that I was at—you know these are people who are doing something that has a very high potential for hurting people. And yet they don't want to see, their object is not to hurt people, their object is to do this without hurting people. So a lot of thought and care and effort and study has been taken so that we can do this and we can get the, you know, the amazing emotional and physical sensation, and yet know that we are not really in that much danger.

At the Leather Archives & Museum in Chicago, I located two archival pieces that suggest the reach of this instrumental approach to leather sex. One is a detailed work sheet on how to tie different types of bondage knots, specifically targeting gay leathermen. This twelve-page pamphlet includes an introduction, sections on bondage safety, and illustrations of various types of knots (modified fisherman's bend, clove hitch, half hitches, cow hitch, and camel hitch). The other item of interest is an outline of what was apparently some type of public presentation on proper paddling techniques. Topics covered in the outline include paddle materials (wood, Lucite, metal, plastic, and leather), sensations (the "thud" vs. the "sting"), areas of impact (buttocks, thighs, back, and genitals), use in the scene (reward or corporal punishment fantasies, including school and parent/child fantasies), and safety issues (deep bruising, soft tissue damage, callusing).[21]

When I first encountered these practices, I interpreted them as a mode of thought that transforms matters of sexual pleasure into a goal-directed and technical activity. Upon further reflection, I wonder if it is not more the opposite. Perhaps it is goal-directed and technical activity that is being transformed into pleasure. Perhaps the elaborate techniques of leather sex actually represent a kind of reenchantment strategy. The technical, mundane, instrumentally rational action is eroticized, producing the decidedly nonrational effects of transcendence and ecstasy. This goal, once achieved, cannot be reduced to a stepping-stone. It cannot be experienced or configured as a means to some other end; the achievement can only be an intense and all-consuming presence. I really do wonder what Weber would say.

Leathermen and Embodied Pleasures

While in the field I assumed a variety of both dominant and submissive roles, but I soon found that with respect to pain, my tolerance was quite low. Consequently I usually ended up topping in any scene that involved pain. Given the safety issues inherent in more exotic practices, I limited myself to the most rudimentary applications (garden-variety punishments like spanking, paddling, nipple torture, light flagellation, pinching sensitive areas of the body with clothespins, etc.). The experience left me with the realization that I would probably never become an acceptable leather master, because while I should have been immersing myself in the numinous connection being forged between me and my submissive partner, I often found myself fascinated instead by the indisputable evidence that the pain I was administering was appreciated, savored, and enjoyed. "Why," I found myself asking, "is this man smiling?" Thus questions about the education and reeducation of the senses consistently led me away from the scene and back to Bourdieu.

S/M leather practices implicate the body in complex series of power exchanges, reenactments, and roles that are undoubtedly steeped in history and tied to the objective power relations of the social worlds beyond the subcultural field of the leatherman. My focus here is on gendered sexuality, and a comprehensive analysis of power relationships is beyond the scope of this study. In this section I pursue the more modest objective of extending some of Bourdieu's ideas regarding the embodied nature of the habitus to a very specific situation unique to S/M culture, specifically, the process by which S/M practitioners come to radically revise their understanding of the relationship between pleasure and pain and the mechanism by which this new understanding is embodied. I concentrate here on the microsocial setting, the face-to-face interactions between leathermen, and how they may facilitate an adaptation of the habitus and its embodied disposition toward pleasure/pain. Of necessity, my thoughts here are somewhat speculative, as Bourdieu (1997, 94) himself admits that embodied principles are "placed beyond the grasp of consciousness, and hence cannot be touched by voluntary, deliberate transformation, cannot even be made explicit; nothing seems more ineffable, more incommunicable, more inimitable." Thus, direct observation of what I am trying to capture is probably impossible, and insightful statements regarding the process cannot be expected from participants.

As it was applied to the Bears, Bourdieu's concept of hexis proves useful in relation to the leathermen, particularly when one considers this more elaborate description:

> Bodily hexis is political mythology realized, *em-bodied*, turned into a permanent disposition, a durable manner of standing, speaking, and thereby of *feeling* and *thinking* . . . given body, *made* body by the transubstantiations achieved by the hidden persuasion of an implicit pedagogy, capable of instilling a whole cosmology, an ethic, a metaphysic, a political philosophy, through injunctions as insignificant as "stand up straight," or "don't hold your knife in your left hand." (Bourdieu 1977, 93–94)

This is not to say that this process of inculcation is limited to such direct verbal instruction. On the contrary, Bourdieu suggests that it is experience (and learning what "goes without saying") that accounts for the greater part of this process. Furthermore, bodily hexis may be acquired through a fairly economical process in that once a few fundamental principles are acquired, they are capable of generating a whole range of dispositions (Bourdieu 1997, 88). Once it goes without saying that pain can be a desired avenue to pleasure, the man who formerly thought it was all about "beating the hell out of a guy" becomes the leather top, learning technique and safety along with the cultivation of a dominant persona. Once it goes without saying that an appreciation of pain occurs in the context of consent and trust, the leather bottom can open himself to a variety of experiences using this same insight.

In applying these ideas to gay leather S/M culture, my thinking proceeds from the assumption that successful initiation into S/M culture involves an adjustment of the habitus, specifically, of an embodied disposition toward pain. My discussion of how this process may be occurring begins with Bourdieu's remarks regarding the circumstances under which the habitus becomes amenable to conscious alteration: "Times of crises, in which the routine adjustment of subjective and objective structures is brutally disrupted, constitute a class of circumstances when indeed 'rational choice' often appears to take over" (Wacquant 1989, cited in Jenkins 1992, 77). During such "times of crises" the naturalized, taken-for-granted adaptation of habitus to field is disrupted and a more deliberate form of strategizing is called for. However, Bourdieu cautions that the form that this conscious strategizing will take is still structured by the dispositions generated by the original habitus. It also goes without saying that, although probably experienced as individual crisis, this upheaval is eminently social in nature. Thus it is important to at least suggest the social conditions that may have opened a space for this radical adaptation of an embodied disposition toward pain. The brief history I have presented here suggests that it was World War II that was the catalyst. On this reading the "greatest generation," in addition to storming the beaches of Normandy and making the world safe for democracy, may have also given us the first gay leathermen, as a small but significant number of traumatized veterans, doubly marginalized by their wounded status and their same-sex interests, sought a way to reconcile themselves to the physical and mental violence they had suffered in combat. For many of these men the crucible of war was no doubt made all the more hellish by the concurrent and probably unwelcome realization of their sexual interest in other men. For at least some of these, leather culture and BDSM must have held an enormous appeal. It not only offered those seeking help an opportunity to work through their pain in a safe, sane, and consensual environment but the appropriation of the unapologetic masculinity of biker culture also promised to let them feel like men again. While this admittedly crude and incomplete explanation may partially explain the initial formation of gay leather BDSM clubs in the postwar years, it does not explain how clubs like the Sentinels sustain themselves. How does the field of leather culture accommodate newcomers?

I argue that the novice gay leatherman enters a field charged with masculine and homoerotic energy, which he finds is extended to S/M practices. The attraction of the field is out of sync with his embodied understanding of pain. Here Adam tries to make sense of his changing disposition toward pain:

I think we associate pain and pleasure as two opposite things, and I think they're actually one and the same. I mean I don't, I think there's maybe 5 percent difference. And when you can bring the pain towards pleasure, that's what it's about. I think that's what it's about. But a lot of people don't want, "No I don't like any pain, I don't." Well, you know what, maybe the first time it's pain, but after that it's pleasure. Or, you know, everybody's at a different level. You know, "No I don't like any pain." Well, but you like pleasure, right? "Oh I love pleasure!" Well you're a pig with pleasure but [*pause*], so what is pain? I mean it's really pretty subjective, I think.

Thus Adam and other novice leathermen must be guided through a period of deliberate reeducation of the body. The field is in fact very responsive to just this dispositional crisis, as the various traditions of apprenticeship within leather culture attest. At any rate, the novice leatherman soon finds he can depend upon the resources of an established tradition of mentorship within the community to guide the adjustment process. I suggest that the social process critical for nurturing an understanding S/M as pleasurable is comparable to the process studied by Becker (1998a) in the 1940s in his study of marijuana smokers. In his landmark study, Becker concludes that in order to experience a marijuana high, a specific socialization process is required. In the case of dope smoking, the subculture is there to offer the novice user an alternative definition of the situation to convince him or her that the altered state of consciousness is not an occasion for panic:

The anxious novice thus has an alternative to defining his experience as "going crazy." He may redefine the event immediately or, having been watched over by others throughout the anxiety attack, decide that it was not so bad after all and not fear its reoccurrence. He "learns" that his original definition was "incorrect" and that the alternative offered by other users more nearly describes what he has experienced. (Becker 1998a, 56)

This alternative definition is evidenced in Hopcke's (2001, 72) observation that "Simply put, I believe S/M provides gay men with an initiation into the body" and in Tucker's (2001, 5) claim that after he "learned" that his initial definition of S/M was incorrect, "I was living fully in my body again for the first time in years." It is also supported by Adam's story.

While Adam has clearly revised his understanding of the relationship between pain and pleasure, he told me of an earlier, unsuccessful attempt to "get into" the leather S/M scene. In the following excerpt it is clear that what was missing during this earlier attempt was careful mentorship through the early phase of initiation, a situation that confused Adam. "I had a scene where this guy almost tortured me, and I said forget it . . ." Here he describes his panicked reaction on his first day back at work as an orderly in a hospital after the incident, when he discovers to his horror that he is bleeding: "And I had my hospital scrubs on. Well that's kind of tacky, so I had to bandage my nipples. And I thought, well this isn't, you know, I mean it was kind of erotic thinking about it, but I thought you know I shouldn't have pain like this, at least my first time."

Adam told me that it took more than fifteen years after this traumatic experience before he was ready to make a second attempt (this time successful) to join an S/M group. With his second attempt he entered on a much more secure footing, as this was a deliberate move that he made along with his partner of ten years. His partner was already connected with the local leather S/M scene, and Adam told me that the turning point came when they decided to install a dungeon in their basement.[22] Thus Adam and his partner were able to invite selected members of the community into their home, establishing a comfort level that allowed Adam to draw on community mentorship. "And we just keep exploring . . . You know, and I think that I could be learning the rest of my life. 'Cause my eventual goal is to become a master, but right now I want to be a boy." That Adam's new, more integrated relationship with the leather S/M community has allowed him to redefine his earlier trauma is evidenced by the following:

Adam: When they know where I'm at, when they're, if they're playing with my nipples and they know the level that I'm comfortable with, and they know the level that is going to cause some more pain or something. When they can, when I know that they can sense where that level is—what that does to my mind, I mean I even give up, I give up more control, when I'm in a situation like that.

Peter: And is it best when they can know that without having to ask you?

Adam: Yeah. And there's a lot of guys like that that know without asking . . . Yeah. Watching you, you know the intuition, and I don't know how they can do it, but some of them, they're [*softly*] WOW!! [*Laughs.*]

Here Adam indicates that the desirable top's intuitive, nonverbal ability to pleasure his partner lends a great deal of erotic energy to the scene. This speaks to the way silence is privileged during intense S/M play and how it focuses attention on the body. Many dungeons and play parties post rules that strictly prohibit conversation. Speaking of the S/M world of the biker clubs of the 1950s, Magister (2001, 97) remarks that "if they had a language, it was the language of their bodies." The passage also speaks to an element that came up repeatedly in my interviews, that is, the intensity of the physical exchange between top and bottom and the high degree of concentration on the physical:

I mean for the most part you shut out everything outside of you. And you may, I mean you have this focus with the person you're interacting with, really intense, and that's really a cool feeling. (Victor)

You know, having somebody completely control you where you can't move and, you know sometimes you'll have a gag in your mouth where, you know, or even breath control where that person, if they don't know what they're doing, could kill you. (Owen)

But as Bourdieu makes clear, adapting the habitus to the new circumstances in the field is structured by the dispositions generated by the original habitus. I suggest that with respect to leather S/M culture, these dispositions are gendered, and at least three such "deep" dispositions structure the process. The first is homoeroticism. This is, in effect, the "carrot" that accounts for the anxious novice's desire to submit himself to the arduous process of initiation into the leather S/M community. This carrot effect is reliant upon the existence of an already-established community of gay leathermen who have intersubjectively constructed S/M as an elaboration of the homoerotic, as an eroticized homage to masculinity (perhaps in some cases seen as masculinity taken to its logical conclusion). The erotic appeal produced by these communities makes the revision of the novice's embodied understanding of pain not only possible but desirable. The second disposition is the tendency to understand this eroticized world in binary terms. The S/M field is uncompromisingly divided into dominant and submissive roles—one must choose.[23] Finally, there is the masculinist assumption that the "best" scenes are those that aggressively seek to push up against the physical and psychological limits of the participants, as Victor intimates when he discusses what he considers a successful bottoming scene:

Victor: Uh huh. I think it's kind of a turn-on too if I know other people may be enjoying the scene too, you know, I like to take it a little bit further just to show that, you know, I can really do this.

Peter: So what would disappoint you about yourself?

Victor: If I couldn't, if really I didn't get very far into the scene.

Peter: And you just had to say your safe word or tell them to stop or whatever.

Victor: Yep. I'll use the safe word and . . .

Peter: Is that the primary concern, the primary thing that you're trying to avoid is having to say no and stop?

Victor: Uh huh. I want to go as far as you can go, and see you test your limits.

Peter: What's the mental effect of that—that seems to be . . .

Victor: A big part of it.

Peter: Yeah—where does it take you?

Victor: [*Pause.*] Well you could, I mean for the most part you shut out everything outside of you. And you may, I mean you have this focus with the person you're interacting with, really intense, and that's really a cool feeling. [*Pause.*] Where does it take me? Is that the question, where does it take me?

Peter: Yeah. It's a hard question to answer.

Victor: Let's see—it takes me . . .

In addition to describing the importance of pushing oneself to the limits of sense experience to achieve transcendence, as Victor's words began to fail him I sensed he was also intensely absorbed in the task of pressing himself into the ineffable, valiantly trying to put into words that which can probably only be expressed in the "language of bodies."

Hypermasculinity and Leather Drag: "Appropriated Effect" or "Reidealization"?

Some mirrors should reflect more before sending back an image.
—JEAN COCTEAU, *BLOOD OF THE POET*

One of the things that consistently impressed me during my time in the field with the Sentinels was the absence of any overt misogyny. In this respect they are similar to the Faeries, and like the Faeries they welcome the presence of women at social functions while generally excluding them from sexual/play environments. At this writing there are no female

167

members of the Sentinels, but some local women are respected by Sentinel members for their knowledge and long association with leather and BDSM. These women are considered friends to the Sentinel men, but again they are (outside of pansexual play spaces) discouraged from participating in Sentinel play parties or scenes. In any event, I do not recall a single disparaging remark made about women during my time in the field. In light of their collective rejection of effeminacy, this prompted questions about the gender politics of gay leather culture. In this section I extend Butler's observations about the performative nature of gender and drag to the hypermasculine drag of leather culture. My empirical evidence concerning leather costuming and accoutrements confirms that much of what Butler has said about men doing feminine drag applies to masculine drag as well. However, my evidence also suggests that, true to Butler's (1993, 122) own admonition, the historical trajectory of masculine drag in gay leather culture is best understood as an "appropriated effect" whose subversive potential has been steadily attenuated over the last three decades.

The notion of the appropriated effect neatly captures Butler's view of agency with respect to making gender trouble. Gendered subjects are not free to step outside of gender to create trouble, but where gender conformity is demanded, "there might be produced the refusal of the law in the form of the parodic inhabiting of conformity that subtly calls into question the legitimacy of the command, a repetition of the law into hyperbole, a rearticulation of the law against the authority of the one who delivers it" (Butler 1993, 122). This passage seems particularly relevant to the hypermasculine self-presentation, or masculine drag, of the leatherman. "Here the performative . . . produces a set of consequences that exceed and confound what appears to be the disciplining intention motivating the law" (122). Thus the possibility exists, from within normative masculinity itself, of subversion through denaturalization.

But again, Butler (1993, 129) acknowledges that a relationship does not necessarily exist between denaturalization and subversion: "Does the denaturalization of the norm succeed in subverting the norm, or is this a denaturalization in the service of a perpetual *reidealization*, one that can only oppress, even as, or precisely when, it is embodied most effectively?" (emphasis added). I argue that while a historical moment may have existed in the late 1960s and very early 1970s within leather culture for "[opening] up the possibility of a reworking of the very terms by which subjectivation proceeds—and fails to proceed" (Butler 1993, 124) with respect to the masculinity of the leatherman, the current situation more closely resembles an "uncritical miming of the hegemonic" (131).

As an example of how denaturalization may accompany the reidealization of normative gender, Butler points to the case of Venus Xtravaganza, the Latino drag queen/preoperative transsexual from the film *Paris is Burning* who is able to pass as a woman:

Clearly, the denaturalization of sex, in its multiple senses, does not imply a liberation from hegemonic constraint: when Venus speaks her desire to become a whole woman, to find a man and have a house in the suburbs with a washing machine, we may well question whether the denaturalization of gender and sexuality that she performs, and performs well, culminates in a reworking of the normative framework of heterosexuality. (Butler 1993, 133)

Likewise we may question whether the masculinity of the leatherman, when it is performed well, represents resistance to or compliance with hegemonic masculinity. An important dispositional difference with respect to female and leather drag that I encountered in my fieldwork may help to answer this question. Whereas the discrepancy between the drag queen's sexed (male) body and her/his presentation of self (as female) directs attention to the surface, to the way that clothing and makeup produce an effect "out there" in the social world in a way that highlights its artifice, leather drag seems to do precisely the opposite in that it draws attention inward, toward a presumed interiority whose authentically masculine nature is "liberated" through drag. But whereas traditional (men doing feminine) drag is always accompanied at some level by an awareness of transgression— of breaking gender rules—masculine drag, while no less performative in nature, is much more likely to be understood as a release, a "calling forth" (in this sense leather acts as a kind of interpellation) of a hitherto obscured or hidden masculine essence.

This process of realizing masculinity through drag was expressed by a number of my interview subjects, in a variety of ways. Eric had his first experience with leather drag when a more experienced leatherman picked him up at a bar and took him back to his apartment. In his description of that evening, he emphasizes how leather enabled a surprisingly convincing performance of masculinity, one that triggered an interior process recognized not only by Eric but by the more experienced man as well:

Eric: What happened was he, he basically flung open his closet and started, you know, putting things on me thinking he was going to see how they look. And I looked in the mirror and he got out his camera and took some pictures and it's like—he said later just seeing the look on my face, like you know, "Wow!" you know, "That's me in the mirror? And I look like this?" That's, he said that was so much better than anything we could have done sexually. You know that was, that one look was what it was about . . . he was watching me kind of discover myself.

Peter: What did you mean by "and I look like this?"

Eric: Well I would not have thought that I could look anywhere near that butch, or that hot, or that whatever. You know, that masculine—that sexy. I never thought of myself as that. *I didn't think I could wear this stuff and pull it off.* (Emphasis added)

For Eric, the realization that he could indeed "wear this stuff and pull it off" draws attention inward, while apparently sparking a great deal of erotic energy around the realization. Adam makes the same connection, with an emphasis that explicitly reveals how leather amplifies his erotic interest in men:

Leather—I put it on and I feel like a different person. You know a different side of me comes out . . . Much more open and honest, well, I'm honest, really honest if I want to get into BDSM stuff, 'cause you gotta be. But I just, I feel more whole when I'm wearing leather, when I'm in a leather scene. 'Cause I'm not hiding anything and [*pause*] I like men. So men in leather just is really—a turn-on.

Later in the interview, Adam's comments indicate an awareness of the performative nature of *some* manifestations of leather drag while at the same time underscoring the authenticity of the drag *he* practices: "And one friend had told me once, if you want to get involved in a leather group in Friendlytown, get involved with the Sentinels, 'cause they're men—who have sex with men. The Red Dragons [another area leather club] are like drag queens." Butler, again drawing on examples of female drag from the film *Paris is Burning*, might explain the distinctions Adam is making here in terms of performative realness and how this is judged through "reading." A reading is a listing of performance flaws, a peer critique that reveals the performer's specific failures to convince an audience. Thus the ideal drag performance is completely real and cannot be read (Butler 1993, 129).[24] Similarly, while Adam can easily read the inferior performance of masculinity as practiced by the Red Dragons, he is unable to read the real leather drag of the Sentinels. Butler goes on to say that "The rules that regulate and legitimate realness (shall we call them symbolic?) constitute the mechanism by which certain sanctioned fantasies, sanctioned imaginaries, are insidiously elevated as the parameters of realness" (130). Lance can easily identify the "sanctioned imaginaries" informing leather realness:

Yes. Um, very much plays into why leather, it's become associated with very masculine, very strong images of a, well, the hero. Um, we don't have a song of Roland, we don't have Beowulf, but we do have stories of the cowboys on the cattle drives, we do have stories of the flying leathernecks. We have our stories of biker gangs, sort of the flip side, the more evil side of the antihero. But this sort of hero person, very strong, courageous, overcoming great odds, the person that we all look up to. *And you put on those clothes and you assume those qualities.* If not completely within yourself at least within how other people perceive you. I personally think that a great deal of our hero worship is also erotic. (Emphasis added)

This passage provides an excellent example of the different dispositional reactions to leather versus female drag, in that Lance is able to identify the exterior effects of leather drag while clearly privileging what he experiences as an internal process of transformation. As Lance continues, the outside world seems to completely disappear, yielding to an intensely erotic and exclusively subjective experience:

You put on the costume, you become the character. As far as how it interacts with my leather, a lot of leather is costume. It allows us to act out feelings and to experience emotions and feelings we wouldn't without because it creates a certain atmosphere or setting. When you add to that an actual BDSM scene where you're going to do something involving your leather and S/M or bondage and discipline, you sort of create a very deep theater in which you're not watching but you're the participant creating it . . . because it reaches very deep inside of you, and if you're doing it well—you know when we say the word "theater" we have the idea of a performance and that's being observed, and even when we talk about that we're participants, we have the conception that we're somehow observing what we're doing. It ceases to be an act of observation and completely an act of participation. Um [*pause*], it gives a great deal of personal release. I'm talking about, you know, bottoms talking about how when they're in bondage they feel most truly free. Because they're complete, you've created a scene where you can be the exact opposite of what our American culture demands you to be, which is the rugged, self-made, successful individualist dependent on no one, no one puts you down, you're standing there on your own pedestal, the hero of your own life story. You go into a BDSM scene, you can put all of that aside and you can completely give in to your feeling of needing or wanting to be absolutely helpless. Absolutely bound.[25]

What is critically important here is, for Lance, the realization of masculinity through the realness of the performance ("you *become* the character"), which enables the ecstasy of absolute submission. Masculine realness offers a powerful, if fleeting, escape from the effeminacy effect ("a great deal of personal release"), which paradoxically allows for an ecstatic rejection of all that normative masculinity implies ("the rugged, self-made, success-ful individualist dependent on no one"). But it is equally clear that, at least for Lance, this is experienced on a deeply personal, perhaps spiritual level. His attention is focused on an inner experience of subjectivity, and there is little connection to the political arena. While we can see how it *might* do so, the ecstatic experience Lance speaks of here, even though it may foster a political insight, does not provoke political action.[26] It certainly does not encourage a critique of masculinity, anymore than it obviates the need to continue performing masculinity.

The lived experiences of these men (Eric, Adam, and Lance) may serve as a metaphor for historical developments within leather culture in the last three decades. Here I review evidence that as they collectively real-ized that they could "wear this stuff and pull it off," leathermen began to invest themselves more seriously in gay masculinity, emphasizing realness while eschewing the more transgressive and parodic possibilities of hyper-masculine drag. One way of tracing this development is by looking at the changing relationship between leather culture and effeminacy. Consider the playful, campy "girl talk" celebrated in the following excerpt from the August 1970 issue of *Wheels!*, the official newsletter of a gay motorcycle club in New York City:

Sufferin' saddlebags, we need a bigger club house. This one is beginning to look like a set for the second act of *Tannhauser!* Our entire wall is now bedecked with the banners of our (ahem) sister clubs . . . Those members of the second city who cherish the genteel virtues of propriety and good taste cannot believe their ears when they hear how Larry K. and Don K. (no relation) (hah!) showed up for the cocktail party at The Marathon [a recent run]. Haven't they heard that hemlines are lower these days?[27]

Less than two decades later, a more mature leather culture had left much of this playful blend of camp and hypermasculinity behind. Some found the new mix of hotter sex with less laughter oppressive. Thus, by the late 1980s, the forerunners of the Bear movement were able to make a subver-sive statement simply by placing a cuddly little teddy bear in their pocket, where he peeped out playfully from a space normally reserved for sexual signaling with a colored hanky (see chapter 4). While campy banter about improper hemlines may have facilitated the celebration of leather sex in the early days, in only a few short decades things had reached a point where parody and camp were reinterpreted as a wet blanket to the leather-man's manly passions (Bersani 1987, 208). My field notes recounting a 1999 visit to a local leather bar provide a sense of this new, gravely serious investment in masculinity:

Shortly after being introduced to a man in his late thirties, I have a rather awkward exchange with my new acquaintance. Commenting on what I thought was his interest in another (much younger) man standing across the bar from us, I am surprised by his vehement denial. When I wonder aloud if perhaps he thinks this guy is too boyish, he responds curtly, "No, not too boyish—too *girlish*. I like *men!*" Later on, this same man expresses his disgust with men who sip their drinks through straws, complaining that it looks "too femmy."

Citing Gramsci, Butler (1993, 132–33) reminds us that hegemonies operate through *rearticulation*: "here is where the accumulated force of a historically entrenched and entrenching rearticulation overwhelms the more fragile effort to build an alternative cultural configuration from or against that more powerful regime." The archival material I have located points to an unruly conflation of female drag, an effeminate camp sensibility, and the parodic production of the hypermasculine image in early leather biker groups. I cannot help but wonder at the possibilities, had this gender chaos been able to sustain itself, for a more truly subversive challenge to the gender order. Alas, this "fragile effort" has all but disappeared as gay leathermen have become convinced by their own performances of masculinity—a social and historical process that has enervated leather culture's transgressive potential even as it has assuaged the leatherman's deep-seated fears of effeminacy.

Phallic Sex and Other Fetishes: Distributing Pleasure across the Body

I was not surprised to find that with respect to sex, phallocentric logic was a powerful structuring force informing many leathermen's experience of sex. This logic most often revealed itself in the eternal, quasi-spiritual significance attributed to the "ritual" of insertive intercourse, even as it trumped more recent anxieties centered around the fluidity of sexual roles:

The suppression of this darker side of men's experience is perhaps one of the most pernicious effects of the patriarchal identification of masculinity with rationality and spirit, serving to cut men off from the lower aspects of what one Jungian analyst, Eugene Monick, has called *Phallos*, the sacred image of the Masculine, and thereby denying men, and gay men in particular, wholeness as men. (Hopcke 2001, 74)

Tonight's top is tomorrow's bottom. We're all more interested that the ritual be enacted than concerned about which role we assume. (White 1980, 268)

This emphasis was apparent in my field notes as well:

After a little dirty talk, Roy begins to massage Jack's asshole with his finger. Roy lubes up one finger and sticks it in, then another. This Jack likes. A lot. Roy continues finger-fucking Jack while others work on his chest, nipples, etc. Jack's excitement level builds until he finally yells to Roy, "Tell me you're fucking me! Tell me you're fucking me!"

I think this provocative excerpt is rich in implications. First, it clearly suggests that pleasure in sex was, in this case, greatly facilitated by a team performance, one that went beyond mere physical manipulation to (at least the request for) a collaborative fiction. Second, the nature of the request indicates that Jack places penetration by the penis (fingers are seen as a substitute and not the "real" thing) at the center of his erotic preferences. This suggests that it is the symbolism of the act, the phallic power of the penis, rather than its physical stimulation that is critical for Jack. Finally, at the same time that the incident underscores the enduring appeal of the phallus, it also demonstrates the malleability of the scene's ability to produce the desired pleasure. Fingers will do for now, but please (oh please!) tell me you're *fucking* me.

On the other hand (and paradoxically), of the three case study communities I studied, this one strikes me on balance as the *least* supportive of phallocentrism. In the context of all of the other powerful forms of eroticization going on at Leather Camp, it becomes possible to regard Jack's desire to be fucked as just another fetish. What I mean to suggest is that in exploding the possibilities for sexual pleasure, both in terms of multiplying sexual practices and expanding the sexualized surface of the body, leathermen may have succeeded in "dephallicizing the cock" (Kelly and Kane 2001, 341) where other communities have failed. Barry tells me that of the entire smorgasbord of sex practices available in the leather community, his favorites remain kissing, sucking, and hugging:

Peter: OK, how important is fucking?

Barry: If it is, if it isn't, don't care.

Peter: You could take it or leave it?

Barry: That's right. It doesn't matter to me . . . I mean I've never been into the fucking scene.

When I asked Victor if garden-variety fucking still holds pride of place in the leather community, he tells me that:

Victor: It still ranks up pretty high. I mean despite doing these other scenes, at least in my mind, the other part's kind of nice to do too [*laughs*] as part of it.

Peter: So does the fucking usually finish the scene?

Victor: Um [*pause*], I would say, in my experience, at least with me it's more finishing a scene.

Adam's response to my question seems to indicate that he attaches no particular importance to standard (genital) penetration; for him it seems to be understood as just another fetish similar to other kink practices: "I think they put less emphasis on fucking, but then what do you call fisting? Or water sports? Or rubber? There's, I mean a lot of guys in the leather community have their own fetish." As Adam continues, he reveals that while he sees a close association between genital penetration and other forms of penetration (such as fisting) as they are practiced in the community, his particular perspective does not privilege genital penetration:

Adam: Um, but there's, fucking goes on, I mean even if there's fisting, there's fucking and there's fisting, and there's fucking and there's fisting. But some guys are into fisting and they only want to fist, so . . .

Peter: Do you think some guys are into fisting as a substitute for fucking?

Adam: Sometimes it's better than a fuck. 'Cause it's different. Talk about trust! And then knowing your own body enough to have that.

Owen's response seems to suggest that there may be an inverse relationship between an interest in kink and traditional fucking. When I ask him to put traditional intercourse in the context of all other sex practices in the leather community, he responds:

Owen: I'd say it's about 99 percent.

Peter: What do you mean 99 percent?

Owen: Oh, I mean, the thing is, like I said, I'm vanilla with sprinkles. I think most people in the leather community are probably much more vanilla than you'd assume by looking at them.

Peter: So you're saying that they do more straight fucking than you might think?

Owen: Oh yeah, of course. Oh yeah, of course. Yeah.

175

Peter: And does that mean it's more a part of the leather sexual culture than the larger gay community, or is it the same, or is it less?

Owen: I think it's probably the same.

Mains (1987, 116) has argued that when safety is defined in terms of viral (HIV) transmission, almost all leather practices are safer than conventional "vanilla" sex practices, and he scolds the medical establishment for condemning many of these alternative practices out of an ignorance of "the full range of human capacities." Eric, on the other hand, is able to fully articulate his thoughts on the decentering of anal intercourse within the leather community and to put it in historical context as well:

OK, and that's another thing that leathermen bring to the table, sexually speaking. That it doesn't always have to be, it doesn't have to be insertive intercourse . . . especially in the face of AIDS—AIDS forced a lot of rethinking of, you know, what was safe and what was not. AIDS forced a lot of exploration for alternate ways of pleasuring ourselves and each other that would be safer, that wouldn't result in passing on the virus. And out of that came a real sexual richness that, you know, I don't think the rest of the wider heterosexual community has any idea about. You know, and again, that's something that we just came up with for ourselves. And I think it makes it much, much richer and more fulfilling and certainly more varied.

———

On balance, while these responses indicate an array of meanings and associations with insertive anal intercourse, my conclusion is that the enthusiastic experimentation with alternative sex practices in gay leather culture *has* in fact achieved a substantial degree of success in decentering the phallocentric logic of anal sex that thrives elsewhere in the gay community. I think the best evidence of this is the fact that more than one member of this community was able to speak of anal intercourse as "just another fetish."

But this world of the decentered phallus, of the desublimated anus, of paddling, hot wax, nipple torture, electricity, fisting, flogging, and all the rest is a *secret* world. I do not mean to suggest that these specific practices are secret; indeed, they seem to be gaining increasing acceptance both in popular culture and in practice. Rather I suggest that the particular ensemble of erotic meanings and associations that surround these and other practices in gay leather culture can only be fully experienced through a process of initiation into the world of gay leather. Part of this initiation includes a wholesale embrace of and homage to hegemonic masculinity through an exaggeration of its form. Perhaps the biggest secret is that unlike Faerie drag, leather drag is deadly serious. The evidence I have presented here suggests that, unlike the Faeries and much like the Bears, gay leathermen *do not* wish to understand this performance as camp, as parody. As Leo Bersani (1987, 208) reminds us, "Parody is an erotic turn-off . . . if you're out to make someone you turn off the camp." Gay leathermen *do not* exaggerate their masculinity because they wish to cultivate an ironic distance from it; quite the opposite is the case. Leather is adored, eroticized, and cathected precisely because it promises membership in a fraternity of real men that had been presumed to be forbidden. As Eric says, "I didn't think I could wear this stuff and pull it off."

So what we have here, ironically, is a sexual culture that truly *subverts* hegemonic masculinity, into which one can only be fully integrated by means of a kind of dispositional pledge of allegiance *in support of* hegemonic masculinity. More precisely, leather culture subverts hegemonic masculinity *sexually* (by successfully decentering "phallus and receptacle" sex) even as it reinforces its *gendered* assumptions (through the exaggeration of gender in hypermasculinity). The Sentinels are the only one of my three case study communities whose sexual culture even approaches Hocquenghem's (1996) liberated "grouping," where the "desiring machine" does in fact "desublimate the anus."

But while Hocquenghem hoped the desiring machine model would be celebrated in gay cultures, it is probably safe to assume that his primary concern was with the liberation of *desire* rather than the creation of *machines*. In this chapter I have offered evidence that the latter has indeed accompanied the former in leather culture. Thus, alongside liberated desire I also found the rationalization of sex, an emphasis on the technical aspects of pleasure production, and the reduction of the body to a pleasure-producing/receiving machine.

The reason I do not believe that the subversive sexual culture of leathermen will ever gain substantial political ground is that, unlike the Bears, leathermen remain feminized by the outside world. The leatherman's deadly serious investment in masculinity is effectively obscured by the stereotype of the leather queen, the mincing effeminate trying way too hard to look like a real man. The stereotype survives because imperfect performances of leather hypermasculinity are out there to be read as evidence of an essential nature that is both feminine and homosexual, the failed performer thereby understood as "overcompensating" for the masculinity that he "naturally" lacks. In defense of the heterosexual matrix, the leather queen comes to stand in for all gay leathermen. Moreover, the stereotype of the leather queen may prove to be particularly robust, as it is more likely to be corroborated in the empirical world than, say, something as inchoately figured as an effeminate Bear. Failed performance is much more frequent in the leather community than it is for Bears because of the element of exaggeration. It is simply easier to fail at leather hypermasculinity than it is to fail at conventional Bear masculinity. It is easier to wear a baseball cap and T-shirt and "pull it off" than it is to wear a leather vest and cap effectively. Those leathermen who pass, who put in near-perfect performances of masculinity that cannot be read, face the same dilemma that people of color encounter when they pass as white. Their difference is rendered invisible, in this case because it is too often assumed in the larger social world that such a convincing performance could only come from a real (and therefore heterosexual) man. And so the "secret" of gay leather culture's sexual subversion is effectively contained.

SIX

Fielding Questions, Fielding Possibilities

In the United States, these are interesting times for scholars of gay and queer identity communities. There is something both exciting and potentially embarrassing about studying identities in an era when they are said to be everywhere collapsing in on themselves. In my analysis of Faeries, Bears, and leathermen I have tried to put the tension between modern and postmodern conceptions of identity to productive use. Readers will decide whether I have done this, or whether it is advisable or even possible to do so. In any case, their reaction does not obviate the need to assess the political impact of the communities I have presented here.

While at this writing some signs are evident that the rabid resurgence of American social conservatism may have reached its apogee, the reactionary tenor of the new century's first decade cannot be denied. Same-sex marriage, sex education, and access to contraception remain potent political issues, and in many quarters the fear of the lust-mad, disease-ridden homosexual out to seduce "our children" shows few signs of abating. The brief career of the metrosexual provides a useful political barometer, indicating oppressively high atmospheric pressure around even the most compliant gender experiments. As a marketing strategy, the metrosexual originally figured as a distinctly heterosexual man who exhibited stereotypically gay consumption habits. But with amazing rapidity the term "metrosexual" has become synonymous with something very like "urban gay." On the other hand, there may be some reason to expect increasing tolerance for sex and gender nonconformists. Can the retirement of the television show *Will and Grace*, a successful mass-media representation of stereotypical male gayness that is carefully homogenized and normalized so as not to threaten mainstream sensibilities, herald a readiness for more diverse, queerer fare? Or have we yet to realize the full effects of "regimes of the normal" (Warner 1999, xxvi)? On the progressive side, Seidman (2003) has written persuasively about the decline of the closet and the salience of sexual orientation as a category of identity, and Connell and Messerschmidt (2005) have recently acknowledged that hegemonic forms of masculinity are not impervious to change. They are influenced "from below" by nondominant masculine forms, like gay masculinities, and by women. On the other hand, in the 2004 elections no fewer than eleven states voted to write prohibitions against same-sex marriage into their constitutions, and gender loomed large in the presidential race as voters were repeatedly asked to compare George W. Bush's straight-shooting, folksy, "boots on the ground" approach with John Kerry's effeminate, patrician, indecisive "flip-flopping." The changes wrought by September 11 present further ambiguities. The new era of constant warfare cannot ignore four decades of feminism, yet how the military assimilates feminism provides little comfort. One only need look at the sharply polarized gender images of rescued prisoner of war Jessica Lynch (helpless victim/America's sweetheart) and military prison guard Lindy England (power-mad dominatrix/ heartless bitch) to see that this assimilation is proceeding on terms that reinstall hegemonic masculinity and reward traditionally gendered women. Given this ambivalent context, the political presence of communities like Faeries, Bears, and leathermen takes on added significance.

As Connell (1995, 144) notes, the question of whether the gay community is best understood as the site of subversion and cultural change or of gender conservatism has not been adequately examined in the United States. She points to the work of two British scholars by way of illustrating the more rigorous treatment of the topic in the United Kingdom: "Gregg Blachford (1981) has argued that gay communities provide a certain resistance, but not a significant challenge, to the culture of male dominance in society as a whole. Jeffrey Weeks (1986), taking a poststructuralist view of social order, sees sexual subcultures as more diverse and having greater potential for change." In the final analysis, are Faeries, Bears, and leathermen resistant to or compliant with hegemonic masculinity? The answer to this question would seem to hinge on the particular reaction each community has taken up with respect to "the effeminacy effect." As I have conceived it, this concept does not simply equate to an attitude toward effeminacy, but rather how these communities negotiate the powerful historical coupling of effeminacy and homosexuality. If it were simply a matter of the community's take on effeminacy, the answers would be greatly simplified. Faeries revel in effeminacy, exaggerate the claims of the effeminacy effect, and from their marginalized location toss the matter back to the cultural center with parodic glee. Like Goldilocks, Bears want to get things just right. The cultural porridge they cook up represents, on the one hand, a spirited rejection of effeminacy (too cold) and, on the other, a suspicion of the exaggerated masculinity of the leatherman (too hot). A normalized Bear identity represents a "just right" compromise with the effeminacy effect, which would otherwise pit their sexual interests and their gender investments against each other. Leathermen reject effeminacy as well, but here the rejection is so spirited that their embellished homage to masculinity serves, in some contexts, to revive the specter of starched chiffon. But the question is not simply a matter of accepting or rejecting effeminacy. The really significant questions have to do with the effects of the various cultural refusals collectively crafted by the unruly subjects of my research. When gay/queer men refuse to recoil from effeminacy, or when they seek to resignify male homosexuality as masculine, what effect does this ultimately have on the larger set of reified gender arrangements that govern the lives of less adventurous souls? Does it ultimately trouble, reinstall, undo, or recuperate gender? Are these communities challenging gender? If so, in what sense?

In their recent *Drag Queens of the 801 Cabaret*, authors Leila Rupp and Verta Taylor (2003) offer a set of criteria that may be of use in determining whether my case study communities can be characterized as oppositional. In evaluating the political character of the drag performers they studied, Rupp and Taylor offer contestation, intentionality, and collective identity as three concrete indices of resistance (Rupp and Taylor 2003, 217). The first, *contestation*, "suggests that the discourse—or symbols, identities, and cultural practices—conveyed by a cultural performance subverts rather than maintains dominant relations of power" (217).

Can these communities be said to be interacting with a larger "audience" (in the same way that the drag queens at the 801 do), or does the dynamic lead inward, so that the "audience" for their identity work is the members themselves? Or are both audiences present simultaneously? If Faeries can be said to perform for an outside audience, it would seem to be a rather select, invitation-only crowd. The Faerie groups that I am familiar with make their most public appearances at gay/queer-friendly events like pride celebrations. As I mentioned earlier, their preference for "sanctuary," while lowering their public profile, may also potentially raise their status as a "movement in abeyance." Bears present a starkly contrasting arrangement; it seems that all the social world is their stage.

Their costumes are not as interesting as the Faeries'—but that is the whole point. Normalization means nothing without the approval of a normalizing regime (Warner 1999, xxvi), and by definition normalization cannot be achieved by retreating from the public sphere. Finally, the relationship between leather identity performers and their audience is complex and multilayered. As I have indicated, a built-in audience exists within the culture, as scenes are typically semipublic and derive a great deal of their erotic effect from this arrangement. But as I have also intimated, in public the leatherman either passes as a more-or-less conventionally masculinized man or may be refeminized if he is perceived as trying too hard.

Clearly, from the perspective of mainstream America, Faeries, Bears, and leathermen have all constructed deeply subversive cultural statements, so in my application, the contestation question shifts slightly to take into account the degree of what might be legitimately termed "audience interaction." By this logic, and in light of my earlier remarks, Faeries score somewhat low on audience interaction, Bears score very high (although this is complicated by the degree to which the Bear man's public appearance as a "regular guy" is or is not accompanied by a concomitant public recognition of his "gayness"), and leathermen score somewhere in the middle.

Intentionality, in Rupp and Taylor's (2003, 218) view, asks the question, "To what extent are [community members] intentionally thinking and acting consciously about goals and strategies for challenging dominant constructions of masculinity, femininity, and the gendered heterosexual family?" In their active embrace of the feminine and the cultural gestures they make toward the idea of a "third gender," Faeries score extremely high in this respect. Likewise, by deliberately infusing homosex with masculine erotic energy on the one hand and by reinterpreting the erotic as only incidentally tied to phallic sex on the other hand, leathermen also score high on intentionality. In that they are consciously cultivating "normality," Bears probably score low on this aspect. The Bear case, however, presents an interesting challenge with respect to intentionality in that their cultural message may *un*intentionally prove troubling. Whether Bears will become the unwitting Trojan Horse of the culture wars, injecting radical sexual difference into the heart of mainstream heteronormative society via an ostensibly regular guy appearance, remains to be seen. But the fact that this possibility can even be seriously considered suggests that when a movement community takes up two incommensurable cultural narratives, it may be their cultural collision and not the conscious intention of movement actors that manifests meaningful change.

The third index of resistance presented by Rupp and Taylor (2003) is *collective identity*. All three communities clearly score high here, and, as I demonstrated in the previous chapters, it is the identities fostered by these communities that define the magnetic center of their respective cultures. But in an analysis of oppositional politics, even this seemingly clear-cut assessment is complicated by my contention that the draw is primarily emotional and not political for members of these groups. This again returns us to problematic aspects of intentionality, as these groups clearly have political implications, whether they are intended by individual members or not. While some are drawn to these communities with political intentions, for most members the draw is emotional.

What, then, can we conclude? Despite a careful application of the criteria, an overall assessment remains ambiguous. If you have been keeping score, you can see that when you add up the assessments across the categories, you end up with something that looks very much like a three-way tie, with each of the communities exhibiting strong oppositional tendencies in some areas and weaker tendencies in others. Of course, this tidy egalitarian outcome obtains if, and only if, one can assume that contestation, intentionality, and collective identity play an exactly equal role in determining a group's political profile. This is surely a matter that is open to debate, and a comparison of the overall oppositional strengths and weaknesses of these three communities is, and probably should remain, an open question. However, I hope that my appropriation of Rupp and Taylor's criteria has provided a helpful framework for advancing such a discussion.

Questions of relative degrees of resistance or compliance become easier to decipher when specific issues are considered. For example, with respect to the decentering of the gendered centrality of penetrative intercourse, all of these communities introduce resistance. Based on the data I encountered in this study, I would put leathermen in the lead here, as they seemed to have introduced at least the suggestion that penetrative intercourse might be viewed within the context of an array of novel pleasures as "just another fetish." Bears sustain noncompliant sexual practices like the "Bear hug" alongside more compliant practices that grant erotic pride of place to penetrative intercourse; thus I would place them at some distance behind leathermen in terms of challenging traditional notions of what constitutes the sexual. My data on Faerie sexuality is sparse, but my rudimentary assessment of "sex magick" suggests that Faeries too are interested in expanding notions of the sexual, probably placing them somewhere between Bears and leathermen in this respect.

In terms of the challenge each community poses to the effeminacy effect, I would place Bears solidly in the lead, as they effectively refute the effeminacy charge, while the specter of starched chiffon puts leathermen at a close second. Faeries deliberately place last in this respect. But simply disrupting the cultural association between effeminacy and homosexuality ignores the more pressing matter of misogyny. Thus it is critically important to assess each community in terms of how (and whether) it disrupts the misogynistic assumptions at the heart of the effeminacy effect. It is important to emphasize here that I encountered no evidence of active, conscious misogyny in any of my case study communities. While the historical material introducing each of the studies at times reflects it, I never encountered deliberate misogyny in my research subjects. The question then reduces to the degree each community is shaped unconsciously by misogyny, and what community members have done in response. Faeries are unquestionably out in front on this issue, as both the feminine essence and consciousness raising are held in high regard among them. Leathermen probably follow based on their attention to states of consciousness associated with pleasure/pain and the evidence I have presented that at least some of these men are "doing gender" as a means of transcending gender. Bears probably place last here, since they foster an unreflective, taken-for-granted perspective on masculinity that leaves the misogynistic character of effeminacy unquestioned.

Finally, one set of resistant practices registers in each of my case study communities, albeit in widely varying ways: anti-ageist or "youth resistant" strategies. Faeries exhibit this in the elevated status given to grannies—the more experienced and older Faeries who assume de facto leadership roles in the group. Bears demonstrate this through the inclusion of older Polar Bears and through (often mistaken and problematic) notions of sexual dominance over younger Cubs. Among gay leathermen the concept of the leather daddy queers mainstream paternal and patriarchal cultural strands while simultaneously recasting age as a positive, desirable attribute.

Divorce Court: Irreconcilable Differences?

If, as I have suggested, the "marriage" of effeminacy and homosexuality was the result of a centuries-long process, consummated only a little over a century ago, then my ethnographic chapters would seem to suggest that this marriage is headed for the rocks. Although, as I have concluded, specific processes are at work that obscure the effects of their reinvestment in masculinity, among leathermen and Bears there can be little doubt that these robust projects are central to their collective identity work. While Faeries embrace the feminine, this approach is accompanied by a kind of satire of the effeminacy effect. In short, it seems that with respect to the marriage of effeminacy and homosexuality, divorce proceedings are well underway. Given this situation, now seems an opportune time to raise some questions of accountability. Could this marriage have been saved? Are the two parties' differences truly irreconcilable? What does it mean when two entities so exquisitely suited to each other cannot get along? And perhaps most important, with whom will effeminacy be consorting in the future?

The response to the first question is refreshingly clear. *Of course* the sanctity of this marriage might have been preserved. If we could simply erase the corrupting influences of gay liberation, second- and third-wave feminism, the civil rights movement, technological advances in birth control, the expansion of wage labor, the urbanization of American society, and the AIDS pandemic and kept Paul Lynde on *The Hollywood Squares*, the marriage of homosexuality and effeminacy would still be in its honeymoon stage. Men with same-sex interests would remain convinced of their nelly natures and preoccupied with the doomed pursuit of Quentin Crisp's "great dark man."

Then again, I am told some marriages are not really worth saving. Divorcing effeminacy from homosexuality creates some opportunities while it forecloses others. Among the less savory opportunities, the divorce allows men with same-sex interests to join with their more conventional fellows as they relentlessly repudiate the feminine. At long last they can retire the angora sweater, lose the lisp and the limp wrist, and trash the old Judy Garland albums. They can become "real men," drive Hummers, hunt, fish, play racquetball, change their own oil, and not wash behind their ears.

Of course, some divorces settle on better terms than others. If the divorce settlement means that more "soldiers"—those now liberated to embrace transgressive gender practices—will be waging the gender wars, gender activists may have good reason to celebrate. On the other hand, it seems that the window of opportunity offered by gay liberation has been slowly closing since activists in the early 1970s staked a claim for reform that included tolerance for both homosexuality *and* effeminacy. In those early days gay men were uniquely positioned to contest their oppression on not only sexual terms but gender terms as well. Instead of undermining or "undoing" gender (Butler 2004), each of the responses taken up in these pages represents an embrace and celebration of gender. Of the three communities presented here, the kind of conscious gender play among the Faeries seems to present the most hopeful case for a revival of the liberationist fight, but as I have suggested, their strategy is not without its limitations. If events proceed more conservatively along the cultural path of least resistance, it may well be that in the coming decades homosexuality and effeminacy will become increasingly detached.

If so, whither effeminacy? If it becomes possible to reconfigure homosexuality *sans* gender implications, if the divorce is finalized and the cultural bonds are permanently torn asunder, what is to become of effeminacy? The long and varied history I have included in this study suggests that the end of the feminized homosexual would likely not signal the end of effeminacy. In an age of increasing militarism, one possibility is close at hand: Peace-loving men may find that the charge of effeminacy transfers quite easily to them. Those who resist military service or who protest military intervention may find their loafers involuntarily lightened. The strategy could be expanded to stigmatize other types of protest masculinities, as it has at various points in America's past (Rotundo 1993, 232–39). Henceforth, environmental, poverty, and animal rights activists may find themselves carrying a greatly increased share of feminine baggage. Another possibility is suggested by the dismantling of the American welfare state. The hyperindividualism and radically antisociological perspective of neoliberalism may provide fertile ground for new configurations of effeminacy. Men who are unwilling to settle for underemployment in minimum wage jobs or unable to find work of any kind may find themselves portrayed as soft and lazy "girlymen." Finally, a new relationship between sexuality and effeminacy may emerge. It seems that Foucault's (1990a) warnings about the oppressive aspects of the oversexualized self have, for the most part, fallen on deaf ears. In an era when sexuality is installed as *the* domain of pleasure and expression, one that is readily taken up and exploited by Madison Avenue, those deemed insufficiently sexual (regardless of orientation) may find themselves cast as the new nancies. None of these scenarios requires an active, organized campaign, nor do any of them necessarily preclude this possibility. I simply mean to suggest, by way of lamenting the closing of a window, a few of the possibilities presented by a social world still devoted to gender difference once effeminacy is cut loose from its homosexual moorings.

Theoretical Conclusions

In chapter 1 I proposed a theoretical "tool kit" approach, citing Bourdieu's (1990, 28) pragmatic relationship with other authors as "craft-masters" and "people you can ask to give you a hand in difficult situations." My analysis has borne out the utility of this approach. In addition to promoting epistemological modesty, it serves to recall the radically perspectival nature of social knowledge, a point perhaps especially relevant to the study of gender and sexuality. As in the Buddhist parable of the five blind men and the elephant wherein each man announces the "truth" about elephants based on his own limited encounter with one small portion of the beast, every theoretical position illuminates some aspects of the phenomena under study while it obscures others. Performativity captures the gender-constitutive practices of my research subjects but fails to capture some of the more concrete aspects of embodiment conveyed by the idea of a gendered habitus. Hegemonic masculinity provides an incisive conceptual tool with which to track the successes and failures of these communities in challenging hierarchical thinking, but it cannot provide the fine-grain detail needed in a study such as this one about exactly how the presence or absence of hegemonic gender shapes the process of identity construction. While I concede that my tool kit approach can never suggest a final, comprehensive understanding of how gender and effeminacy are shaping these communities, it is helpful in maintaining and foregrounding the complexity and dynamism of sex and gender studies. For myself, at the very least this approach prevents me from falling too much in love with one particular line of thought and falling too much under the spell of an inevitably partial approach. In what follows I summarize what I have gained from each of the theoretical tools I have employed.

Performativity and Gender Trouble

In my examination of Faerie culture I used my data to argue that there is nothing inherently transgressive in parodic practices like drag, a point that Butler (1993, 125) readily concedes. What is new here is the identification of the social processes whereby drag's subversive potential is mitigated, even in an ostensibly "radical" community like the Faeries. For Calliope, whose drag means so much more than just "performing for the squirrels," masculinity is a problem he confronts on a daily basis, one that has become a central tension in a truly transgressive existence. But Calliope's more engaged deployment of drag is not the dominant mode within Faerie culture, and while a great deal of subversive potential exists here, a substantive challenge to hegemonic masculinity is sequestered at present in the safe space of Faerie sanctuary.

Similarly, with respect to the Bears, an enthusiastic embrace of normative masculinity might—but as this study suggests, currently does not—effectively disrupt the logic of the heterosexual matrix to produce gender trouble. For the most part, through a sustained performative effort only slightly more conscious than that of heterosexual men, Bears seem to have successfully attained regular guy status. My data strongly suggest that in their day-to-day lives, most Bears easily "pass" for straight men. That little if any disruptive intent or potential is seen in this move is suggested by a definition I recently encountered on a Bear Web site, contributed by Richard Bulger, one of the most prominent figures in the national Bear community:

Bear \\`bar\ 2 a: A gay man whose **disposition is rooted in contemporary male culture** (*decidedly **not** contemporary gay male culture*) that emphasizes and **celebrates secondary male characteristics such as beard and body hair.** (Emphases in original)[1]

While this might be read as eschewing contemporary gay male culture on political grounds, by now it should be clear that the evidence does not support such a reading. What Bulger is rejecting here is not the political lassitude of gay male culture but the feminized subject that the culture enables, or at least fails to renounce. Still, by successfully normalizing gay masculinity, Bear culture in some respects represents the most powerful *potential* threat to the logic of the heterosexual matrix. My data suggest that this potential will, for the foreseeable future, remain dormant.

Whereas Faerie culture is revealing for what it suggests about the transgressive potential of drag, my observations in the leather sadomasochism (S/M) community reveal something important about drag practitioners themselves: drag can work to undermine rather than reinforce an awareness of gender performativity. I have shown how traditional (men doing female) drag can raise awareness of gender as a surface phenomenon, and I have also demonstrated that in the case of leather drag something quite different occurs. Typically, the leatherman's consciousness is drawn inward, toward the discovery of a masculinity previously obscured, presumably by the feminizing propaganda of a homophobic culture. Thus this potentially transgressive move (putting on the clothing of the "outlaw biker") is revealed as a reinscription of hegemonic masculinity. Again, there is nothing here that Butler would necessarily disagree with; my study's particular contribution lies in the empirical approach that allows me to identify the specific situations and processes at work in the leatherman's lived experience of drag.

Embodied Masculinity

In this study I have applied Bourdieu's ideas regarding embodiment and hexis to two specific areas: the embodiment of Bear masculinity and the adjustment of the embodied disposition toward pain that allows for its eroticization within gay leather S/M culture. With respect to Bears, I have demonstrated that many of Bourdieu's (2001) ideas from *Masculine Domination*—in that work applied to embodied gender among the Kabyle—can be productively applied to illuminate aspects of Bear culture. Just as in the larger culture the masculine is defined in binary opposition to the feminine, so Bears define their more "authentic" masculinity against that of the feminized gay "twink," whose shaved and toned body seeks to minimize rather than celebrate male secondary sex characteristics. The existence of an elaborate set of associations between the icon of the bear and masculinity (wildness, strength, independence) helps to explain the extraordinary success of Bear identity. Acceptance into Bear community is itself a form of masculine initiation, one not open to women or twinks, and the community allows its members to reject the negative assessment of the larger Bear body coming from the mainstream gay community as it reinforces this same body as phallic signifier. My observations of leather S/M community have led me to some speculative conclusions about how even the body's most basic dispositions may be altered under duress, in this case the way the disposition toward pain can be revised through the longing to join a fraternity of real men. This perspective on the habitus highlights the process in terms of the immediate microsocial setting and face-to-face interactions and suggests a number of intriguing research possibilities (see below).

Sexual Innovation

Does sexuality in these communities more closely resemble the heteronormative "dyad of phallus and receptacle" mentioned above, or have innovations within these cultures (and the "grouping" of dissident desires within these communities) actually helped gay men to escape the oedipalization of sex and allowed them to "dephallicize the cock?" The data are inconclusive on this point—clearly both conceptions exist simultaneously in these communities. The leather case is perhaps most promising in this respect, and the dearth of data on Faerie sexuality makes it difficult to compare them with Bears on this point.

Hegemonic Masculinity

Finally, with respect to Connell's (1995) notion of hegemonic masculinity, a few brief remarks are in order. Faeries consciously reject the authoritarian logic of hegemonic masculinity and foster an alternative notion of consensual power. Here the important empirical point is how and to what extent this alternative vision is realized in practice. As I have indicated, this ideological commitment is only partially fulfilled, yet it remains a central tenet of the Faerie vision. The countervailing force here is, of course, the move toward sanctuary and away from active engagement with hegemonic power relations on the outside. In their rejection of hierarchical power relations Faeries, do indeed, as Genet's quote at the start of chapter 3 suggests, act as "harbingers of new beauty." The question remains as to whether it is a beauty that can ever be realized outside of Faerie space.

Bears highlight and complicate the concept of "complicit masculinity." Connell (1995, 79–80) assigns this term to the majority of men who do not meet the exacting standards of hegemonic masculinity yet comply with hegemonic logic because it benefits them indirectly. "The number of men rigorously practicing the hegemonic pattern in its entirety may be quite small. Yet the majority of men gain from its hegemony, since they benefit from the patriarchal dividend, the advantage men in general gain from the overall subordination of women." Connell goes on to articulate the patriarchal dividend in terms of heteronormative benefits. "Marriage, fatherhood, and community life often involve extensive compromises with women rather than naked domination or an uncontested display of authority" (79–80). Thus, though they are not actively constructing hegemonic masculinity, Connell argues, most heterosexual men are tacitly in compliance with it. Bear men also demonstrate this type of compliance, but in place of the heteronormative aspects of the patriarchal dividend, they demand acceptance as regular guys, which in turn may disrupt the subordinating logic of hegemonic masculinity. Here the significant point is that while complicit masculinity normally buttresses the established hierarchy of masculinities, in this case it carries the potential to turn back on the very system that produces it.

Finally, the way that leather clubs articulate the relationships between power, masculinity, and the erotic poses a seriously disruptive challenge to the hierarchical logic of hegemonic masculinity. In order to rank order different types of masculinities, clear distinctions between them must be maintained. The erotic logic of leather culture replaces these simplistic categorical assumptions with an inside-out logic suggesting the presence of homosexual desire always and already at the heart of hegemonic authority relations (Namaste 1994). Leathermen make explicit that which remains safely implicit in the everyday workings of hegemonic power, demonstrating and enacting the way that power relations among men are infused with desire and the way that this always risks exceeding the bounds of the homosocial and traversing into the homosexual.

Postmodern Community

Each of my case study communities acts as an "identity cove" to shelter participants against the storms of postmodernism: the saturation and population of the self; multiphrenia; fractured, discontinuous, and contradictory identities. The dynamics of the identities forged in these communities underscore some of Gergen's (1991, 140) points about the relational self, wherein he suggests that one of the hallmarks of contemporary identity formation is "the reconstruction of self as relationship." But it is decidedly contrary to his observations regarding the "collage" community, "a community in which homogeneity in life patterns gives way to a multiplicity of disjunctive modes of living" (212). Furthermore, I see evidence in all three of my cases of a rejection of "fractional relationships," those "built around a limited aspect of one's being" (178). In yielding three distinctly different examples of postmodern community, some glimmer of hope is provided by this study, which to some extent is in accordance with Gergen's (1991) optimistic suggestions at the conclusion of *The Saturated Self.* Against the oft-cited fears of social chaos, multiphrenetic alienation, and moral relativism associated with the postmodern, we find here three caring communities, each in its own way undeniably postmodern, yet each providing clear identity anchors with sustained (albeit unconventional) moral guidance for its members.

Implications for AIDS Research

I turn now to the specific implications of the study for AIDS prevention, policy, and education. Perhaps the most important implication of the study is how it clearly reveals the deficiencies in what has come to be known as the "condom code," whereby wearing a condom "every time" for anal sex is recommended as the primary method of preventing HIV infection. By contrast, this study problematizes the practice of anal intercourse by emphasizing its heteronormative (phallus and receptacle) character and placing it in the context of a variety of alternative sex practices. Consequently it raises questions about the presumed centrality and "natural" character of penetrative intercourse. Moreover, the perspective I have sustained throughout this study examines the possibilities for decentering (without prohibiting) anal intercourse, a practice that continues to anchor the sexual lives of many gay/queer men even as it continues to provide the most efficient means of HIV transmission. I have presented evidence that in at least one community (leather), anal intercourse is understood by some participants as "just another fetish." This suggests that it may be possible to extend this insight to the larger gay community in ways that would expand, rather than diminish, the possibilities for pleasure. But even as I make this hopeful suggestion, my data hint at important constraints preventing the widespread adoption of the "anal intercourse as fetish" perspective. In any case, the most recent statistics on rising rates of HIV infection strongly suggest that without continuing attention to the issues raised here, without efforts to raise consciousness of the restrictions of putatively natural sex, current patterns are unlikely to change. And unless current patterns change, the popular equation between same-sex activity and pathology will be not only sustained but also strengthened.

Furthermore, whatever the limitations of the current study, the approach I adopt here is likely to be much more productive than those that emphasize prohibition (no sex without a condom, no sex outside your primary relationship, etc.). I am not the first person to observe that in the context of a late capitalist culture where pleasure is at a premium, prohibition is ultimately counterproductive. Indeed, Butler (1990) maintains that the prohibiting laws and taboos are themselves productive of pleasure. Thus any perceived prohibition of barebacking (anal intercourse without condoms) is only likely to enhance the pleasure that the practice affords. Based on my findings I propose instead a deliberate strategy of pleasure production, one that resists the logic of prohibition and celebrates the social construction of pleasure-in-community instead. In both the Bear and leather case studies, it is abundantly clear that a variety of cultural and sexual practices have been developed and sustained intersubjectively, as the community, not just individuals within it, enables the experience of new pleasures.

Another implication of the study is that if such a reimagining of gendered sexual pleasures is to occur, we will need to pay much more attention to those communities at the margins of the margins—those queer communities marginalized even within the already marginalized gay, lesbian, bisexual, and transsexual community. The data on the communities I have studied here, especially when contrasted with Connell's (1995) "very straight gay," suggest that this is where we need to look for guidance in the development of an innovative collective sexual imagination. The study also suggests that no single alternative exists to a heteronormative sexual imagination, but rather a rich field of possibilities provides a range of collective sexual imaginings. Again I want to emphasize that what I am speculating on here is imagination *in community*, the construction of pleasure *in community*. My case studies suggest (but do not exhaust) the possibilities for such imaginings.

More Questions

I conclude by revisiting some of the points of convergence in the study where gender has intersected with other significant social categories. My emphasis here is on generating new questions.

At the intersection of gender and race, I have demonstrated how whiteness is encoded in the particular historical construction of effeminacy anchoring the communities I have studied, and how in the Faerie and Bear cases the communities' use of racialized symbols may be contributing to the reproduction of whiteness. However, I have largely ignored questions of race and gendered desire. My data have not allowed me to attend to the various ways in which men's attraction to other men is shaped by race. As Chodorow (1994, 38) observes, "Those who are called or consider themselves heterosexual are, in all likelihood, tall-blond-Wasposexual, short-curly-haired zaftig-Jewishosexual, African-American-with-a-southern-accentosexual, erotically excited only by members of their own ethnic group or only by those outside of that group." Surely, self-identified gay and queer men are subject to these same racialized currents—for many, sexual desire is shaped in powerful ways by race, gay/queer men included—but questions as to just what is entailed in this process have not been adequately addressed here. Furthermore, my analysis suggests that whiteness, as the "default" or taken-for-granted racial category, allows the white men in my study to focus their identity production on gendered matters: masculinity and effeminacy. A comparative study with gay/queer men of color might be instructive in revealing how whiteness is able to "get out of the way" and render itself invisible with respect to producing desire in this process. By what mechanisms, and in what specific situations, is race among white men taken for granted? What types of situations highlight whiteness, and to what effect? Most important, how and where do other concerns mitigate the salience of gender for gay/queer men of color?

At the intersection of gender and class, I have demonstrated the critical role of social class in Western constructions of effeminacy. In the same way that whiteness obscures the influence of race on sexuality and foregrounds gender, perhaps the emphasis on gender is obscuring some enduring class implications that circulate along with contemporary constructions of effeminacy. If this is true, it suggests that I may have neglected some important class effects in this analysis. For example, what does it mean that most of the men in my study are middle class, and how might this affect their various collective responses to the effeminacy effect?

Perhaps the most intriguing junction we have encountered is the three-way intersection of gender, history, and the body. Through what she calls "body reflexive practices" Connell (1995, 65) observes that "bodies are addressed by social process and drawn into history." Throughout my work I have been startled by the rapidity of this process. Of my three case study communities, the oldest (leather) is perhaps sixty years old. In that brief period, the body reflexive practices of Faeries, Bears, and leathermen have produced distinct somatic tendencies as each of these communities takes up a separate historical response to the effeminacy effect. Interestingly, this process is most prominent among Bears, the youngest of the three communities. The meteoric rise of Bear culture since the late 1980s has enabled heavier and hairier men to radically reconstruct themselves, representing an opportunity reflected in new ways of talking, walking, and interacting with other men. Their case, along with the others, provides strong empirical support for the idea that history is capable of producing embodied dispositions in astonishingly short order. What I find particularly interesting here is that despite the obvious evidence of their historical production, Faeries, Bears, and leathermen have all constructed naturalizing narratives for themselves, in effect placing themselves *outside* of history. For Faeries, this is reflected in the essentialist notion of the fae spirit, for Bears it is encoded in the elaborate analogy with bears in the wild, and for leathermen it is exhibited in the "authentic" self that is revealed through leather drag. I wonder, is this illusion of the natural self a predominantly masculine fantasy? Is it possible, for example, that the renaturalizing tendencies I have documented here are an extension of the traditionally American masculinity narrative of "self making?" What might an analysis of mainstream masculinities, and the naturalizing tendencies therein, look like if subjected to the kind of analysis I have attempted here?

Finally, while I have devoted significant attention to the crossroads of gender and pleasure, many more questions are left to ask at this intersection. Most of my analysis along these lines has been devoted to an exploration of how gender structures the enjoyment of penetrative intercourse and how each of the study communities has devised limited strategies that challenge the centrality of penetrative intercourse with new pleasures. I have merely skimmed the surface here, but my data suggest some preliminary conclusions. First, prohibition seems merely to increase the erotic appeal of penetrative intercourse rather than diminish it; second, the limited successes in decentering the erotic appeal on intercourse—for example, the Bear hug and various S/M practices—I have documented here all draw on strategies that supplement rather than supplant intercourse with novel erotic practices; and third, these strategies all entail, to some degree, challenging genitally centered understandings of pleasure by disbursing pleasures across the body. Specific areas requiring further study include the process of sexual innovation, how and whether innovate practices are supported and extended at the microsocial level, how these microsocial settings generate desire for innovative pleasures, how this microsocial process is structured by macrosocial arrangements, and how the experience of new pleasures is facilitated by their collective construction as natural. With respect to gender's role in this process, I find the pansexual community remarkable for what it is able to ignore. That community, which I mention briefly in chapter 5, on leather culture, is a fascinating example of a "degendered" sexual culture. Here sexual orientation and gender take a back seat to a shared erotic interest in specific practices and techniques. As one of my interview subjects suggested, a typical pansexual "play party" might include men, women, transsexuals, heterosexuals, lesbians, gay men, married people, or singles. We need to know much more about the nature of the desire generated in these communities and the processes that facilitate this desire, what distinguishes these pansexual "players" from the gay/queer identified subjects of this study, and what all these factors might mean for the deliberate redirection of gendered pleasures and the degendering of traditional pleasures.

Notes

1. The term is Judith Butler's (1990), referring to practices or speech acts that challenge and disrupt the taken-for-granted relationships between genitals, sex, gender, and sexual orientation.

2. Those familiar with Connell's work on hegemonic masculinity are encouraged to skip this note; it is intended for those seeking more information on this basic concept. In a recent reassessment of the concept of hegemonic masculinity, Connell and Messerschmidt (2005, 846) reaffirm their faith in its constitutive components: "The fundamental feature of the concept remains the combination of the plurality of masculinities and the hierarchy of masculinities. This basic idea has stood up well in 20 years of research experience." Connell is best known for developing the concept through a series of empirical studies she conducted in the early 1980s. Rather than trying to develop an exhaustive typology that included all of the various masculinities and their characteristics (a futile task, since, according to Connell, these multiple masculinities are always changing), she tried to theorize the relationships between different masculinities. Thus the concept seeks to avoid reifying masculinity by deemphasizing the specific properties of particular masculinities ("real men don't eat quiche," etc.) and emphasizing how the relationships between these various masculinities are socially organized. The term "hegemonic" draws on the work of the famous Italian political theorist Antonio Gramsci (1971). Hegemony "refers to the cultural dynamic by which a group claims and sustains a leading position in social life" (Connell

1995, 77). This position is held not by force but through the consent (and often the active participation) of those involved. Thus hegemonic masculinity is whatever form of masculinity a society upholds as the cultural ideal—the kind of man all "real men" want to be. Connell argues that this dominant form of masculinity is largely shaped by institutionalized power arrangements in the top levels of business, government, and the military. While hegemonic masculinity designates the form of masculinity that is likely to dominate in a particular society, within groups of men a definite "pecking order" is in place that evaluates masculinities that deviate in significant ways from the ideal (hegemonic) form. The most obvious example of a subordinate masculinity is the cultural stigmatization of gay men. This line of thinking equates male homosexuality with femininity, which, according to some gay theorists, accounts for the ferocity of some homophobic attacks (Connell 1995, 78). However, gay masculinity is not the only form of subordinate masculinity. Heterosexual men and boys who deviate in significant ways from the ideal are also stigmatized, which again registers a symbolic blurring with femininity. Connell (1995, 79) provides a list of derisive terms used to illustrate this connection: wimp, nerd, turkey, sissy, lily liver, jellyfish, yellowbelly, candy ass, pushover, cream puff, panty waist, mama's boy, dweeb, geek, etc. This process of feminization extends to the body through the notion of "body reflexive practices" (Connell 1987, 1995).

3. For example, Messner (1997) has examined how masculinities are reinterpreted in communities emerging from the mythopoetic men's movement, the Christian Promise Keepers, men's liberation, and feminist men's movements. Taylor and Whittier (1992) researched collective identity formation in social movement communities, concentrating on lesbian feminism. Affected by shifts in two related but distinct movements (gay liberation and liberal feminism), they argue that lesbian feminism functions as a movement abeyance structure, attracting more committed radical feminists unwilling to compromise with the liberal mainstream. Their findings also highlight the importance of gender in identity construction, in that feminism is deemed central to lesbian activism. These findings also suggest that in lesbians' relationship to gay men, gender may trump sexual orientation (Taylor and Whittier 1992, 121–22). Kessler (1998) and Preves (2003) have investigated identity construction among the intersexed, highlighting the challenges intersexed individuals face in a culture devoted to binary models of sex and gender. Kessler demonstrates how the presence of the intersexed reveals the constructed nature of gender and the sexed body, while Preves shows how the intersex community enables "intersex pride" and a platform from which to protest medical interventions. In her investigation of women in racist movement organizations, Blee (2002, 2004) examines gendered identity construction among women of the Ku Klux Klan and other right-wing extremist groups. While Blee sees these groups as contrary to their

interests, she shows how these women are able to negotiate the tension their presence in these groups often elicits and to craft identities that align women's rights rhetoric with racial and religious bigotry. Using a symbolic interactionist approach in her study of animal rights activists, Einwohner (2002) demonstrates how external claims made by those outside the movement affect the identity work taking place within it. Wilkins (2004a, 2004b) investigates identity construction among young women in youth cultures to demonstrate how they create identity opportunities through the violation of traditional norms of femininity. Goth women exercise this option through the cultivation of a more active feminine sexuality, while "Puerto Rican wannabes" establish a unique identity space for themselves primarily through racial and class transgressions.

4. For more on embracing the self in the research process, see Krieger (1985).

5. On the other hand, these situations may present a risk of what one ethnographer has identified as "over-rapport." See Miller (1952).

6. My thanks to Lisa Disch for bringing this point to my attention.

CHAPTER TWO

1. As Gregor (1985, 182) explains, the spirited misogyny of the Mehinaku culture may be linked to child-rearing practices: "The key to Mehinaku masculinity is the extraordinarily intense and sensual period of intimacy with the mother during the first years of life. At a time when male children in most cultures have discovered the differences between themselves and their mothers, a Mehinaku boy is still basking in an undiminished maternal warmth. With the arrival of a new sibling, he is evicted from the mother's hammock, and given (at best) second place at the breast. His conflicting feelings of anger and dependency are generalized to all women and become the basis of devaluing women and accepting the culture of masculinity. The boy's transition to manhood, however, is dearly bought. A part of him, as 'Tapir Woman' suggests, continues to yearn for the lost union with the mother. He must, however, be vigilant against such regressive and forbidden urges."

2. For a history of the current polarized view of gender in the West and its antecedent, see Laqueur (1990).

3. In *The Naked Civil Servant*, Quentin Crisp (1983, 1) provides an example of effeminacy experienced as master status: "As soon as I put [makeup] on, the rest of my life solidified around me like a plaster cast. From that moment on, my friends were anyone who could put up with the disgrace; my occupation, any job from which I was not given the sack; my playground, any café or restaurant from which I was not barred or any street corner from which the police did not move me on."

4. Personal correspondence, July 2006.

5. Gaudio (1996).

6. Here I present only the briefest of summaries of several excellent studies of ancient Greek and Roman effeminacies. The best of these appear in Dover (1989), Williams (1999), and Halperin (1990, 2002a).

7. Clearly, my working definition is derived from Foucauldian notions of discipline and normalization. Insofar as I have undertaken this study to identify possible areas of resistance and rereading in the historical record, my objectives are in line with various modes of queer theorizing. However, I am not so queer here as to apply the notion of effeminacy to the performative practice of masculinity (Butler 1990) on bodies sexed female (see Halberstam 1998). Such practices undoubtedly have a rich and complex history, but I would argue that conscious, reflexive identifications of such performative practices as *masculine* (as opposed to butch) are very recent. Thus, as a disciplinary device deployed in the service of a normalized masculinity, my history of effeminacies focuses on bodies sexed male. For an analysis of butch/femme relationships within contemporary lesbian cultures, see Weston (1996); for a more specific focus on femme identity, see the collection of essays edited by Newman (1995).

8. Greenberg (1988, 292) reports complaints of what I would term moral effeminacy from eleventh- and twelfth-century clerics: "The young men of the royal court had begun to wear long hair and women's clothing, and adopted effeminate mannerisms; it was this the monks found offensive." Ordericus Vitalis, a cleric in England at the time of the Norman conquest, "deplored the court of William Rufus, son of the Conqueror, where 'the effeminate predominated everywhere and reveled without restraint.'" He notes that such passages condemn homosexuality only incidentally: "their deepest preoccupation is with men dressing and acting like women" (Greenberg 1988, 293). Kimmel (1996, 176–77) presents evidence that Christ himself had to be rescued from charges of effeminacy as part of the "Muscular Christianity" movement of the late nineteenth and early twentieth centuries in England and the United States. The goal of the Muscular Christians was to transform Jesus from a "thin reedy man with long bony fingers and a lean face with soft, doelike eyes and a beatific countenance" into a "brawny carpenter, whose manly resolve challenged the idolaters, kicked the money changers out of the temple, and confronted the most powerful imperium ever assembled."

9. As Bray (1982, 82) explains, the molly house raids were sponsored in London by the Societies for the Reformation of Manners, "a crusading religious organization which played an important role in prosecuting sodomites, prostitutes and sabbath-breakers." As to the specific animus that led to the raids and the extent of punishment meted out to molly house patrons, Bray explains that this was not a matter of a change in the legal standing of such behavior, but rather in its increasing visibility: "There was now a continuing culture to be fixed on and an extension of the area in which homosexuality could be expressed and therefore recognized; clothes, gestures, language,

particular buildings and particular public places—all could be identified as having specifically homosexual connotations . . . it was this that brought upon it the persecution which for so long had been often no more than an unrealized potential. Its visibility was its bane" (Bray 1982, 92).

10. It occurs to me that this quaint historical example may serve to clarify some of Butler's (1993) ideas on the materiality of the body. Extending the notion of performativity from its more familiar association with drag to child-bearing serves to illustrate Butler's point that the body that is undeniably "there" at moments like childbirth is also coconstructed by performative practices. As Bech (1995, 188) remarks in his review of Butler's (1993) *Bodies That Matter*, "In this way, the 'material' i.e. the allegedly non-constructed sex and body, is inescapably co-constructed by the discursive; discourses establish a 'domain of intelligibility,' a framework for what can at all be spoken of and conceived as the sex and the body." From this perspective, the molly house birthing dramas can be seen as highlighting performative aspects of even the most "material" of bodily experiences.

11. This emphasis on morality should not be interpreted to mean that the level of hostility toward homosexual behaviors had necessarily increased. As Bray (1982, 92) notes, "It is not that homosexuality was more fiercely disapproved of. There is no evidence whatsoever of any absolute increase in hostility to homosexuality. The vitriolic condemnations of it to be read in the sixteenth- and seventeenth-century literature are not one whit less vicious than those of the following century. Indeed it is difficult to see how those of the eighteenth century could be any more violent. The change is not absolute but rather in the extent to which people actually came up against that hostility; and the reason for the change is not in the hostility but in its object. There was now a continuing culture to be fixed on."

12. Thus it would seem that, in terms of advancing less restrictive understandings of gender and masculinity, the effeminate practices within the molly houses did little more than move an outraged "general public" toward a renewed investment in normative masculinity. For a critique of drag and gender parody as a transgressive political strategy, see Lloyd (1999).

13. Laqueur (1990) demonstrates that scientists moved from viewing the male and female bodies as essentially the same (with the female form being a "less developed" form of the male) to one that emphasized the radical differences in their sexed bodies and dispositions.

CHAPTER THREE

1. Although the vast majority of those attending the Faerie functions I observed were male, a small number of women attended as well. For example, of the approximately fifty-five attendees at the ten-day gathering, four were women. Of these, all had attended a gathering previously and were well known to at least some members of the community. From what I could

tell, no major issues arose involving women's participation. Identification as a Faerie was not limited to men, and women received the same welcome extended to everyone else.

2. At this writing an active movement is taking place among members of the community I studied to establish a permanent Faerie space within a nearby city, which would include a communal living arrangement. Other communities have made similar efforts with some success.

3. I am loath to dredge up this distressing episode, the memory having mercifully settled to the very depths of my subconscious. However, in the interest of full disclosure I must admit that this latter episode probably left lasting psychological scars. To be precise I dressed that Halloween as *samurai* Barbara Bush; my disguise combined characteristics of the esteemed former first lady (wig, pearls, makeup) and the John Belushi character from the old *Saturday Night Live* skits (a friend's judo robe and a plastic samurai sword). My intention was to craft a persona puzzling enough to prompt inquiries from handsome young men ("So, big boy, what are you supposed to be?") and provide an opening for a variety of erotically charged flirtations throughout the evening. Imagine my horror when I discovered that my features were entirely legible, as I learned after being greeted several times from forty paces with a dismissive, "Oh look, here comes samurai Barbara Bush." Sensing my consternation, my beloved partner, Steve, tried to break the news to me gently, "Petie, you really, really look like her." This frightened me.

4. *RFD*'s evolving subcultural profile is reflected in a running joke about the magazine's title. Ostensibly a way to suggest its rural readership (Rural Free Delivery), the meaning of the initials is constantly being revised. With each new issue readers might discover that the magazine's title is "Really Feeling Divine," "Rustic Faerie Dreams," "Radical Faeries Digest," "Religious Fanatics Descend," and even, during the Gulf War, "Rutting for Disarmament" (Rodgers 1993, 17).

5. It is interesting, from a life-history perspective, to consider how this idea of "a life in exile" resonates with Faerie essentialism and the notion of a Faerie diaspora (see "What Is a Faerie?" below).

6. Here again it is interesting to speculate on how this dispersal of authority, which in the homophile days was a matter of practicality, came to be recast in Faerie culture in more philosophical and gendered terms. In both cases the commitment to decentralized authority contrasted with the reality of Hay's charismatic leadership.

7. The name marks another anticipation of Faerie culture. "Mattachine" is drawn from a number of secret sects that emerged in Europe during the fifteenth century to preserve the festivities associated with the Christian Feast of Fools (itself based on the festival of Saturnalia of Roman antiquity). Driven underground by both church and state prohibitions against the festivities, the all-male Mattachine Society (known as Mattasins in France, Mattaccino in Italy, and Mattachino in Spain) emphasized social satire

through a dance with staffs that parodied warfare and hypermasculine posturing. Timmons' (1990, 130) description includes "the flamboyant costumed jester who ridicules the false pretenses of society by his critical mocking cloaked in comic antics and graceful dances." A contemporary Faerie gathering might be described in very similar terms. Note also the link with the notion of the Faerie diaspora, in that the original Mattachines were a culture driven underground.

8. As a white man attending Howard University (a historically black college), Kilhefner most likely received an extensive education about racism in American society and brought these insights to his pioneering work with the Radical Faeries. However, my research did not yield any direct evidence of this.

9. A notable exception from my field notes proves this rule regarding generally lowered identity volume outside the sanctuary. In Brekhus's (2003) terms, Lotus was perhaps the most high-density/high-duration Faerie I encountered during my fieldwork. Prior to a trip home from the sanctuary, he asked if I could give him a ride and if we could make a few stops along the way. "I let him know that I'd like to leave as soon as possible, since we have several 'errands' (his) to attend to on the way down (we need to stop off at a bank and fax a notarized copy of something to his roommate in town). Before I know it I am saying goodbye to everyone. I'm a bit surprised to see that Lotus has chosen to dress in a 'do rag' and a 'granny' skirt for the trip home. I make no mention of this, but I'm back in my "boy drag" (I've packed my skirt and yellow housedress). We stop in the first town, but the first bank doesn't have a notary. While Lotus is in the first bank, I get us some coffee. After we finally take care of business at a second bank, he returns to the car jubilant because the bank workers really liked his skirt." Again, this incident is distinguished by the fact that it was so unusual. My general impression was that most Faeries do not maintain such high-identity volume off of sanctuary land.

10. Hay (1987) further shows his hand when he reinvokes the binary with his concept of the "hag." He explains that these are "the proud and free women of the wildwood" (279) roughly analogous to Faeries. The clear indication is that men become Faeries and women become hags. Not surprisingly, few proud and free women found the moniker appealing.

11. This note is intended for those seeking some background on Butler's theoretical treatment of gender. Those familiar with her work will find nothing new here. In her best-known work, *Gender Trouble* (1990), Butler argues against the line of thinking originally advanced by Simone de Beauvoir (1989) and celebrated in the identity politics that informs much of second-wave feminism. In Butler's view, gender is not simply a cultural artifact constructed on the bedrock of two distinct, unconstructed sexes that exist as uncontestable biological categories. On the contrary, the startling alternative she advances is that both sex and gender are constructed categories;

sex is "always already" gender. From this perspective, Beauvoir's notion of "becoming" a woman implies an a priori sexual subjectivity that is then "gendered" through a socialization process. This is precisely the assumption that Butler (1990, 7) wishes to challenge: "It would make no sense, then, to define gender as the cultural interpretation of sex, if sex itself is a gendered category." Critics have charged that while this theoretical reconfiguration opens up exciting avenues of thought, it leaves the concept of gender largely undefined. Mary McIntosh (1991, 114) remarks that "If, as Butler claims, 'The ostensible natural facts of sex are discursively produced by various scientific discourses,' what follows is not that sex was 'gender all along,' but that both 'sex' and 'gender' are meaningless." Butler (1993) responds by arguing that gender is only meaningless in terms of substance; indeed, one of her central claims is that gender is all surface and no substance. It consistently (and falsely) presents itself as the natural consequence of biological sex. Butler's point is that the apparent interiority of gender is derived not from nature but from performativity. This concept, drawn from the work of British linguistic philosopher J. L. Austin (1962, 1970), defines a class of speech utterances that qualify as actions in and of themselves. Simply by way of producing the utterance, the thing described is brought into being (e.g., "I bet ten dollars," or "I hereby christen this ship," or "I now pronounce you man and wife"). Butler draws an analogy between this linguistic production of action through utterance and the discursive production of gender through repeated, historically sedimented gender performances (involving dress, movement, gestures, voice, and habits in addition to language) such that "There is no gender identity behind the expressions of gender; that identity is performatively constituted by the very 'expressions' that are said to be its results (Butler 1990, 25). As we move through the world in gendered ways, we are not simply expressing an essential truth about ourselves that is a natural consequence of biological sex; we are, conversely, actively reinforcing and perpetuating the illusion that gender possesses just this interiority and connection to the natural. This way of moving in the world obscures not only the constructed nature of the connection between sex and gender but also the primacy of gender in sexual subjectivity. The example Butler offers of gender performativity par excellence is drag. Drag reveals the performative nature of gender through parody, but Butler takes pains to remind us that what drag mocks is itself a parody. Thus the relation between a drag gender performance and more traditional gender performances is not one of copy to original but rather one of copy to copy. In this way traditional gender performances lose some of their claim to authenticity, because as Hood-Williams and Harrison (1998, 80) observe, "The true, the genuine, the serious performative is always at risk of potential ruin from the parodic or non-serious."

12. Morgensen (2005) is critical of precisely this type of cultural appropriation in his research on a different Faerie community. From the inception of the

Faerie movement he argues that "Hay and his followers racialized radical faerie culture as a normatively white imaginary of indigeneity, whose participants could become more like indigenous people than the inheritors of settlement most otherwise were destined to be. Such claims offered gay men, and, in masculinist extrapolations, all lesbian, bi, and trans people authentic cultural roots as well as belonging to all nations born on stolen land" (Morgensen 2005, 258).

13. Hay clearly made connections between an evolving understanding of himself as a gay man and his political convictions, as he spoke of "newer levels of Marxist perceptions which were emerging in me as gay values" (Timmons 1990, 255).

14. The popularity of the idea was not confined to Hay and his immediate friends, as evidenced by this passage from Timmons (1990, 257): "Harry's ideas captured the imagination of many who found in the concept of subject-subject consciousness a deeply felt yet unspoken truth. The argument that there existed a gay reservoir of untapped potential was refreshing to those for whom ghetto liberation had grown hollow. Continuing his tendency to take up the baton of such thinkers as Walt Whitman and Edward Carpenter, Harry posed that homosexuals carried an intermediary consciousness and that once this was made clear, a new era would begin." Also in evidence is this passage from a Faerie sexual manifesto: "Always take hold of your sex with love . . . I don't wish to compete with them, trick, trip or trounce them. I don't think of them as objects to acquire. They are shining substance of my own godbody flesh" (Broughton 1991, 44).

15. Hay regularly said that the exploitive or sadistic people one ran into in gay bars the world over "were simply not really gay" (Timmons 1990, 270).

16. More on clones from Timmons (1990, 253): "In the sexually active age-bracket, the clone was athletic, square-jawed, and swinging. His trumpeted masculinity was almost caricatured: Muscles, mustaches, mirrored 'cop' sunglasses, bomber jacket, and boots became a veritable uniform for the scores of gay men so identified. (The gay painter Buddha John Parker christened this rampant new breed as 'male impersonators.') Fashions, urban hot-spots, and, in that pre-AIDS decade, sex itself were steadily packaged by ever-creative marketers. Because their gay identities had been delayed, clones were perfect consumers, ever living out long-suppressed fantasies. This emphasized such a restless materialist outlook that many gay men complained that the chase from object to object tainted their ability to achieve intimacy in relationships. The dubious ideal of the clone was, in reality, only a high-profile minority of homosexuals; nevertheless it was widely emulated." On the other hand, many gay men of this period reveled in this sexual carnival of equal-opportunity objectification, as I suggest below. For more on the gay clone, see Levine (1998).

17. The fact that designating someone as a "granny" suggests an elevated social status is an indication of the Faeries' rejection of ageism. My experience in

the field indicates that the community pays more than lip service to this idea, as there seemed to be no substantive divisions among Faeries based on age. There are probably several reasons for Faeries' reverence for age. First, it is consistent with the broader Faerie commitment to egalitarianism. The fact that Harry Hay was nearly seventy years old at the first Faerie gathering in 1980 probably also plays a part. Perhaps the most potent explanatory factor is the demographic profile of the majority of the membership. Many Faeries are baby boomers, and I suspect this reverence for age is part of a strategy to redefine the aging process, a concern shared by the generation as a whole. Each of my case study communities exhibited this tendency to redefine older men in positive terms, and each is composed primarily of baby boomers. I return to this point in Chapter 6.

18. At this writing the literature on drag and gender resistance is expanding rapidly. It all started with Esther Newton's groundbreaking pre-Stonewall study of drag queens, *Mother Camp* (1972). In the last decade, much of the work in this area problematizes drag as a resistant process. For a sampling, see Brubach and O'Brien (1999), Schacht (2000, 2002), and Tewksbury (1994). For a more focused analysis of the potential political deployment of drag, see Rupp and Taylor (2003). For a theoretical treatment, see Butler (1990, 1993). Finally, for examinations of the disruptive potential of masculine drag, see Halberstam (1998) and Troka, Lebesco, and Noble (2003).

19. See Pickett (2000) for an excellent photo documentary.

20. I am grateful to an anonymous reviewer for this insight.

21. Timmons (1990, 249) reports that the words were recited at the first Faerie gathering by "a young, hardened street person from San Diego," who attributed them to Genet. I have been unable to verify the source.

CHAPTER FOUR

1. The Web site is http://www.resourcesforbears.com/CLUBS/US.html.

2. In what follows, sources or commentary not specifically attributed to a member of the Friendly Bears should be understood as applying to or coming from the broader national community of Bears or writers commenting on the same.

3. Again, my prior association with the Friendly Bears made the observation of sexual activity relatively unproblematic. I was an occasional participant in these parties before I began my research, so formal observation entailed simply introducing a higher degree of methodological rigor to a familiar activity. As was the case at other (nonsexual) observation sites, I recorded extensive field notes as soon after leaving the site as possible. The sexual nature of observations made confidentiality an especially important issue, but I saw little reason for additional concern. As a sex-positive community, play parties like the ones observed in this study have been a central component of Bear culture since its inception (Wright 1997d), and many Bears are frank about participating in them. However, I found a range of attitudes

about this type of activity among the Friendly Bears. Two of my interview subjects characterized themselves as "vanilla" (conservative) in their sexual tastes. In addition, in his study of Bear erotica, McCann (2001) characterized Bear culture as sexually conservative. The conservative characterization did not go unchallenged, however. One of my subjects (Travis) described Bear culture as "almost no holds barred." Another (Franklin) confessed his bewilderment at the popularity of open (nonmonogamous) relationships among Bears.

4. This recalls Gergen's (1991, 74) concept of multiphrenia, which he describes as "a result of the populated self's efforts to exploit the technologies of relationship." Bears, far more than my other two case study communities, put these technologies at the center of their group interactions. The Bear code, the flourishing online aspects of the community, and the proliferation of Web sites featuring individual Bear profiles (including pictures and profiles) speak to this core method of interaction. However, all this frenetic technology-based communication is comfortably nestled within certain central assumptions about Bear culture: a rejection of body fascism, a gregarious interest in other Bears that extends beyond sexual interest, and a commitment to a conventionally masculine presentation of self.

5. Les Wright has dedicated a good portion of his career to chronicling and preserving Bear culture. In addition to editing two wide-ranging volumes of essays on Bears (1997, 2001), he also runs the Bear History Project and a collection of Bear memorabilia, the Bear Icons Project.

6. It seems to me that the emphasis here is clearly on recuperation, in that the concept "bear" succeeded so stunningly where "husky" did not (or in Bourdieu's [2001] terminology, "husky" lacked the elaborate gender homology that "bear" suggested), possibly by linking Bear culture to the various back-to-nature moves that had been staged at various points in American history (see above). Perhaps the strongest appeal was the fact that these earlier movements were launched by (presumably) heterosexual men. In this way the Bear reaction can be seen as almost the antithesis of the angry drag queens who rose up at Stonewall. By demanding acceptance of their feminized bodies, the drag queens emphasized the connection between a marginalized effeminacy and stigmatized homosexuality: "We demand acceptance because our exclusion is based on an unjustifiable intolerance of difference." The Bear movement, on the other hand, seeks to emphasize a connection between a naturalized homosexuality and a normative masculinity: "We demand acceptance because we've been misperceived—we're *not* different."

7. It would be difficult to exaggerate the extent of Bear commodification. As an example, in *The Bear Book II*, Jack Fritscher's foreword appears with the byline, "by www.JackFritscher.com." At this writing the Web site is active and features promotions for Fritscher's books.

8. I found no evidence of this iconography in my research on the Faeries.

9. For example, Fritscher, in reference to real bears, says, "They think bears are fat, but bears are big, they're not fat" (Suresha 2002b, 94).

10. Wilgoren cites the specific example of Boston, where the Girth and Mirth chapter thrived from 1986 to 1991 and then headed into a "downhill spiral" just as Bear groups began to be seen as a viable alternative (Suresha 2002b, 74). Again, one reason for the out-migration from Girth and Mirth may be the more successful strategy employed by the Bears in eroticizing and masculinizing the bigger body by linking it with nature and a return to the wild.

11. It is important to remember that Kelly and Kane (2001) are referring to an early phase of the pandemic when wasting syndrome was common. Ironically, many of the treatments used at this writing include steroids, which can actually enhance the body's bulk and muscle composition.

12. The exclamation "woof!" is used by Bears as a physical complement (see chapter 1). Thus a man who is woofy would be considered an attractive Bear.

13. This has important implications for Brekhus's (2003) concept of identity-potent settings as well. In a sense, the most potent identity setting for Bears is the everyday social world shared by all. It is here that the Bear strategy of concentration on identity dilution is tested. Are they able to pass as just regular guys? In a narrower sense, events like the Bear Camp I attended and the various Bear runs sponsored by clubs across the country do serve as more potent identity settings. Still, I would argue that of my three case study communities, setting matters least for Bears. The more potent identity settings are much less likely to produce radically altered presentations of self for Bears, but they are likely to encourage more open demonstrations of affection for their fellows, including amorous physical contact (as in the group "Bear hug" described below).

14. The habitus occupies a central place in Bourdieu's thought. Along with the concepts of "field" and "capital," it forms the backbone of Bourdieu's perspective on the social world. Over time Bourdieu has provided various "shorthand" descriptions of the habitus, including "cultural unconsciousness," a "habit-forming force," a "set of basic, deeply-interiorized master-patterns," a "mental habit," and a "generative principle of regulated impro-visations" (Swartz 1997, 101). The important concept to remember is that the habitus represents not only a set of cognitive understandings or orienta-tions toward the world but also the *embodiment* of these understandings. Bourdieu highlights as an indicator of social class, often operating subcon-sciously, the fact that habitus is evident in how a person presents physically. He offers an expanded definition of habitus in a frequently cited passage that is typical of a writing style that has been characterized as diabolical: "[Habitus is a] system of durable, transposable dispositions, structured structures predisposed to function as structuring structures, that is, as prin-ciples which generate and organize practices and representations that can

be objectively adapted to their outcomes without presupposing a conscious aiming at ends or an express mastery of the operations necessary in order to attain them" (Bourdieu 1990b, 53). Habitus is *durable* in that it represents a set of dispositions that individual actors use to orient themselves toward the world and upon which they draw in performing various actions. As such they are (for the most part) inculcated in childhood and fairly resistant to change. Elsewhere Bourdieu has implied that subsequent experiences of individuals or dramatic changes in objective conditions may transform the habitus, but he does not seem to provide much detail as to exactly when or how this happens. The dispositions of the habitus are *transposable* in that they allow the actor to transfer a set of dispositions to a widely varying set of circumstances. The best illustration of this point that I encountered used an analogy to handwriting, a disposition to form letters in a particular way. Handwriting is a transposable disposition in that I will write in roughly the same fashion whether I am using pen and paper or writing a message in wet sand using a stick. Surely gender dispositions display this same type of durability. I would suggest that while the socially constructed nature of these gendered dispositions is relatively easy to identify with respect to gendered habits and attitudes, it is less apparent when considering the durability of the body's gendered capacities for pleasure. How gender socialization structures embodied pleasures is a neglected topic within childhood socialization research (probably in large part due to cultural anxieties associated with children's sexuality), but the few empirical studies that exist suggest that the gendered disciplining of the body's sensations begins at birth (Tauber 1979; Rubin, Provenzano and Luria 1974).

Furthermore, habitus is transposable with respect to gender through the application of the basic principles of phallocentricism. This application allows the gendered individual to adapt to novel situations (e.g., the man who has lost his way on a road trip can use his gendered habitus to interpret a specific situation and determine whether or not he may permit himself to stop and ask for directions) and, absent the countervailing influence of a dissident sexual community, how he ought to experience new sensations (e.g., phallocentrism might permit a man who identifies as "straight" to enjoy being fellated by another man under certain circumstances but would never allow him to enjoy the role of fellator). The habitus is a *structuring structure* in that it provides an improvisational framework to guide an individual actor's choice of actions. The habitus has also been described as *generative* in nature in that it generates a set of possible actions or ideas in response to circumstances occurring within a particular set of objective relations (in this case, patriarchal relations informed by phallocentrism).

The habitus is a *structured structure* in that it is formulated under a specific set of objective conditions. As such, it serves, in Bourdieu's thought, the link between objective social conditions and actual human practice. Three points are in order here. The first is that the way the habitus is constructed tends to reproduce existing objective relations; it is developed from the internalization of a particular social class or group with regard to their understanding of their own objective life chances. The second point to be made is that this process is not a deliberate one. Finally, the habitus operates *outside of language*: "The schemes of the habitus, the primary forms of classification, owe their specific efficacy to the fact that they function below the level of consciousness and language, beyond the reach of introspective scrutiny or control by the will" (Bourdieu 1990, 32).

15. I deal with only three of these in this section: "rites of institutions," the "symbolic remaking of anatomical differences," and "the rites affecting the masculinization of boys and feminization of girls." The significance of the fourth subprocess, the "symbolic coding of the sexual act," is elaborated in the next section on Bear sexual culture.

16. During my time in the field I also observed more than one man who literally growled during sexual activity, something I have not observed outside of the Bear community.

17. Connell (1995, 143–63) makes a similar point with her concept of "the very straight gay."

18. Again, several accounts characterize Bear culture as sexually conservative, including McCann (2001) and two of my interview subjects, who characterized themselves as "vanilla" (conservative) in their sexual tastes. This cultural feature may be easily obscured by what follows, in that many of the settings I observed included open sexual displays, and many of my interview subjects were very explicit in their discussions of Bear sexuality. The conservative characterization did not go unchallenged, however, as I indicate in note 3 above.

19. Hocquenghem's work is of particular relevance to this study because his theoretical focus is on gay men (indeed, his work has been criticized by some who complain that his approach renders lesbianism invisible), and his work explicitly links desire with social structure through capitalism and the family. Furthermore, he is provocative in his elaboration of Gilles Deleuze and Felix Guattari's work in *Anti-Oedipus* (1977) through his conception of "the sublimated anus." As an alternative to the oedipal images of sexuality and the erotic that they wish to critique, Deleuze and Guattari propose the notion of an ensemble of "desiring machines" beyond the reach of the Oedipus complex. Paradoxically, this idea is perhaps best captured through Freud's concept of polymorphous perversity: "Infinite types and varieties of relationships are possible; each person's machine parts can plug into and unplug from machine parts of another" (Weeks 1996, 31). Deleuze and Guattari see the oedipal perspective on sexuality not so much as something Freud discovered but rather as a useful social construction and powerful method of social control. Its disciplinary function acts to restrict perceptions of "normal" sex to the phallocentric, genital sex practiced by heterosexual, married couples. "Psychoanalysis, by accepting the familial frame-

work, is trapped *within* capitalist concepts of sexuality . . . So Freudianism plays a key role under capitalism: it is both the discoverer of the mechanisms of desire, and the organizer, through its acceptance of the Oedipus complex, of its control" (Weeks 1996, 31–32; emphasis in original). In this view, familial order is maintained by the father acting as family despot, juxtaposed with the image of the mother as representative of earth and country. "Thus the privatized 'individual' that psychoanalysis studies within the Oedipal family unit is an artificial construct, whose social function is to trap and control the disorder that haunts social life under capitalism" (Weeks 1996, 32). Using these ideas as a point of departure, Hocquenghem goes on to argue that "homosexuality expresses an aspect of desire which is fundamentally polymorphous and undefined, which appears nowhere else, and that is more than just sexual activity between members of the same sex. *For the direct manifestation of homosexual desire opposes the relations of roles and identities necessarily imposed by the Oedipus complex* in order to ensure the reproduction of society (Weeks 1996, 35; emphasis added). In what follows I argue that in fact the roles and identities assumed in gay sexual relationships reproduce certain heteronormative patterns and that in many instances the pleasure experienced in sex is a direct result of the structuring effects of hegemonic masculinity. Hocquenghem, on the other hand, sees the pleasures afforded by gay sex as directly attributable to a rejection of the phallus. On this view gay men revel in their dissident sexual status through "the operation of a desiring machine 'plugged into the anus'" (Weeks 1996, 39). In "Capitalism, the Family and the Anus" (chapter 4 of *Homosexual Desire*) Hocquenghem (1996, 93) demonstrates the significance of such a move by mapping the connections between private pleasures and social structures, theorizing that "Capitalist ideology's strongest weapon is its transformation of the Oedipus complex into a social characteristic, and internalization of oppression which is left free to develop." His major insight here is that "Whereas the phallus is essentially social, the anus is essentially private" (96). Capitalism organizes the desiring function of the anus out of its cosmology, leaving it with nothing but an eminently private, excremental function. Here Hocquenghem notes that "Freud sees the anal stage as the stage of formation of the person" (96). However, under capitalism the formation of persons must include the production of a sense of inviolable individuality, along with the "proper" understanding of both money and ownership. Here, what Hocquenghem calls the "sublimated anus" (95) is crucial because, like money, "Your excrement is yours and yours alone; what you do with it is your business" (97). Furthermore, "Control of the anus is the precondition of taking responsibility for property. The ability to 'hold back' or to evacuate the faeces is the necessary moment of the constitution of the self" (99).

It is through this reading of the Oedipus complex that bourgeois familial socialization comes to be seen as a critical ideological component of capitalism.

To escape this "Oedipus hex," as it were, Hocquenghem (1996, 110) proposes what he calls homosexual "groupings," communities of dissident sexual desire where "the desiring 'grouping' of the anus, would cause the collapse of both the sublimating phallic hierarchy and the individual/society double-bind." Perhaps more than any of his contemporaries, Hocquenghem seems to have recognized the revolutionary potential inherent in gay liberation, advocating nothing short of just such a "revolution of desire." My argument is that despite gay liberation and, subsequently, the powerful disruptions of the AIDS pandemic, Hocquenghem's revolution of desire has only partially materialized. In the chapters that follow I present evidence that indicates more specifically that Hocquenghem has not adequately problematized the liberation of the sublimated anus as a site of pleasure (one that escapes oedipalization). On the other hand, I consider my three case study communities as at least partially successful examples of (or at least analogous to) Hocquenghem's homosexual groupings.

20. Burt's status among the Friendly Bears is significant here, given his resistant sexual philosophy. In addition to being a longtime member, Burt served for several years as an officer of the club. The overwhelming impression I received from my time in the field is that he is an admired, a highly respected, and a beloved member of this community.

21. Insofar as power and dominance are understood as desirable attributes, this assumption about the relationship between older Bears and younger Cubs challenges ageism, as is the case with the Faeries' reverence for grannies. Furthermore, the fact that "Polar Bear" (an older Bear with gray or white hair) is a widely recognized identity subcategory in this community suggests that Bears are age inclusive. Again, my time in the field suggests that this is more than an ideological commitment; it is, at least among the Friendly Bears, part of their everyday interactions.

22. For an extended critique of the normalization of gay culture, see Warner (1999).

CHAPTER FIVE

1. To be more precise, the Sentinels sponsor either a campout or a "run" every summer. The term "run" comes from the club's roots in motorcycle (biker) culture, where these types of events usually involved a long trek on a motorcycle to visit another club. Most leathermen no longer ride motorcycles, but the terminology is used by gay leather clubs across the country. A run will typically attract more men (approximately a hundred) from a wider geographical area than a campout (which is primarily attended by club members and their friends). Sentinel runs take place every other year and include more formally organized activities, including opening and closing ceremonies. The event I attended was a campout with approximately twenty-five men in attendance.

2. In this chapter I use the terms "leather" and "leather culture" to indicate broad cultural formations centered on the fetishization of leather. As subsets of the leather community, my particular focus in this chapter is on gay leather sadomasochism or, more precisely, gay leather bondage, discipline, and sadomasochism. Sadomasochism typically involves the eroticization of power role plays and pain. Bondage and discipline typically do not involve pain; here the emphasis is on restraint, submission, and trust. "Kink" is a term employed to describe a wide variety of nonnormative sex practices, including (but not limited to) role playing, spanking, flogging, whipping, paddling, nonpermanent piercings, and use of electricity. All of these practices are informed by the motto "safe, sane and consensual." By convention, coercion in leather scenes is prohibited. Training in leather practice includes education regarding the possible risks involved (including, but by no means limited to, the risk of HIV transmission) and how to minimize them. This motto is not peculiar to the Sentinels but is a norm informing leather culture generally.

3. Brekhus's (2003) work is especially useful here. It is probably safe to describe gay men who only occasionally indulge a fetishistic or "hobby" interest in leather as exhibiting low-identity dominance (low duration, low density). Men who are more seriously invested in leather (but not BDSM practices) probably qualify as exhibiting somewhat higher-identity dominance (high duration, low density) and leathermen drawn to extensive involvement in BDSM as registering high-identity dominance (high duration, high density).

4. Of course, sadomasochism has a history that precedes the formation of identity categories like "gay" by many centuries. The Leather Archives & Museum in Chicago distributes a timeline dating S/M back to antiquity, including references to the Marquis de Sade (1740–1814) and Britain's Hellfire Club (c. 1760).

5. During my time in the field I found evidence that despite the protean changes in gay male leather culture since the 1950s, many of the clubs still provide refuge for this same kind of war-wounded masculinity. Billy, the man mentioned in the opening to this chapter, strongly identifies with his status as a Vietnam veteran. He told me shortly after we met that he had been damaged by Agent Orange (for more on Billy, see below). Two other men I encountered while studying this community, although clearly in better mental and physical shape than Billy, also related strongly with their status as Vietnam vets. I found no connection whatsoever with military service in Faerie or Bear communities.

6. This material is drawn from a timeline provided by the Leather Archives & Museum in Chicago.

7. Here Harris (1997) conflates leather and S/M rather unproblematically. Not all men who like to dress in and/or eroticize leather are into S/M.

8. Tom of Finland is an artist famous for his homoerotic drawings of masculine icons such as policemen, sailors, soldiers, and motorcyclists. The term

"vanilla sex" is used to denote conventional, mainstream sexual activity. Included here would be garden-variety intercourse, fellatio, and mutual masturbation.

9. Of course all fetishes (sexual and nonsexual) are social to the extent that they are crafted from the psychic and symbolic raw materials gleaned from individual social experience. However, not all fetishes are closely affiliated with supportive communities, as is the case with leather.

10. For more on the feminist critique of S/M, see Linden (1982). For arguments in support of S/M from a feminist perspective, see Duggan and Hunter (1995) and Rubin (2003). For an argument that positions S/M as neither feminist nor antifeminist, see France (1984).

11. This view of the body as quasi machine recalls Haraway's (1991) cyborg and can be related to the eroticization of the motorcycle as machine in the early motorcycle clubs. For more on this perspective and how leather S/M facilitates an instrumental view of sex as mechanical process, see the section below titled "Hanging a Sling in the Iron Cage: Rationalization and the Production of Erotic Pleasure."

12. This provocative title is an interesting example of Hocquenghem's (1996) "desublimation of the anus."

13. This is somewhat at odds with my earlier remarks about the pansexual movement. See my discussion of the pansexual movement below.

14. While this may strike readers as escapist logic that simply denies the social reality that all gay men are feminized, this notion has a long history. Halperin (2002a) documents a masculinist reading of homosexuality as he comments on the *Erôtes*, a third- or fourth-century Greek dialogue concerning the relative merits of boys versus women as sex partners for adult males. In the debate between Charicles of Corinth, who favors women, and Callicratidas of Athens, who prefers boys, Halperin demonstrates that it is Charicles who is feminized. Conversely, Callicratidas's preference for boys "makes him more of a man; it does not weaken or subvert his male gender identity but rather consolidates it" (Halperin 2002a, 94). Moreover, this idea, to the extent that it succeeds within gay leather cultures, resurrects the eighteenth-century effeminate who becomes "womanlike" as a result of his sexual interest in women (see chapter 2).

15. While the pansexual leathermen I interviewed expressed no reservations about playing in mixed-sex spaces, others are not so accepting. I learned that at some events billed as pansexual, three separate play areas are established: men only, women only, and mixed space. I recently attended an all-male workshop in leather techniques hosted by a trainer well known on the national leather scene. He confessed after conducting a number of workshops for pansexual groups that "It's good to be back with men again."

16. This also suggests a certain generational tension between older and younger leathermen and may serve as another example of baby boomer anxiety

on the part of older leathermen. However, my time in the field indicates that among leathermen into S/M and bondage/discipline, training and experience matter a great deal. Furthermore, the admiration for the leather "daddy" suggests the same kind of associations with power and dominance that enhances the status of older Bears.

17. This document was obtained from the Leather Archives & Museum in Chicago.

18. My thanks to Karla Erickson for noting the charming parallels between these first three narratives of corruption/decline and anxieties attending the incursion of postmodernism in the academy, particularly in the social sciences and humanities. They represent a powerful challenge to traditional notions of academic expertise and credentialing, the disruption of "top down" power arrangements in many departments, the fluidity/instability of professional identity, and questions regarding the nature of "real" or "legitimate" scholarship and research.

19. According to an intriguing entry, part of a timeline I uncovered at the Leather Archives & Museum in Chicago, fisting was "invented" in a San Francisco basement in 1962. I have little information beyond this documentation, but this tantalizing bit of knowledge has some intriguing implications for the social construction of pleasure. An investigation of how this practice came to be understood as pleasurable, and how various dissident sexual communities have collectively nurtured and sustained this pleasure, would go a long way toward explaining how desire is generated socially.

20. Some of my interview subjects made an explicit distinction between sadomasochism and kink. As I mentioned at the beginning of this chapter, the latter is the general term subsuming a variety of fetishes and specialized sex practices.

21. Not surprisingly, there is also a detailed set of rules that governs interactions between dominants and submissives. A few examples can be found in a 1976 issue of *Drummer* magazine, entitled "Advice to a New Slave": "Obey your Master fully, immediately and silently (except for "Yes, Sir")," "Never question your Master in public," "Every statement or question directed to your Master should contain the word 'Sir,'" "Chairs and couches are forbidden to you from now on."

22. This illustrates the importance of the dungeon as what Brekhus (2003) would call an identity-potent setting. Furthermore, I suspect this potency is directly related to the degree of identity dominance exhibited by the individual leatherman (see note 3). The low-dominance hobbyist will be relatively unaffected (and may even be repelled) by the dungeon. The dungeon may spark some increase in identity density for the casual leather enthusiast, but for the invested leatherman actively participating in BDSM, the dungeon is a highly potent identity space.

23. This dichotomous organization of serious leather sex scenes into bottoms and top refers, of course, to individual scenes. As I mentioned earlier,

sometimes a great deal of fluidity is seen from one scene to the next, with the bottom from one scene topping in the next. Occasionally, an exchange of dominant and submissive roles may occur within a single scene; however, if this occurs, it is clearly recognized by the participants, who adjust their behavior accordingly. The point remains that despite the importation of significant role fluidity in leather culture, individual scenes continue to be structured by the dominant/submissive binary.

24. More on realness from Butler: "'Realness' is not exactly a category in which one competes; it is a standard used to judge any given performance within the established categories. And yet what determines the effect of realness is the ability to compel belief, to produce the naturalized effect. This effect is itself the result of an embodiment of norms, a reiteration of norms, an impersonation of a racial and class norm, a norm that is at once a figure, a figure of a body, which is no particular body but rather a morphological ideal that remains the standard that regulates the performance but that no performance fully approximates" (Butler 1993, 129). For more on authenticity in a very different setting, see Grazian (2003).

25. Lance's words suggest that the moment of connection between a leather top and a bottom can be interpreted as profoundly therapeutic. Against what Gergen (1991) sees as the fracturing of the self and the multiphrenetic demands of contemporary life, for the leatherman this moment of intense connection stands, both symbolically and realistically, as a temporary moment of pure concentration and powerfully enhanced connection.

26. Of course, the mere existence of leather culture has political implications, and I do not mean to suggest that in keeping a low political profile this culture does not present the larger culture with a set of political challenges. I am speaking here in the more narrow political sense of active political organizing and social protest. While many in the leather community are active with respect to a variety of gay, lesbian, bisexual, and transsexual issues, I see little evidence of the kind of aggressive political action sparked by religious fundamentalism, another type of profoundly moving and highly subjective experience. In any event, I do not mean to minimize the importance of the challenges that the mere existence of leather culture represents.

27. From the July 1970 issue of *Wheels!* describing a recent production of *Oh Sinderella!* at the club's recent run: "It was amazing that Sinderella ever made it to the ball considering all those toys, etc. The costume for the fairy godmother was not to be believed. (Loved the second ugly stepsister!)" Notes on the after-dinner entertainment included the following: "Material was presented from *Dames at Sea; New Girl in Town; Apple Tree;* and *Fade Out, Fade In . . .* plus a spectacular version of *Movie Star . . .* Special mention must be given to the infamous Swampy Sisters (Swampy, Stella, and Samantha) who forgot their Nair! . . . The patriotic finale was unbelievable! Red, white, and blue streamers (well, it WAS the 4th of July) and then

Swampy appeared from atop one of the walls of the set dressed to represent the Statue of Liberty." For more evidence of this playful attitude toward gay hypermasculinity as recently as the early 1980s, see Henley (1982).

CHAPTER SIX

1.   The Web site is http://www.columbusbears.org/ (accessed August 2002).

References

Almaguer, Tomas. 1991. "Chicano Men: A Cartography of Homosexual Identity and Behavior." *Differences* 3 (2): 75–100.

Austin, J. L. 1962. *How to Do Things with Words*. Oxford, UK: Clarendon Press.

———. 1970. *Philosophical Papers*. Oxford, UK: Clarendon Press.

Barebackjack.com. 2001. Home page. http://www.barebackjack .com (accessed November 12, 2001).

Bean, Joseph W. 2001 (1991). "The Spiritual Dimensions of Bondage." In *Leatherfolk: Radical Sex, People, Politics and Practice*, ed. Mark Thompson, 257–66. Los Angeles: Alyson Publications.

Beauvoir, Simone de. 1989 (1952). *The Second Sex*. New York: Alfred A. Knopf.

Bech, Henning. 1995. "Sexuality, Gender and Sociology." *Acta Sociologica* 38:187–92.

Becker, Howard. 1998a. "The Social Basis for Drug-Induced Experience." In *Inside Social Life*, ed. Spencer Cahill, 52–58. Los Angeles: Roxbury.

———. 1998b. *Tricks of the Trade: How to Think about Your Research While You're Doing It*. Chicago: University of Chicago Press.

Becker, Howard S. 1997 (1963). *Outsiders: Studies in the Sociology of Deviance*. New York: Simon and Schuster.

Becker, J. 1973. "Racism in Children's and Young People's Literature in the Western World." *Journal of Peace Research* 10 (3): 295–303.

Bederman, G. 1995. *Manliness and Civilization*. Chicago: University of Chicago Press.

Behar, Ruth. 1993. *Translated Woman: Crossing the Border with Esperanza's Story*. Boston: Beacon Press.

Bersani, Leo. 1987. "Is the Rectum a Grave?" In *AIDS: Cultural Analysis, Cultural Activism*, ed. Douglas Crimp, 197–222. Cambridge, MA: MIT Press.

Bérubé, Allan. 1989. "Marching to a Different Drummer: Lesbian and Gay GI's in World War II." In *Hidden from History: Reclaiming the Gay and Lesbian Past*, ed. Martin Duberman, Martha Vicinus, and George Chauncey, Jr., 383–94. New York: NAL Books.

Blachford, Gregg. 1979. "Looking at Pornography: Erotica and the Socialist Morality." *Radical America* 13 (1): 7–18.

———. 1981. "Male Dominance and the Gay World." In *The Making of the Modern Homosexual*, ed. Kenneth Plummer, 184–210. London: Hutchinson.

Blee, Kathleen M. 2002. "The Gendered Organization of Hate: Women in the U.S. Ku Klux Klan." In *Right-Wing Women: From Conservatives to Extremists Around the World*, ed. Paola Bacchetta and Margaret Power, 101–14. New York: Routledge.

———. 2004. "Women and Organized Racism." In *Home-Grown Hate: Gender and Organized Racism*, ed. Abby L. Ferber, 49–74. New York: Routledge.

Bologh, Roslyn Wallach. 1990. *Love or Greatness: Max Weber and Masculine Thinking—A Feminist Inquiry*. London: Unwin Hyman.

Bond, E. M. 1909. "The Cowman's Carnival." *Sunset* (August).

Bourdieu, Pierre. 1977. *Outline of a Theory of Practice*. Cambridge, UK: Cambridge University Press.

———. 1990a. *In Other Words: Essays towards a Reflexive Sociology*. Palo Alto, CA: Stanford University Press..

———. 1990b. *The Logic of Practice*. Cambridge, UK: Polity Press.

———. 1997. "The Goffman Prize Lecture: Masculine Domination Revisited." *The Berkeley Journal of Sociology* 41:189–203.

———. 2001. *Masculine Domination*. Stanford, CA: Stanford University Press.

Brannon, Robert. 1976. "The Male Sex Role: Our Culture's Blueprint of Manhood, and What It's Done for Us Lately." In *The Forty-Nine Percent Majority: The Male Sex Role*, ed. Deborah S. David and Robert Brannon, 1–48. Reading, MA: Adddison Wesley.

Braun, Virginia. 2005. "In Search of (Better) Sexual Pleasure: Female Genital 'Cosmetic' Surgery." *Sexualities* 8 (4): 407–24.

Bray, Alan. 1982. *Homosexuality in Renaissance England*. Boston: Gay Men's Press.

Brekhus, Wayne H. 2003. *Peacocks, Chameleons, Centaurs: Gay Suburbia and the Grammar of Social Identity*. Chicago: University of Chicago Press.

Briggs, C. L. 1986. *Learning How to Ask: A Sociolinguistic Appraisal of the Role of the Interview in Social Science Research*. Cambridge, UK: Cambridge University Press.

Bronski, Michael. 2001 (1991). "A Dream Is a Wish Your Heart Makes: Notes on the Materialization of Sexual Fantasy." In *Leatherfolk: Radical Sex, People, Politics and Practice*, ed. Mark Thompson, 56–64. Los Angeles: Alyson Publications.

Broughton, James. 1991. "The Holiness of Sexuality." *RFD* 68:43–46.

Brubach, Holly, and James Michael O'Brien. 1999. *Girlfriend: Men, Women, and Drag*. New York: Random House.

Burawoy, Michael. 1991. "The Extended Case Method." In *Ethnography Unbound: Power and Resistance in the Modern Metropolis*, 271–87. Berkeley: University of California Press.

Burkhart, Geoffrey. 1996. "Not Given to Personal Disclosure." In *Out in the Field: Reflections of Lesbian and Gay Anthropologists*, ed. Ellen Lewin and William L. Leap, 31–48. Urbana, IL: University of Illinois Press.

Burnside, John. 1989. *"Who Are the Gay People? And Other Essays*. San Francisco: Vortex Media.

Butler, Judith. 1990. *Gender Trouble: Feminism and the Subversion of Identity*. London: Routledge.

———. 1993. *Bodies that Matter: On the Discursive Limits of Sex*. New York: Routledge.

———. 2004. *Undoing Gender*. New York: Routledge.

Canada, Geoffrey. 1998. "Learning to Fight." In *Men's Lives*, 4th edition, ed. Michael S. Kimmel and Michael Messner, 122–26. Boston: Allyn and Bacon.

Caradoc. 1977. "Sharing the Mysteries." *RFD* 12:25–27.

Chauncey, George. 1994. *Gay New York: Gender, Urban Culture, and the Making of the Gay Male World, 1890–1940*. New York: Basic Books.

Chen, Chiung Hwang. 1996. "Feminization of Asian (American) Men in the U.S. Mass Media: An Analysis of the Ballad of Little Jo." *Journal of Communicative Inquiry* 20 (2): 57–71.

Chodorow, Nancy. 1994. *Femininities, Masculinities, Sexualities*. Lexington: University Press of Kentucky.

Circle of Loving Companions. 1975. "The Gays—Who Are We? Where Do We Come From? What Are We For?" *RFD* 5:38–41.

Cohn, Carol. 2000. "Wars, Wimps, and Women: Talking Gender and Thinking War." In *The Gendered Society Reader*, ed. Michael S. Kimmel and Amy Aronson, 362–74. New York: Oxford University Press.

Collins, Patricia Hill. 1990. *Black Feminist Thought: Knowledge, Consciousness, and the Politics of Empowerment*. New York: Routledge.

———. 2005. *Black Sexual Politics*. New York: Routledge.

Connell, R. W. 1987. *Gender and Power*. Stanford, CA: Stanford University Press.

———. 1995. *Masculinities*. Berkeley: University of California Press.

———. 2002. "The History of Masculinity," In *The Masculinity Studies Reader*, ed. Rachel Adams and David Savran, 245–61. Malden, MA: Blackwell.

Connell, R. W., and James W. Messerschmidt. 2005. "Hegemonic Masculinity: Rethinking the Concept." *Gender & Society* 19 (6): 829–59.

Corber, Robert J. 1997. *Homosexuality in Cold War America*. Durham, NC: Duke University Press.

Cory, Donald Webster. 1951. *The Homosexual in America: A Subjective Approach*. New York: Ayer.

Coser, Lewis A. 1977. *Masters of Sociological Thought*. Fort Worth, TX: Harcourt Brace Jovanovich.

Crisp, Quentin. 1983 (1968). *The Naked Civil Servant*. New York: Penguin Books.

Crow, Chenille. 1977. "The Clarity of St. Therese." *RFD* 12:34.

D'Emilio, John. 1983. *Sexual Politics, Sexual Communities: The Making of a Homosexual Minority in the United States, 1940–1970.* Chicago: University of Chicago Press.

D'Emilio, John, and Estelle B. Freedman. 1988. *Intimate Matters: A History of Sexuality in America.* New York: Harper and Row.

Davis, Simone Weil. 2002. "Loose Lips Sink Ships." *Feminist Studies* 28 (1): 7–35.

Deleuze, Gilles, and Felix Guattari. 1977. *Anti-Oedipus: Capitalism and Schizophrenia.* New York: Viking.

Denizet-Lewis, Benoit. 2003. "Double Lives on the Down Low." *New York Times Magazine,* August 3, 28–33.

Donahue, Bob, and Jeff Stoner. 1997. "The Natural Bears Classification System: A Classification System for Bears and Bearlike Men, Version 1.10." In *The Bear Book: Readings in the History and Evolution of a Gay Male Subculture,* ed. Les K. Wright, 149–56. New York: Harrington Park Press.

Douglas, J. 1985. *Creative Interviewing.* Beverly Hills, CA: Sage.

Dover, K. J. 1989 (1978). *Greek Homosexuality.* Cambridge, MA: Harvard University Press.

Dowling, Linda. 1993. "Esthetes and Effeminati." *Raritan* 12 (3): 52–68.

Drummer. 1976. "Drummer Goes to a Slave Auction." *Drummer* 1 (6): 12.

Duberman, Martin. 1993. *Stonewall.* New York: Plume.

Duggan, Lisa, and Nan D. Hunter. 1995. *Sex Wars: Sexual Dissent and Political Culture.* New York: Routledge.

Einwohner, Rachel L. 2002. "Bringing the Outsiders In: Opponents' Claims and Construction of Animal Rights Activists' Identity." *Mobilization* 7 (3): 253–68.

Englebert, C. 1977. "Footing a Foundation Alone." *RFD* 12:22.

Erber, Nancy. 1996. "The French Trials of Oscar Wilde." *Journal of the History of Sexuality* 6 (4): 549–88.

Espiritu, Yen Le. 2004. "All Men Are Not Created Equal: Asian Men in U.S. History." In *Men's Lives,* 6th edition, ed. Michael S. Kimmel and Michael A. Messner, 39–47. Boston: Pearson.

Eyerman, Ron, and Andrew Jamison. 1991. *Social Movements: A Cognitive Approach.* University Park: Pennsylvania State University Press.

Feirstein, Bruce. 1982. *Real Men Don't Eat Quiche.* New York: Pocket Books.

Floyd, Van Lynn. 1997. "Front Range Bears: A History." In *The Bear Book: Readings in the History and Evolution of a Gay Male Subculture,* ed. Les K. Wright, 187–90. New York: Harrington Park Press.

Foucault, Michel. 1990a (1978). *The History of Sexuality,* vol. I. New York: Vintage Books.

———. 1990b (1985). *The Use of Pleasure.* Vol. II of *The History of Sexuality.* New York: Random House.

———. 1995 (1977). *Discipline and Punish: The Birth of the Prison* New York: Vintage Books.

France, Marie. 1984. "Sadomasochism and Feminism." *Feminist Review* 16:35–42.

Fritscher, J. 2002. "Bearness's Beautiful Big Blank: Tracing the Genome of Urso-masculinity." In *Bears on Bears*, ed R. Suresha, 77–96. Los Angeles: Alyson Books.

Fritscher, Jack. 2000. "I am Curious (Leather)." In *The Leatherman's Handbook* by Larry Townshend, 9–22. Los Angeles: L. T. Publications.

Froelich, Mitch. 2001. "Houston Area Bears." In *The Bear Book II: Further Readings in the History and Evolution of a Gay Male Subculture*, ed. Les K. Wright, 233–42. New York: Harrington Park Press.

Fung, Richard. 2004. "Looking for My Penis: The Eroticized Asian in Gay Video Porn." In *Men's Lives,* 6th edition, ed. Michael S. Kimmel and Michael A. Messner, 543–52. Boston: Pearson.

Gamson, Joshua. 1995. "Must Identity Movements Self-Destruct? A Queer Dilemma." *Social Problems* 42 (3): 391–407.

———. 1996. "The Organizational Shaping of Collective Identity: The Case of Lesbian and Gay Film Festivals in New York." *Sociological Forum* 11 (2): 231–61.

———. 1997. "Messages of Exclusion: Gender, Movements and Symbolic Boundaries." *Gender & Society* 11 (2): 178–99.

———. 2000. "Sexualities, Queer Theory, and Qualitative Research." In *Handbook of Qualitative Research,* 2nd edition, ed. Norman K. Denzin and Yvonna S. Lincoln, 347–65. Thousand Oaks, CA: Sage.

Gan, Dave. 2001. "An Asian Bear in Minnesota." In *The Bear Book II: Further Readings in the History and Evolution of a Gay Male Subculture*, ed. Les K. Wright, 129–34. New York: Harrington Park Press.

Garner, Anna, Helen M. Sterk, and Shawn Adams. 1998. "Narrative Analysis of Sexual Etiquette in Teenage Magazines." *Journal of Communication* 48 (4): 59–78.

Gaudio, Rudolph. 1996. "Funny Muslims." Paper presented at the Fourth Berkeley Women and Language Conference, Berkeley, CA, April 19–21.

———. 1998. "Male Lesbians and Other Queer Notions in Hausa." In *Boy Wives and Female Husbands: Studies of African Homosexualities*, ed. Stephen O. Murray and Will Roscoe, 115–28. New York: St. Martin's Press.

———. 2001. "White Men Do It Too: Racialized (Homo)sexualities in Postcolonial Hausaland." *Journal of Linguistic Anthropology* 11 (1): 36–51.

Gergen, Kenneth. 1991. *The Saturated Self: Dilemmas of Identity in Contemporary Life*. New York: Basic Books.

Gilligan, Carol. 1982. *In a Different Voice*. Cambridge, MA: Harvard University Press.

Gilmore, David D. 1990. *Manhood in the Making: Cultural Concepts of Masculinity*. New Haven, CT: Yale University Press.

Gleason, Maud W. 1990. "The Semiotics of Gender: Physiognomy and Self-Fashioning in the Second Century C.E." In *Before Sexuality: The Construction of Erotic Experience in the Ancient Greek World*, ed. David M. Halperin, John J. Winkler, and Froma I. Zeitlin, 389–415 . Princeton, NJ: Princeton University Press.

Goecke, Tim. 2001. "East Coast Bear Hugz." In *The Bear Book II: Further Readings in the History and Evolution of a Gay Male Subculture*, ed. Les K. Wright, 185–90. New York: Harrington Park Press.

Gramsci, Antonio. 1971. *Selections from the Prison Notebooks*. New York: International Publishers.

Grazian, David. 2003. *Blue Chicago: The Search for Authenticity in Urban Blues Clubs*. Chicago: University of Chicago Press.

Greenberg, David F. 1988. *The Construction of Homosexuality*. Chicago: University of Chicago Press.

Gregor, Thomas. 1985. *Anxious Pleasures: The Sexual Lives of an Amazonian People*. Chicago: University of Chicago Press.

Halberstam, Judith. 1998. *Female Masculinity*. Durham, NC: Duke University Press.

Halperin, David M. 1990. *One Hundred Years of Homosexuality*. New York: Routledge.

———. 2002a. *How to Do the History of Homosexuality*. Chicago: University of Chicago Press.

Halperin, David. 2002b. "The Democratic Body: Prostitution and Citizenship in Classical Athens." In *The Masculinity Studies Reader*, ed. Rachel Adams and David Savran, 69–75. Malden, MA: Blackwell.

Haraway, Donna. 1991. *Simians, Cyborgs, and Women: The Reinvention of Nature*. New York: Routledge.

Harris, Daniel. 1997. *The Rise and Fall of Gay Culture*. New York: Hyperion.

Hay, Bob. 1997. "Bears in the Land Down Under." In *The Bear Book: Readings in the History and Evolution of a Gay Male Subculture*, ed. Les K. Wright, 225–38. New York: Harrington Park Press.

Hay, Harry. 1980. "Toward the New Frontiers of Fairy Vision: subject-SUBJECT Consciousness." *RFD* 24:29–34.

———. 1987. "A Separate People Whose Time Has Come." In *Gay Spirit: Myth and Meaning*, ed. Mark Thompson, 279–91. New York: St. Martin's Press.

Hay, Harry, and Don Kilhefner. 1979. "A Call to Gay Brothers: A Spiritual Conference for Radical Faeries." *RFD* 20:20.

Hemry, Mark. ed. 2001. *Tales from the Bear Cult*. San Francisco: Palm Drive Publishing.

Henley, Clark. 1982. *The Butch Manual*. New York: Sea Horse Press.

Hennen, Peter. 1996. "The Strange Case of Dr. Sagarin and Mr. Cory: A Biographical Approach to Document Analysis." Unpublished manuscript.

Herdt, Gilbert H. 1981. *Guardians of the Flutes*. New York: McGraw Hill.

Hermsen, L. 1977. "When the Sun Stands Still." *RFD* 12:9.

Hill, Scott. 1997. "Aroused from Hibernation." In *The Bear Book: Readings in the History and Evolution of a Gay Male Subculture*, ed. Les K. Wright, 65–82. New York: Harrington Park Press.

Hocquenghem, Guy. 1996 (1972). *Homosexual Desire*. Durham, NC: Duke University Press.

Hood-Williams, John, and Wendy Cealy Harrison. 1998. "Trouble with Gender." In *The Sociological Review*, 73–94. Malden, MA: Blackwell.

Hopcke, Robert H. 2001 (1991). "S/M and the Psychology of Gay Male Initiation: An Archetypal Perspective." In *Leatherfolk: Radical Sex, People, Politics and Practice*, ed. Mark Thompson, 65–76. Los Angeles: Alyson Publications.

Hughes, Everett Cherrington. 1945. "Dilemmas and Contradictions of Status." *American Journal of Sociology* 50:353–59.

Hyslop, Seumas. 2001. "The Rise of the Australian Bear Community since 1995." In *The Bear Book II: Further Readings in the History and Evolution of a Gay Male Subculture*, ed. Les K. Wright, 269–83. New York: Harrington Park Press.

Jackson, Peter. 1989. *Male Homosexuality in Thailand*. Elmhurst: Global.

Jackson, Stevi, and Sue Scott. 1997. "Gut Reactions to Matters of the Heart: Reflections on Rationality, Irrationality, and Sexuality. *The Sociological Review* 45 (4): 551–75.

Jenkins, Richard. 1992. *Pierre Bourdieu*. London: Routledge.

Johnston, Hank, Enrique Laraña, and Joseph R. Gusfield. 1994. "Identities, Grievances, and New Social Movements." In *New Social Movements: From Ideology to Identity*, ed. Enrique Laraña, Hank Johnston, and Joseph R. Gusfield, 3–35. Philadelphia, PA: Temple University Press.

Jordan, Ellen, and Angela Cowan. 1998. "Warrior Narratives in the Kindergarten Classroom: Renegotiating the Social Contract?" In *The Gendered Society Reader*, ed. Michael S. Kimmel and Amy Aronson, 127–40. New York: Oxford University Press.

Kampf, Ray. 2000. *The Bear Handbook*. New York: Harrington Park Press.

Katz, Jonathan. 1992. *Gay American History: Lesbians and Gay Men in the U.S.A.* New York: Meridian.

Kelley, Robin D. G. 2004. "Confessions of a Nice Negro, or Why I Shaved My Head." In *Men's Lives*, 6th edition, ed. Michael S. Kimmel and Michael A. Messner, 335–41. Boston: Pearson.

Kelly, Elizabeth A., and Kate Kane. 2001. "In Goldilocks's Footsteps: Exploring the Discursive Construction of Gay Masculinity in Bear Magazines." In *The Bear Book II: Further Readings in the History and Evolution of a Gay Male Subculture*, ed. Les K. Wright, 327–50. New York: Harrington Park Press.

Kessler, Suzanne J. 1998. *Lessons from the Intersexed*. New Brunswick, NJ: Rutgers University Press.

Kessler, Suzanne J., and Wendy McKenna. 1978. *Gender: An Ethnomethodological Approach*. Chicago: University of Chicago Press.

Kimmel, Michael. 1996. *Manhood in America: A Cultural History*. New York: Free Press.

Kiser, Edgar, and Michael Hechter. 1991. "The Role of General Theory in Comparative-Historical Sociology." *American Journal of Sociology* 97:1–30.

Krieger, Susan. 1985. "Beyond 'Subjectivity': The Use of the Self in Social Science." *Qualitative Sociology* 8 (4): 309–24.

Kulick, Don. 2002. "The Gender of Brazilian Transgendered Prostitutes." In *The Masculinity Studies Reader*, ed. Rachel Adams and David Savran, 389–407. Malden, MA: Blackwell.

Lancaster, Roger N. 1987. "Subject Honor and Object Shame: The Construction of Male Homosexuality and Stigma in Nicaragua." *Ethnology* 27 (2): 111–25.

Laqueur, Thomas. 1990. *Making Sex: Body and Gender from the Greeks to Freud*. Cambridge MA: Harvard University Press.

Laraña, Enrique, Hank Johnston, and Joseph R. Gusfield. 1994. *New Social Movements: From Ideology to Identity*. Philadelphia, PA: Temple University Press.

Laslett, Barbara. 1990. "Unfeeling Knowledge: Emotion and Objectivity in the History of Sociology." *Sociological Forum* 5:413–33.

Levine, Martin P. 1998. *Gay Macho: The Life and Death of the Homosexual Clone*. New York: New York University Press.

Licata, Salvatore J. 1981. "The Homosexual Rights Movement in the United States." *Journal of Homosexuality* 6:161–89.

Linden, Robin Ruth, ed. 1982. *Against Sadomasochism: A Radical Feminist Analysis*. Palo Alto, CA: Frog in the Well.

Lloyd, Moya. 1999. "Performativity, Parody, Politics." *Theory, Culture and Society*. 16 (2): 195–213.

Locke, Philip. 1997. "Male Images in the Gay Mass Media and Bear-Oriented Magazines: Analysis and Contrast." In *The Bear Book: Readings in the History and Evolution of a Gay Male Subculture*, ed. Les K. Wright, 103–40. New York: Harrington Park Press.

Loe, Meika. 2004. *The Rise of Viagra: How the Little Blue Pill Changed Sex in America*. New York: New York University Press.

Lofland, John, and Lyn H. Lofland. 1995. *Analyzing Social Settings*. Belmont, CA: Wadsworth Publishing.

Lofstrom, Jan. 1997. "The Birth of the Queen/The Modern Homosexual: Historical Explanations Revisited." *Sociological Review* 45:24–41.

Louie, Kam. 2002. *Theorising Chinese Masculinity: Society and Gender in China*. Cambridge, UK: Cambridge University Press.

Lucie-Smith, Edward. 1991. "The Cult of the Bear." In *The Bear Cult*, 6–8. Swaffam, England: GMP Publishers.

Magister, Thom. 2001 (1991). "One among Many: The Seduction and Training of a Leatherman." In *Leatherfolk: Radical Sex, People, Politics and Practice*, ed. Mark Thompson, 91–105. Los Angeles: Alyson Publications.

Mains, Geoff. 1984. *Urban Aboriginals*. San Francisco: Gay Sunshine Press.

_____ . 1987. "Urban Aboriginals and the Celebration of Leather Magic." In *Gay Spirit: Myth and Meaning*, ed. Mark Thompson, 99–117. New York: St. Martin's Press.

_____ . 2001a (1991). "The Molecular Anatomy of Leather." In *Leatherfolk: Radical Sex, People, Politics and Practice*, ed. Mark Thompson, 37–43. Los Angeles: Alyson Publications.

_____ . 2001b (1991). "The View from a Sling." In *Leatherfolk: Radical Sex, People, Politics and Practice*, ed. Mark Thompson, 233–42. Los Angeles: Alyson Publications.

Marks Ridinger, Robert B. 1997. "Bearaphernalia: An Exercise in Social Definition." In *The Bear Book: Readings in the History and Evolution of a Gay Male Subculture*, ed. Les K. Wright, 83–88. New York: Harrington Park Press.

Marshall, Barbara L. 2006. "The New Virility: Viagra, Male Aging and Sexual Function" *Sexualities* 9 (3): 345–62.

Mazzei, George. 1979. "Who's Who in the Zoo: A Glossary of Gay Animals." *The Advocate*, July 26, 42.

McCann, Thomas. 2001. "Laid Bear: Masculinity with All the Trappings." In *The Bear Book II: Further Readings in the History and Evolution of a Gay Male Subculture*, ed. Les K. Wright, 305–25. New York: Harrington Park Press.

McCann, Tommy. 1997. "Atlantic Crossing: The Development of the Eurobear." In *The Bear Book: Readings in the History and Evolution of a Gay Male Subculture*, ed. Les K. Wright, 251–60. New York: Harrington Park Press.

McIntosh, Mary. 1991. "Gender Trouble: Feminism and the Subversion of Identity." Review. *Feminist Review* 38:113–14.

Messner, Michael A. 1997. *Politics of Masculinities: Men in Movements*. Thousand Oaks, CA: Sage.

Mey, Pierre de. 1997. "A French Bear Asks: Are Bears an American Thing?" In *The Bear Book: Readings in the History and Evolution of a Gay Male Subculture*, ed. Les K. Wright, 261–68. New York: Harrington Park Press.

Miller, Neil. 1995. *Out of the Past: Gay and Lesbian History from 1869 to the Present*. New York: Vintage Books.

Miller, S. M. 1952. "The Participant Observer and 'Over-Rapport.'" *The American Sociological Review* 17 (2): 97–99.

Mirchandani, Rekha. 2005. "Postmodernism and Sociology: From the Epistemological to the Empirical." *Sociological Theory* 23 (1): 86–115.

Moon, Michael. 1996. "Introduction." In *Homosexual Desire* by Guy Hocquenghem, 9–21. Durham, NC: Duke University Press.

Morgensen, Scott. 2005. "Rooting for Queers: A Politics of Primitivity." *Women & Performance* 29, 15 (1): 251–89.

Namaste, Ki. 1994. "The Politics of Inside/Out: Queer Theory, Poststructuralism, and a Sociological Approach to Sexuality." *Sociological Theory* 12 (2): 220–30.

Newman, Leslea, ed. 1995. *The Femme Mystique*. Boston: Alyson Publications.

Newton, Esther. 1972. *Mother Camp*. Chicago: University of Chicago Press.

Noble, John O. 2001. "The Bears Come to Rochester." In *The Bear Book II: Further Readings in the History and Evolution of a Gay Male Subculture*, ed. Les K. Wright, 243–48. New York: Harrington Park Press.

Oliver, Mary Beth. 2003. "African American Men as 'Criminal and Dangerous': Implications of Media Portrayals of Crime on the 'Criminalization' of African American Men." *Journal of African American Studies* 7 (2): 3–18.

Petersen, Alan. 1998. "Sexing the Body: Representations of Sex Differences in Gray's Anatomy, 1858 to the Present." *Body & Society* 4 (1): 1–15.

Pickett, Keri. 2000. *Faeries: Visions, Voices and Pretty Dresses*. New York: Aperture.

Pierce, Jennifer. 1995. *Gender Trials*. Berkeley: University of California Press.

Plous, S., and T. Williams. 1995. "Racial Stereotypes from the Days of American Slavery: A Continuing Legacy." *Journal of Applied Social Psychology* 25: 795–817.

Plummer, Ken. 1995. *Telling Sexual Stories: Power, Change and Social Worlds*. London: Routledge.

Preston, John. 2000. "Introduction." In *The Leatherman's Handbook* by Larry Townsend, 27–29. Los Angeles: L. T. Publications.

———. 2001 (1991). "What Happened?" In *Leatherfolk: Radical Sex, People, Politics and Practice*, ed. Mark Thompson, 210–20. Los Angeles: Alyson Publications.

Preves, Sharon. 2003. *Intersex and Identity: The Contested Self*. New Brunswick, NJ: Rutgers University Press.

Quadagno, Jill, and Stan J. Knapp. 1992. "Have Historical Sociologists Forsaken Theory?" *Sociological Methods and Research* 20:481–507.

Rey, Michael. 1988. "Parisian Homosexuals Create a Lifestyle, 1700–1850." In *'Tis Nature's Fault*, ed. R. P. Maccubbin. Cambridge, UK: Cambridge University Press.

Rodgers, William. 1993. *The Politics of Vision: The Radical Faerie Movement and the Creation of a Contemporary Gay Spirituality*. Unpublished manuscript.

Rofes, Eric. 1997. "Academics as Bears: Thoughts of Middle-Class Eroticization of Workingmen's Bodies." In *The Bear Book: Readings in the History and Evolution of a Gay Male Subculture*, ed. Les K. Wright, 89–99. New York: Harrington Park Press.

Roscoe, Will. 1996. "Writing Queer Cultures: An Impossible Possibility?" In *Out in the Field: Reflections of Lesbian and Gay Anthropologists*, ed. Ellen Lewin and William L. Leap, 200–211. Urbana, IL: University of Illinois Press.

Rotundo, E. Anthony. 1993. *American Manhood: Transformations in Masculinity from the Revolution to the Modern Era*. New York: Basic Books.

Rowson, Everett K. 1991. "The Effeminates of Early Medina." *Journal of the American Oriental Society* 111 (4): 671–93.

Rubin, Gayle. 2001 (1991). "The Catacombs: A Temple of the Butthole." In *Leatherfolk: Radical Sex, People, Politics and Practice*, ed. Mark Thompson, 119–41. Los Angeles: Alyson Publications.

———. 2003. "Samois." In *Encyclopedia of Lesbian, Gay, Bisexual, and Transgender History in America*, ed. Marc Stein. New York: Charles Scribner's and Sons.

Rubin, J., F. Provenzano, and Z. Luria, Z. 1974. "The Eye of the Beholder: Parents' Views on Sex of Newborns." *American Journal of Orthopsychiatry* 44:512–19.

Rupp, Leila J., and Verta Taylor. 2003. *Drag Queens at the 801 Cabaret*. Chicago: University of Chicago Press.

Sahin, Mehmet Ali. 2001. "A Bear Voice from Turkey." In *The Bear Book II: Further Readings in the History and Evolution of a Gay Male Subculture*, ed. Les K. Wright, 253–61. New York: Harrington Park Press.

Salamone, Frank A. 2005. "Hausa Concepts of Masculinity and the '*Yan Daudu*." In *African Masculinities: Men in Africa from the Late Nineteenth Century to the Present*, ed. Lahoucine Ouzgane and Robert Morrell. New York: Palgrave Macmillan.

Schacht, Steven. 2000. "Gay Female Impersonators and the Masculine Construction of 'Other.'" In *Gay Masculinities*, ed. Peter M. Nardi, 247–68. Thousand Oaks, CA: Sage.

———. 2002. "Four Renditions of Doing Female Drag: Feminine Appearing Conceptual Variations of a Masculine Theme." *Gendered Sexualities* 6:157–80.

Sedgwick, Eve Kosofsky. 1990. *Epistemology of the Closet*. Berkeley: University of California Press.

Seidman, I. E. 1991. *Interviewing as Qualitative Research*. New York: Teachers College Press.

Seidman, Steven. 1988. "Transfiguring Sexual Identity: AIDS & the Contemporary Construction of Homosexuality." *Social Text* 19/20:187–205.

———. 1989. "Constructing Sex as a Domain of Pleasure and Self-Expression: Sexual Ideology in the Sixties." *Theory, Culture & Society* 6:293–315.

———. 1993. "Identity and Politics in a 'Postmodern' Gay Culture: Some Historical and Conceptual Notes." In *Fear of a Queer Planet*, ed. Michael Warner, 105–42. Minneapolis: University of Minnesota Press.

———. 1994. "Symposium: Queer Theory/Sociology: A Dialogue." *Sociological Theory* 12 (2): 166–77.

———. 2001. "From Identity to Queer Politics: Shifts in the Social Logic of Normative Heterosexuality in Contemporary America." *Social Thought and Research* 24 (1,2): 2–12.

———. 2003. *Beyond the Closet: The Transformation of Gay and Lesbian Life*. New York: Routledge.

Sharman, Peter. 2001. "A Short History of the Brisbears." In *The Bear Book II: Further Readings in the History and Evolution of a Gay Male Subculture*, ed. Les K. Wright, 249–50. New York: Harrington Park Press.

Silver, Carole G. 1999. *Strange and Secret Peoples: Fairies and Victorian Consciousness*. New York: Oxford University Press.

Silverstein, C., and Felice Picano. 1992. *The New Joy of Gay Sex*. New York: Harper Perennial.

Sinfield, Alan. 1994. *The Wilde Century: Effeminacy, Oscar Wilde and the Queer Moment*. New York: Columbia University Press.

Smith, Allen C., and Sherryl Kleinman. 1998. "Managing Emotions in Medical School." In *Inside Social Life*, 2nd edition, ed. Spencer Cahill, 67–78. Los Angeles: Roxbury Publishing.

Sommer, Matthew H. 2002. "Dangerous Males, Vulnerable Males, and Polluted Males: The Regulation of Masculinity in Qing Dynasty Law." In *Chinese*

Femininities/Chinese Masculinities, ed. Susan Brownell and Jeffrey N. Wasserstrom, 67–88. Berkeley, CA: University of California Press.

Stein, Arlene and Ken Plummer. 1994. " 'I Can't Even Think Straight': 'Queer' Theory and the Missing Sexual Revolution in Sociology." *Sociological Theory* 12 (2): 178–86.

Stein, David. 2001 (1991). "S/M's Copernican Revolution: From a Closed World to an Infinite Universe." In *Leatherfolk: Radical Sex, People, Politics and Practice*, ed. Mark Thompson, 142–56. Los Angeles: Alyson Publications.

Steward, Samuel M. 2001 (1991). "Dr. Kinsey Takes a Peek at S/M: A Reminiscence." In *Leatherfolk: Radical Sex, People, Politics and Practice*, ed. Mark Thompson, 81–90. Los Angeles: Alyson Publications.

Stoltenberg, John. 1989. *Refusing to Be a Man: Essays on Sex and Justice*. New York: Penguin.

Straightacting.com. 2002. Survey. http://www.straightacting.com (accessed January 12, 2002).

Suresha, Ron. 1997. "Bear Roots." In *The Bear Book: Readings in the History and Evolution of a Gay Male Subculture*, ed. Les K. Wright, 41–49. New York: Harrington Park Press.

Suresha, Ron (ed.) 2002a. *Bearotica*. Los Angeles: Alyson Books.

Suresha, Ron Jackson. 2002b. *Bears on Bears: Interviews and Discussions*. Los Angeles: Alyson Books.

Swartz, David. 1997. *Culture and Power: The Sociology of Pierre Bourdieu*. Chicago: University of Chicago Press.

Swidler, Ann. 1986. "Culture in Action: Symbols and Strategies." *American Sociological Review* 51 (2): 273–86.

Tauber, M. A. 1979. "Parental Socialization Techniques and Sex Differences in Children's Play." *Child Development* 50:225–34.

Taylor, Verta. 1989. "Social Movement Continuity: The Women's Movement in Abeyance" *American Sociological Review*. 54:761–75.

Taylor, Verta, and Nancy E. Whittier. 1992. "Collective Identity in Social Movement Communities: Lesbian Feminist Mobilization." In *Frontiers in Social Movement Theory*, ed. Aldon Morris and Carol McClurg Mueller. New Haven, CT: Yale University Press.

Teal, Donn. 1995. *The Gay Militants: How Gay Liberation Began in America, 1969–1971*. New York: St. Martin's Press.

Tewksbury, Rick. 1994. "Gender Construction and the Female Impersonator: The Process of Transforming 'He' to 'She.' " *Deviant Behavior: An Interdisciplinary Journal* 15:27–43.

Thompson, Mark. 1987. "This Gay Tribe: A Brief History of Fairies." In *Gay Spirit: Myth and Meaning*, ed. Mark Thompson, 260–78. New York: St. Martin's Press.

——— . 2001 (1991). "Erotic Ecstasy: An Interview with Purusha the Androgyne." In *Leatherfolk: Radical Sex, People, Politics and Practice*, ed. Mark Thompson, 284–93. Los Angeles: Alyson Publications.

Tiefer, Lenore. 2006. "The Viagra Phenomenon." *Sexualities* 9 (3): 273–94.

Tilly, Charles. 1984. *Big Structures, Large Processes, Huge Comparisons*. New York: Russell Sage.

Timmons, Stuart. 1990. *The Trouble with Harry Hay*. Boston: Alyson Publications.

Toothman, Larry. 2001. "A Short History of Bear Clubs in Iowa: The Bear Paws of Iowa and The Ursine Group." In *The Bear Book II: Further Readings in the History and Evolution of a Gay Male Subculture*, ed. Les K. Wright, 215–32. New York: Harrington Park Press.

Townsend, Larry. 2000. *The Leatherman's Handbook*. Beverly Hills, CA: L. T. Publications.

Treelove, D.-T. 1975. "Spring, Spirit, and Faggotry." *RFD* 3:42–44.

Troka, Donna Jean, Kathleen Lebesco, and Jean Bobby Noble, eds. 2003. *The Drag King Anthology*. New York: Harrington Park Press.

Trumbach, Randolph. 1977. "London's Sodomites: Homosexual Behavior and Western Culture in the 18th Century." *Journal of Social History* 11 (1): 1–33.

———. 1989. "The Birth of the Queen: Sodomy and the Emergence of Gender Equality in Modern Culture." In *Hidden From History: Reclaiming the Gay and Lesbian Past*, ed. Martin B. Duberman, Martha Vicinus, and George Chauncey Jr. New York: New American Library.

———. 1991. "Sex, Gender, and Sexual Identity in Modern Culture: Male Sodomy and Female Prostitution in Enlightenment London." *Journal of the History of Sexuality* 2 (2): 186–203.

———. 1998. *Sex and the Gender Revolution*, vol. I. Chicago: University of Chicago Press.

Truscott, Carol. 2001 (1991). "S/M: Some Questions and a Few Answers." In *Leatherfolk: Radical Sex, People, Politics and Practice*, ed. Mark Thompson, 15–36. Los Angeles: Alyson Publications.

Tucker, Scott. 2001 (1991). "The Hanged Man." In *Leatherfolk: Radical Sex, People, Politics and Practice*, ed. Mark Thompson, 1–14. Los Angeles: Alyson Publications.

Tyler, Melissa. 2004. "Managing between the Sheets: Lifestyle Magazines and the Management of Sexuality in Everyday Life." *Sexualities* 7 (1): 81–106.

Wacquant, Loic D. 1989. "Towards a Reflexive Sociology: A Workshop with Pierre Bourdieu." *Sociological Theory* 7 (1): 26–63.

Walker, Mitch. 1987. "Visionary Love: The Magickal Gay Spirit-Power." In *Gay Spirit: Myth and Meaning*, ed. Mark Thompson, 210–36. New York: St. Martin's Press.

Warner, Michael. 1999. *The Trouble with Normal: Sex, Politics, and the Ethics of Queer Life*. New York: Free Press.

Weber, Max. 1964 (1947). *The Theory of Social and Economic Organization*. New York: Free Press.

———. 1998 (1946). *The Protestant Ethic and the Spirit of Capitalism*. Los Angeles: Roxbury.

Webster, John. 1997. "Kiwi Bears." In *The Bear Book: Readings in the History and Evolution of a Gay Male Subculture*, ed. Les K. Wright, 239–50. New York: Harrington Park Press.

Weeks, J. 1996 (1972). "Preface to the 1978 Edition." In *Homosexual Desire* by G. Hocquenghem, 23–47. Durham, NC: Duke University Press.

Weeks, Jeffrey. 1986. *Sexuality*. New York: Routledge

West, Candace, and Don H. Zimmerman. 1987. "Doing Gender." *Gender and Society* 1:125–51.

Weston, Kath. 1996. *Render Me, Gender Me*. New York: Columbia University Press.

White, Edmond. 1980. *States of Desire*. New York: Dutton.

Wilkins, Amy C. 2004a. " 'So Full of Myself as a Chick': Goth Women, Sexual Independence, and Gender Egalitarianism." *Gender & Society* 18 (3): 328–49.

———. 2004b. "'Puerto Rican Wannabes: Sexual Spectacle and the Marking of Race, Class, and Gender Boundaries." *Gender & Society* 18 (1): 103–21.

Williams, Craig A. 1999. *Roman Homosexuality: Ideologies of Masculinity in Classical Antiquity*. New York: Oxford University Press.

Williams, Walter L. 1996. "Being Gay and Doing Fieldwork." In *Out in the Field: Reflections of Lesbian and Gay Anthropologists*, ed. Ellen Lewin and William L. Leap, 70–85. Urbana, IL: University of Illinois Press.

Winton, Mark A. 1989. "The Social Construction of the G-Spot and Female Ejaculation." *Journal of Sex Education and Therapy* 15 (3): 151–62.

Wittman, Carl. 1975a. "In Search of the Gay Tarot." *RFD* 3:33–37.

———. 1975b. "Loving Dance." *RFD* 4:31–34.

Wray, Matt. 1994. "Unsettling Sexualities and White Trash Bodies." Paper presented at *White Trash: Reading Poor Whites*. Sponsored by the American Studies Working Group at the University of California, Berkeley, Oct. 10, 1994.

Wright, Les. (ed.) 1997a. *The Bear Book: Readings in the History and Evolution of a Gay Male Subculture*. New York: Harrington Park Press.

———. (ed.) 2001. *The Bear Book II: Further Readings in the History and Evolution of a Gay Male Subculture*. New York: Harrington Park Press.

Wright, Les K. 1990. "The Sociology of the Urban Bear." *Drummer* 140:53–55.

———. 1997b. "A Concise History of Self-Identifying Bears." In *The Bear Book: Readings in the History and Evolution of a Gay Male Subculture*, ed. Les K. Wright, 21–39. New York: Harrington Park Press.

———. 1997c. "Introduction: Theoretical Bears." In *The Bear Book: Readings in the History and Evolution of a Gay Male Subculture*, ed. Les K. Wright, 1–17 . New York: Harrington Park Press.

———. 1997d. "The Bear Hug Group: An Interview with Sam Ganczaruk." In *The Bear Book: Readings in the History and Evolution of a Gay Male Subculture*, ed. Les K. Wright, 201–5. New York: Harrington Park Press.

Wu, Cuncun. 2003. "Beautiful Boys Made Up as Beautiful Girls: Anti-Masculine Taste in Qing China." In *Asian Masculinities: The Meaning and Practice of*

Manhood in China and Japan, ed. Kam Louie and Morris Low. London: Routledge Curzon.

Wylie, Phillip. 1996 (1942). *Generation of Vipers*. New York: Dalkey Archive.

Young, Ian. 1995. *The Stonewall Experiment: A Gay Psychohistory*. London: Cassell.

Index